P9-DGM-198

m 39.95

Cruising Guide to British Columbia Vol. 2

DESOLATION SOUND

and the Discovery Islands

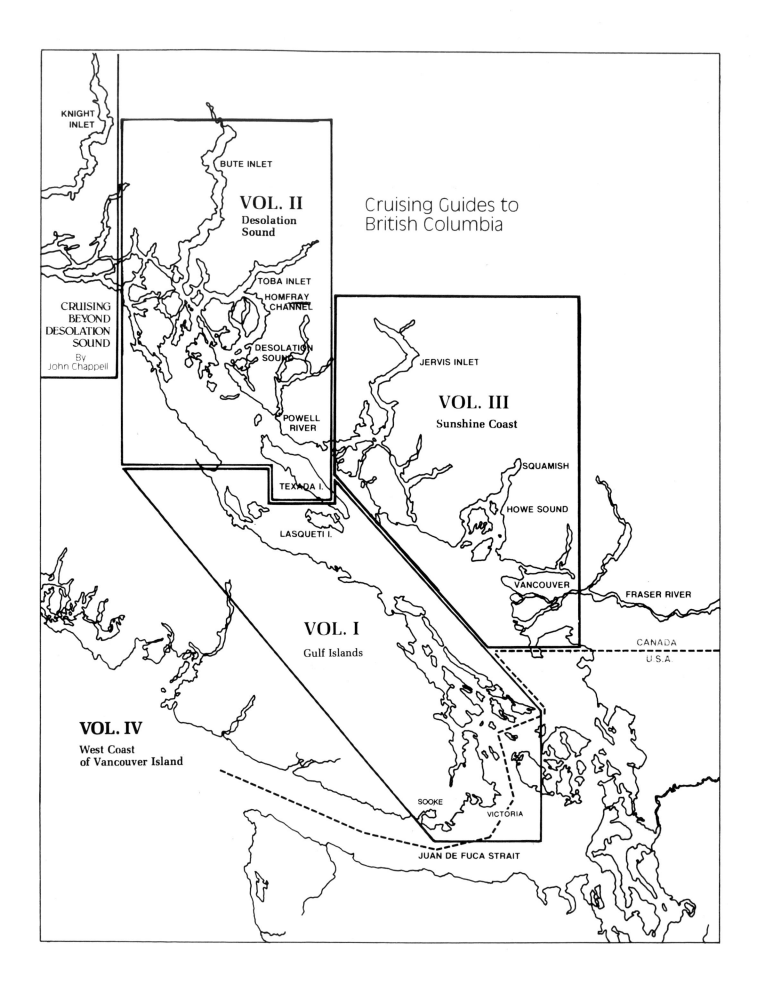

KNIGHT
INLET

BUTE INLET

VOL. II
Desolation
Sound

Cruising Guides to
British Columbia

TOBA INLET

HOMFRAY
CHANNEL

CRUISING
BEYOND
DESOLATION
SOUND
By
John Chappell

DESOLATION
SOUND

JERVIS INLET

VOL. III

Sunshine Coast

SQUAMISH

POWELL
RIVER

HOWE SOUND

TEXADA I.

LASQUETI I.

VANCOUVER

FRASER RIVER

VOL. I

Gulf Islands

CANADA
U.S.A.

VOL. IV

West Coast
of Vancouver Island

SOOKE

VICTORIA

JUAN DE FUCA STRAIT

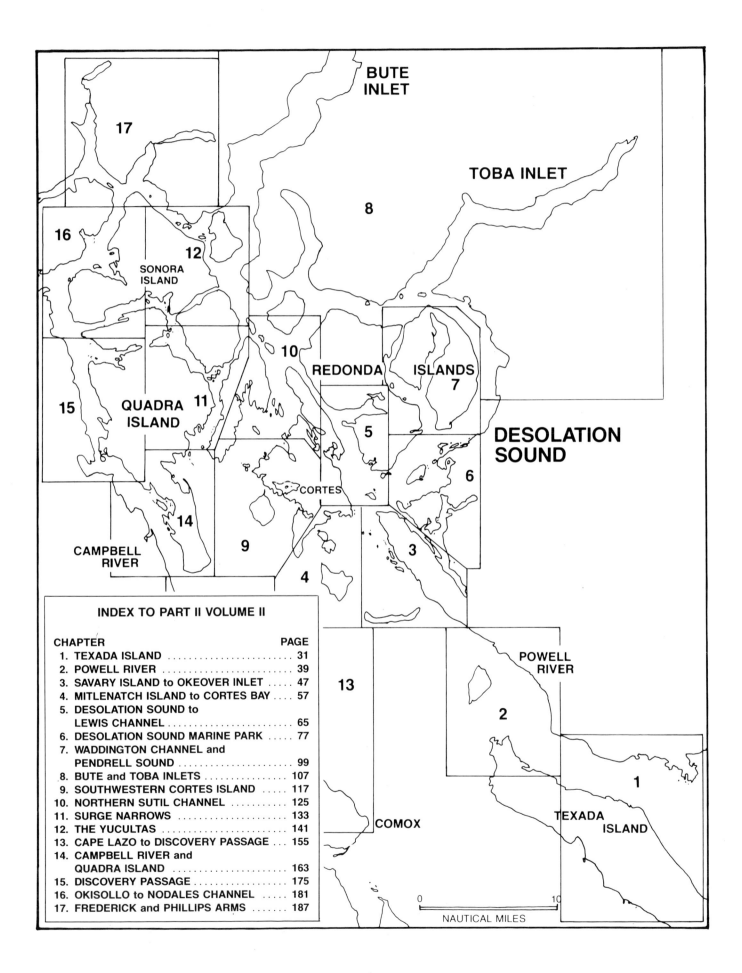

BUTE
INLET

TOBA INLET

17

16

12

SONORA
ISLAND

8

10

REDONDA   ISLANDS
7

DESOLATION
SOUND

15

QUADRA
ISLAND

11

5

6

14

CORTES

CAMPBELL
RIVER

9

3

4

POWELL
RIVER

13

2

1

COMOX

TEXADA
ISLAND

INDEX TO PART II VOLUME II

0   10

NAUTICAL MILES

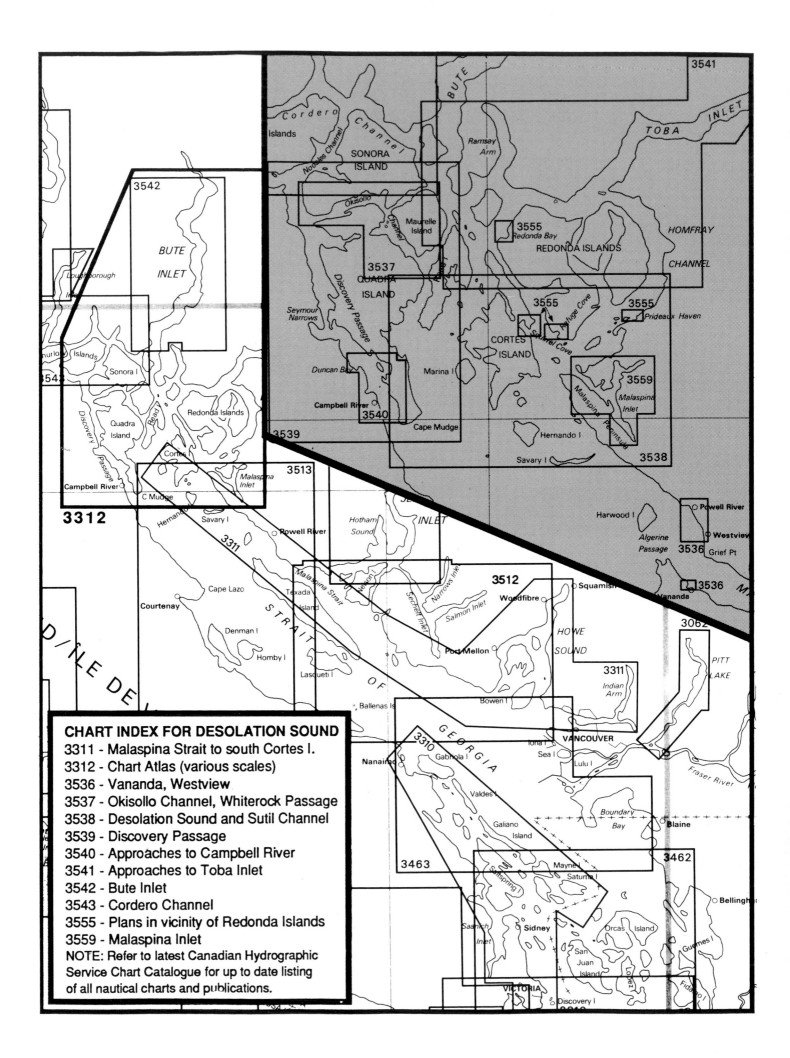

CHART INDEX FOR DESOLATION SOUND
3311 - Malaspina Strait to south Cortes I.
3312 - Chart Atlas (various scales)
3536 - Vananda, Westview
3537 - Okisollo Channel, Whiterock Passage
3538 - Desolation Sound and Sutil Channel
3539 - Discovery Passage
3540 - Approaches to Campbell River
3541 - Approaches to Toba Inlet
3542 - Bute Inlet
3543 - Cordero Channel
3555 - Plans in vicinity of Redonda Islands
3559 - Malaspina Inlet
NOTE: Refer to latest Canadian Hydrographic
Service Chart Catalogue for up to date listing
of all nautical charts and publications.

Cruising Guide to British Columbia Vol. 2

DESOLATION SOUND

and the Discovery Islands

by Bill Wolferstan

Whitecap Books
Vancouver/Toronto

This is my Father's world;
I rest me in the thought
Of rocks and trees, of skies and seas,
His hand the wonders wrought.

— *Maltbie D. Babcock*

Canadian Cataloguing in Publication Data

Wolferstan, Bill, 1942-
    Cruising guide to British Columbia
    Includes bibliographies and indexes.
    Contents: v. 1. Gulf Islands and Vancouver
Island from Sooke to Courtenay — v. 2.
Desolation Sound
    ISBN 0-921061-10-2 (v. 1). — ISBN
0-921061-23-4 (v.2). — ISBN 0-921061-11-0 (set)

    1. Yachts and yachting - British Columbia -
Guide-books. 2. British Columbia - Description
and travel - 1981-   - Guide-books.*
I. Title.
FC3817.4.W643   917.11'34   C87-10587-6
F1087.W643

Copyright© 1987, by Bill Wolferstan and Whitecap Books Ltd.,
1086 W. 3rd Street, North Vancouver, B.C., V7P 3J6. No part of
this book may be reproduced or transmitted in any form by any
means without express permission from the publisher, except
by a reviewer, who may quote brief passages in a review.

First paperback edition 1989

CONTENTS

Introduction and Addendum to the New Edition

This Cruising Guide is divided into two parts. The first briefly summarizes background information on cruising conditions and facilities, geography and history of the Desolation Sound-Discovery Islands area of the British Columbia coast. The second part is made up of seventeen separate chapters which describe in detail the coasts and islands from northern Malaspina Strait to Johnstone Strait.

Since the first edition of this book was published in 1980 there have been few major changes in this area. However, many formerly deserted bays and coves are now occupied by new shellfish or finfish farming operations. The government has endeavoured to ensure that space is allowed for emergency boat anchorage or moorage and access to crown foreshore in most of these coves. In addition, they have designated the major boat anchorages as no aquaculture areas.

Major changes to the list of marinas and marine resorts on the map on page 26 include: Brimacombes' fishing resort (286-2061) in Big Bay, Stuart Island; and Brown's Bay Marina (286-3135) just north of Seymour Narrows in Discovery Passage (formerly Adam's Resort, page 178, Chapter 15). There is a new fishing pier/promenade south of the Campbell River Government Wharf and Discovery Harbour, a new marina, is planned for construction north of the Quadra ferry dock. The Royal Savary Lodge (6) has been removed and Dodman's Store (13) at Surge Narrows is no longer operating. Taku Resort (28) is now private. For current information on marine facilities please refer to the annual Pacific Yachting Cruising Services Directory.

Charts and Nautical Publications

Up-to-date Canadian Hydrographic Service charts, *Sailing Directions and Small Craft Guides* are essential for safe navigation of the coast. Some of the charts listed in this guide may no longer be available. Please refer to the 1988 chart index on page 4 or the most recent Canadian Hydrographic Service Catalogue of Nautical Charts. The large yellow *Sailing Directions* (Volume 1, B.C. Coast [south portion]) is required for the waters north of Campbell River and Cortes Island. The *Small Craft Guides* are green and similar to the *Sailing Directions* but are designed especially for use by smaller vessels. Volume 1 covers the Gulf Islands and Vancouver Island north as far as Campbell River and Volume 2 covers the mainland coast north to Cortes Island.

Canadian Tide and Current Tables are required for times of high and low water, slackwater and maximum velocities of the current in the tidal passes. Volume 5 (green) covers the Strait of Georgia and Volume 6 (blue) is required for the Discovery Islands and Desolation Sound. Other useful publications such as the *List of Lights, Buoys and Fog Signals* and *Radio Aids to Marine Navigation* are listed in the annual CHS Catalogue.

Acknowledgments

The author wishes to thank the many people, friends and acquaintances who have assisted him in many ways towards the final completion of this guide. In particular: Hubert and Pat Havelaar, George and Kay Wood, Brian and Joan Robertson, Alex and Clio Matheson, Al Fairhurst, Jamie Alley, Elizabeth Owen, Cathi and Gary Robinson, Brock Friesen, David and Jennifer Oliver, George McNutt, Al Nairne, Gerry Kidd, Graeme Matheson, Rex Armstead, Paul Burkhart and the staff of PACIFIC YACHTING, the B.C. Provincial Archives, the Victoria Public Library, the B.C. Maritime Museum and the Canadian Hydrographic Service.

Part One

Introduction to
DESOLATION SOUND
and the Discovery Islands

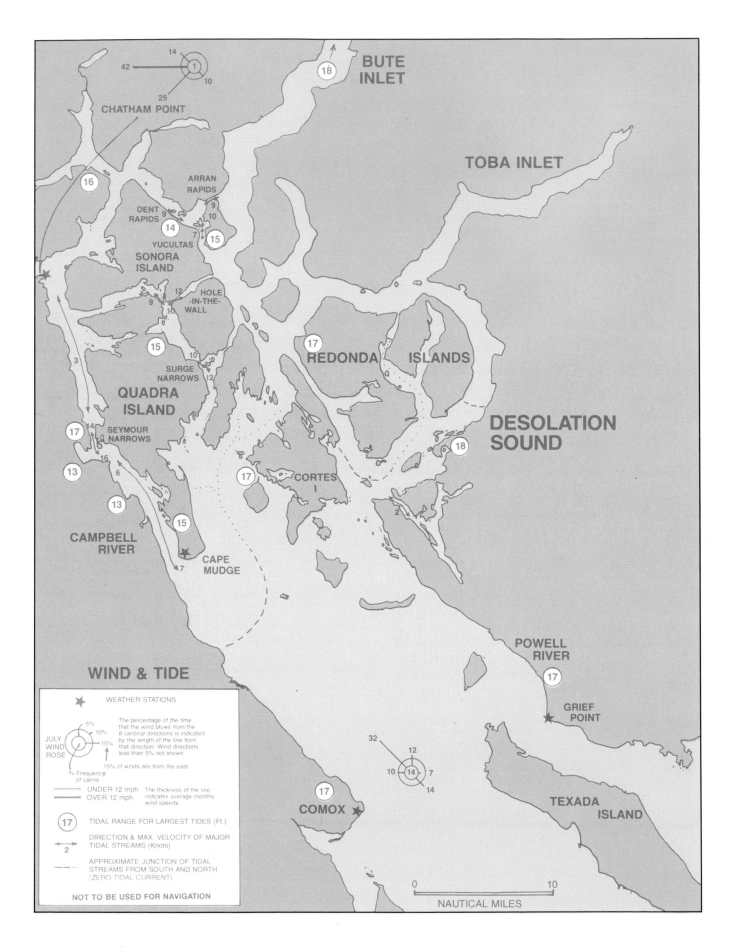

BUTE INLET

TOBA INLET

CHATHAM POINT

ARRAN RAPIDS

DENT RAPIDS

YUCULTAS

SONORA ISLAND

HOLE -IN-THE- WALL

REDONDA   ISLANDS

DESOLATION SOUND

SURGE NARROWS

QUADRA ISLAND

SEYMOUR NARROWS

CORTES

CAMPBELL RIVER

CAPE MUDGE

POWELL RIVER

GRIEF POINT

WIND & TIDE

COMOX

TEXADA ISLAND

WEATHER STATIONS

JULY WIND ROSE

5%
10%
15%

The percentage of the time that the wind blows from the 8 cardinal directions is indicated by the length of the line from that direction. Wind directions less than 5% not shown.

15% of winds are from the east.

% Frequency of calms

——— UNDER 12 mph
——— OVER 12 mph

The thickness of the line indicates average monthly wind speeds.

(17) TIDAL RANGE FOR LARGEST TIDES (Ft.)

2 DIRECTION & MAX. VELOCITY OF MAJOR TIDAL STREAMS (Knots)

- - - APPROXIMATE JUNCTION OF TIDAL STREAMS FROM SOUTH AND NORTH (ZERO TIDAL CURRENT)

NOT TO BE USED FOR NAVIGATION

0   10
NAUTICAL MILES

WIND AND TIDE

Weather conditions (wind, sea and visibility) are recorded regularly at the weather stations indicated on the map and broadcast several times a day on local radio stations with a synopsis of the expected conditions over the next 24 hour period.

In the summer months of June, July and August the mean maximum daily temperature varies from about 19°C (66°F) in those areas most exposed to the moderating influence of colder oceanic waters (such as Chatham Point), to around 22°C (72°F) at the heads of Inlets and in the Texada-Powell River area. The average amount of precipitation varies from about 4 inches (in the 3 summer months) in the central Strait of Georgia — Gillies Bay, Cape Lazo; to over 8 inches at the heads of Inlets and at Chatham Point (10 inches). The number of days with rain in the three summer months varies from 20 in the central Strait of Georgia to 28 at the heads of Inlets.

Fog

Fog is uncommon in the Strait of Georgia in the summer months. Occasionally, fog from Johnstone Strait spills past Chatham Point down Discovery Passage and up into Cordero Channel. This fog seldom penetrates beyond the tidal rapids at Seymour Narrows and the Yucultas.

Winds

Wind roses for the major weather stations on the map give an indication of the percentage frequency of wind direction for the month of July. The prevailing, good weather summer westerly can blow from almost any direction within the twisting channels of the Discovery Islands north of the Strait of Georgia. Diurnal (onshore-offshore) wind patterns are also a major influence with up-inlet (south or southwest) winds being strongest and most consistent during the afternoon and down-inlet (north or northeast) winds blowing at night. Winds in this area tend to be light in the summer months. The Southern Strait of Georgia southeasterly, which brings rain and unsettled weather, can also be a "dry" or onshore diurnal wind along the Sunshine coast or at the north end of the Strait of Georgia. In winter, the strongest winds are southeasterly gales (northern Strait of Georgia) or "Squamish" winds — outbreaks of interior winds spilling out through mainland inlets with considerable force.

Tides

The maximum tidal range (rise and fall of the water) varies from only a few feet within tidal lagoons to over 18 feet at Prideaux Haven. This maximum range is seldom reached but is approached during spring tides (about once or twice a month) and is about 50% more than the mean rise and fall of the tide. The tidal range within enclosed basins or inlets guarded by tidal rapids is generally less than in open, unrestricted channels. This applies to such places as upper Okisollo Channel and the south half of Discovery Passage, where the maximum tidal range varies from 13 feet at Gowlland Harbour and Menzies Bay to 15 feet at Quathiaski Cove (a mile to the south of Gowlland Harbour) and 17 feet at Seymour Narrows (a mile north of Menzies Bay).

Currents

The rise and fall of tides results in currents flooding into and ebbing out of the Strait of Georgia via Juan de Fuca Strait to the south and Johnstone Strait to the north. The approximate location where the two tidal streams meet is indicated by a dashed line on the map. The actual meeting place may vary over several miles with changes in barometric pressure and local wind conditions. The strength of the flood and ebb tidal streams within the Strait of Georgia and other unrestricted channels and inlets seldom exceed 2 knots. Tidal rapids occur where channels narrow, particularly between the northern Discovery Islands. Nine of the most prominent of these rapids are indicated on the map. Such rapids should be negotiated only at times of slack water.

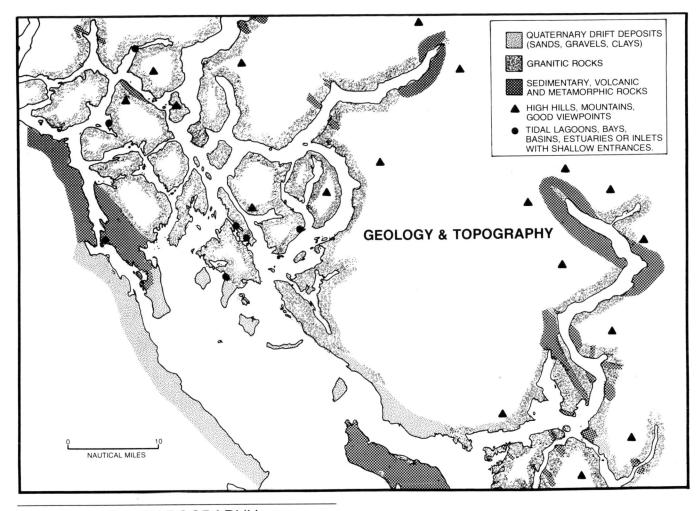

GEOLOGY & TOPOGRAPHY

Legend:

- QUATERNARY DRIFT DEPOSITS (SANDS, GRAVELS, CLAYS)
- GRANITIC ROCKS
- SEDIMENTARY, VOLCANIC AND METAMORPHIC ROCKS
- ▲ HIGH HILLS, MOUNTAINS, GOOD VIEWPOINTS
- ● TIDAL LAGOONS, BAYS, BASINS, ESTUARIES OR INLETS WITH SHALLOW ENTRANCES.

0 10
NAUTICAL MILES

GEOLOGY AND TOPOGRAPHY

The outstanding topographic features of the British Columbia coast are the many fiord inlets. These fiords rank in size and scenic grandeur with the world famous fiord coastlines of Norway; Southern Chile; and New Zealand.

The geology of the mainland coast is dominated by the igneous (mainly granitic) shorelines. Fractures or joints in these rocks have influenced the orientation of valleys and ridges to give a pronounced NW-SE trend to the topography with transverse and subordinate patterns forming a roughly rectangular network.

The fiord system is a product of intense glaciation of the mountainous coastline. The pre-glacial valleys were occupied by Pleistocene ice and served as escape routes for ice flowing westward to the sea from the high area of accumulation along the crest of the mountains. The moving ice eroded the valley walls to their present steep profiles and the great thickness of ice and rock bebris caught up within the glacier eroded the bottoms of trunk valleys to considerable depths below sea-level. Then as the ice left the valleys (about 10,000 years ago) they were invaded by the sea to produce the drowned fiord system of today. Small remnants of these glaciers can still be found at the higher elevations, mainly on NE-facing slopes.

Glaciation within what is now the Strait of Georgia was intense. Ice pouring westward from the Coast Mountains and eastward from the Vancouver Island Ranges coalesced in the Strait to form a glacier which moved south escaping to the sea via Juan de Fuca Strait. When this glacier melted, the ground-up sands, gravels, boulders and clays were deposited as ground moraines or as outwash plains, of which Marina, Hernando, Savary and Harwood Islands are remnants. Other glacial deposits (drift) can be found between Comox and Campbell River, at the south ends of Quadra and Cortes Islands, and between Powell River and Thunder Bay. These deposits (and other marine or riverine deposits) are easily eroded and generally form low, shallow coastlines of constantly changing depths with the most extensive fine sand beaches.

Along the boundary of the granitic (and at some places within the granitic zone) we find sedimentary, volcanic and metamorphic rocks of varying degrees of texture and erodibility. These rocks are mainly greywackes, limestones, cherts, mixed with volcanic lavas and fragmental rocks. The foliated metamorphic rocks are mainly sedimentary rocks which have been greatly altered by extreme heat and pressure. They are particularly resistant to erosion and occur on the coast mainly as roof pendants in the mountains and near the heads of inlets.

(adapted from Holland, 1976)

13

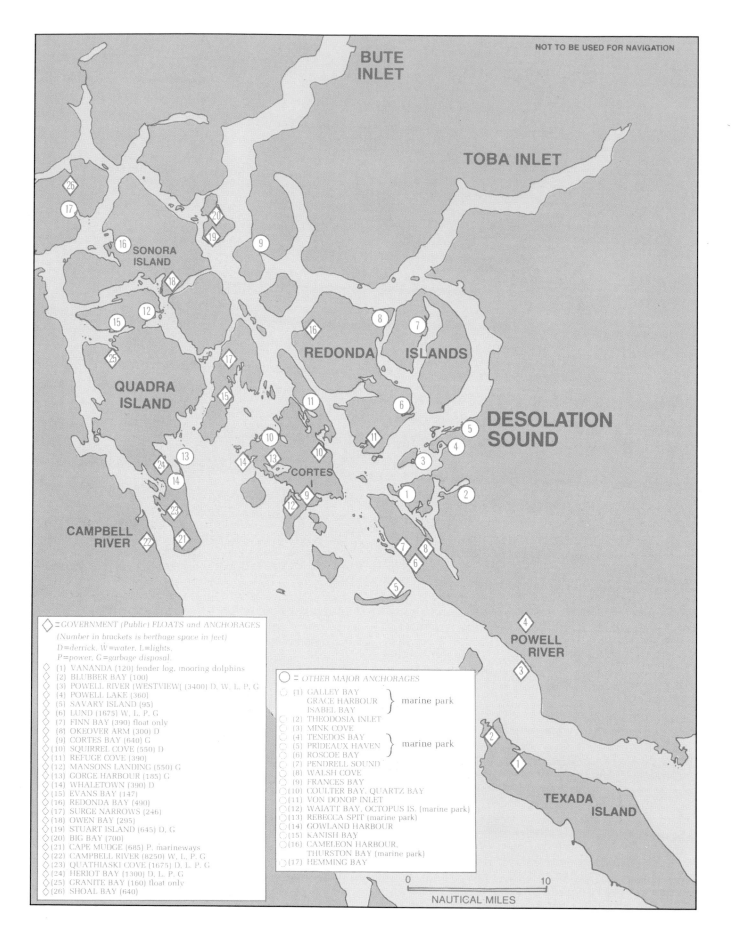

BUTE INLET

TOBA INLET

SONORA ISLAND

REDONDA ISLANDS

DESOLATION SOUND

QUADRA ISLAND

CORTES

CAMPBELL RIVER

POWELL RIVER

TEXADA ISLAND

◇ =GOVERNMENT (Public) FLOATS and ANCHORAGES
(Number in brackets is berthage space in feet)
D=derrick, W=water, L=lights,
P=power, G=garbage disposal.

◇ (1) VANANDA (120) fender log, mooring dolphins
◇ (2) BLUBBER BAY (100)
◇ (3) POWELL RIVER (WESTVIEW((3400) D, W, L, P, G
◇ (4) POWELL LAKE (360)
◇ (5) SAVARY ISLAND (95)
◇ (6) LUND (1675) W, L, P, G
◇ (7) FINN BAY (390) float only
◇ (8) OKEOVER ARM (300) D
◇ (9) CORTES BAY (640) G
◇ (10) SQUIRREL COVE (550) D
◇ (11) REFUGE COVE (390)
◇ (12) MANSONS LANDING (550) G
◇ (13) GORGE HARBOUR (185) G
◇ (14) WHALETOWN (390) D
◇ (15) EVANS BAY (147)
◇ (16) REDONDA BAY (490)
◇ (17) SURGE NARROWS (246)
◇ (18) OWEN BAY (295)
◇ (19) STUART ISLAND (645) D, G
◇ (20) BIG BAY (700)
◇ (21) CAPE MUDGE (685) P, marineways
◇ (22) CAMPBELL RIVER (8250) W, L, P, G
◇ (23) QUATHIASKI COVE (1675) D, L, P, G
◇ (24) HERIOT BAY (1300) D, L, P, G
◇ (25) GRANITE BAY (160) float only
◇ (26) SHOAL BAY (640)

◯ = OTHER MAJOR ANCHORAGES

◯ (1) GALLEY BAY
       GRACE HARBOUR   } marine park
       ISABEL BAY
◯ (2) THEODOSIA INLET
◯ (3) MINK COVE
◯ (4) TENEDOS BAY
◯ (5) PRIDEAUX HAVEN   } marine park
◯ (6) ROSCOE BAY
◯ (7) PENDRELL SOUND
◯ (8) WALSH COVE
◯ (9) FRANCES BAY
◯ (10) COULTER BAY, QUARTZ BAY
◯ (11) VON DONOP INLET
◯ (12) WAIATT BAY, OCTOPUS IS. (marine park)
◯ (13) REBECCA SPIT (marine park)
◯ (14) GOWLAND HARBOUR
◯ (15) KANISH BAY
◯ (16) CAMELEON HARBOUR,
        THURSTON BAY (marine park)
◯ (17) HEMMING BAY

0   10
NAUTICAL MILES

FLOATS AND ANCHORAGES

Government floats available for transient moorage can be identified by their brightly painted red railings and are usually located in coves or harbours which also serve as major anchorages. They provide access to shore, and in some cases (see list) water, power and lights are available on the floats. Garbage disposal facilities and derricks (for lifting masts or engines) are sometimes located on the wharves above the floats. Moorage fees are payable at most government floats. Rafting up alongside other boats is a requirement during busy periods and no obstructions should be placed to hinder other vessels coming alongside. Canadian fishing vessels generally have priority over other vessels at these floats, but in summer when most are away, the floats provide convenient temporary moorage for transient recreational small craft.

Anchorages

Other major anchorages are listed and identified by circles on this map. Like the government floats, these anchorages are located in coves or harbours which are generally safe in all weathers. Each Chapter in Part II describes these anchorages in some detail. In addition a number of temporary anchorages are described and indicated by asterisks (*) on the maps. These temporary (conditional) anchorages may be suitable for overnight anchorage and be fairly well protected from most winds or seas. Some are usable only when tidal conditions permit (they may dry at low water) or when there are no onshore winds. For every temporary anchorage indicated or described there may be four or five others, just as suitable, awaiting discovery in the vicinity.

Garbage Disposal

Garbage disposal is a growing problem on the coast, especially in those areas which do not have facilities to cope with the seasonal tourist rush.

Yachtsmen and other small craft operators are in an excellent position to recycle their wastes. Ideally, all garbage should be kept and reused in some way. The alternatives in order of priority are:

1) Separate, store and return to a recycling depot all cans, bottles, packaging, paper and other unwanted (non-biodegradable) items.
2) Burn anything burnable (at low tide, on foreshore).
3) Sink anything sinkable (in waters over 100 fathoms).
4) Chop up finely and dispose overboard (at least a mile from land) refuse which is biodegradable. Large banana peels, grapefruit halves, etc. tend to float, look unsightly and cannot be swallowed whole by those great scavengers — the seagulls and crows.
5) Use garbage disposal facilities only where they are regularly maintained.

On no account should garbage be depostited ashore or afloat, whether wrapped in paper or plastic bags, except as noted in (5). When garbage facilities are used, one should ensure that metal or plastic lids are securely fastened over the garbage container, otherwise seagulls and crows will quickly peck their way through and redistribute the contents.

Discovery Passage islands abound in the eyries of bald eagles

WILDLIFE

by Clio Matheson

Birds haunt a sailor, accompanying him on his journeys, moving, like him, in three dimensions, often seen but seldom acknowledged, though an awareness and understanding of their habits can add immeasurably to the pleasure of days at sea. The similarity between the way a bird uses the air, and a sailor the sea, is very great; like sailing, the act of

Great Blue Heron

flight breaks a passage through the air to close behind in a swirling, curling wake. Air is the second element of the four, water the last, yet they are so alike in their behavior, great translucent masses that run sweetly over level plains or roll into turbulence against immovable rock. Both ships and birds are at their mercy, helped or hindered by wind and tide, blown clear by gales, the less adapted crushed and killed.

Crows seen cavorting across a cliff face are doing it there because there the wind changes and makes such games possible; such a wind can fill an empty sail or take one all aback. The sight of gulls strewn like confetti on a green field no longer means a gale or stiff blow at sea, because the Weather Report has taken such ancient knowledge from us in favour of satelite pictures, maps full of swirls and arrows, or weathermen who (at least in this changeable climate) will happily tell us from the depths of their windowless broadcasting rooms that it is raining when it isn't. For small boat sailors on this coast a lot of forecasting can be done by watching the birds.

I'll never forget when we were fogbound in the Bering Sea looking for our landfall. The sea was still, grey and soundless, the fog muffling everything; carried by the tide we came to a raft of duck, and then, black on the pewter water, murres, finally, glimmering through the fog, we saw splashes of white guano at their nest sites and so made our landfall. Each species as we came to it was a signpost saying it is here somewhere! Listen for it! Look for it!

16

In such a brief summary of the birds and mammals of the part of the coast included in this book, one cannot mention all the species, but only pick out those most commonly seen or most entertaining in their habits. Ideally, all boats should carry a good bird book or field guide.

One of the birds most easily identified and evocative of still grey days at the water's edge is the *Great Blue Heron*, common throughout the coast. He is a stately bird with a 70 inch wingspan, often seen stalking along the shingle or standing deep in speculation on a rock, sometimes one may be encountered ambling long-legged down a wayside ditch hunting frogs. Another entertaining bird is the *Dowitcher*, tiny, (10 inches from nose to tail) with an extremely long bill, they cluster in little groups at the waters edge, particularly in sandy places and their bills dip in and out like a bevy of tiny sewing machines. The *Black Oystercatcher* too, is a bird of the water's edge, scarlet eyed and billed; with vivid pink legs and a penetrating pipe they hunt molluscs on the rocky islets. Dark, plump, with a triangle at the tip of its white tail and stubby yellow legs, the *Surfbird* winters on the coast but breeds and summers in the mountains above the timberline.

Duck are divided into four groups of which the Aythyinae or diving ducks (also called sea duck, or bay duck) are found most often in the Straits and islands. All dive, whereas the puddle ducks or surface feeding ducks (Anatinae) rarely do. The hind toe has a paddle-like flap which is lacking in surface feeders and their method of takeoff is quite different because their legs are closer to the tail and they patter along the surface of the water before getting airborne. There are 17 different species, and they feed on small aquatic animals and plants, molluscs and crustaceans.

The most beautiful and striking to my mind is the *Harlequin Duck*, approached quietly from a small boat or canoe they are fairly tame — we have got to within 15 feet of them on an overcast day. They are differently marked, male and female. A small duck, the male is blue-grey with chestnut sides oddly patterned with white lines and spots; the female is dusky with three round white patches on the head. They have a squeaky voice that is "spelt" by ornithologists as 'gua gua gua' and ' ek ek ek ek' though to my ear it just sounds like a squeak.

Scoters are heavy-set, blackish ducks often seen flying low over the sea in a stringy formation; the three species are similar. The *White Winged Scoter* is the largest, it has a tick of white just below the eye, an orange bill with a black nob and a squarish white patch on the rear edge of the spread wing, (if swimming you'll have to wait for him to spread his wings to see the spot). The *Surf Scoter*, also called a skunk duck, is black with one or two white patches on crown and nape, a gaily patterned bill of orange, black and white. The *Common Scoter* is sometimes called the American or black scoter; he is the only American duck with entirely black plummage, this, with a bright, butter-coloured nob on the bill are distinctive. They have a charming call, melodious and cooing on the part of the male, growls from the female. In the case of the scoters I have described only the males, because they are so distinctive; the plumage of the females differs and is comparatively drab.

Mergansers are the fishermen of the duck family with elegant, slender outlines, a spiky, saw-edged bill and in most cases a crest; their food is chiefly fish. There are three types, the *Hooded, Common* and *Redbreasted,* of which the Redbreasted is the most arresting to look at, with his rakish, crested, black head glossed over with bottle green, wide white collar and waterline of dusky red as though he'd had a haul out and his bottom painted, the bill and feet are red. Ringing out across still waters and deserted bays the call of the *Loon* means Canada to me, just as that of the *Fish Eagle* on the Zambezi brings back the warmth of Africa. There are four species, the *Common, Yellowbilled, Arctic* and *Red Throated.* The are all heavybodied birds with short, stubby tails, and their feet set so far back that they seldom are seen on land except at the nest site. They can dive to a depth of 200 feet or merely sink their bodies under water so that only their heads surface like a periscope. They eat small fish and other aquatic animals. Often confused with the *Loon,* the *Cormorants* are common near harbours and marinas, particularly where there are free standing piles for them to perch on in their characteristic cruciform attitude with wings held out to dry. There are four species in the West, all black birds. The differences between them, while striking enough, need a very good pair of binoculars to discover, for in general they are differences of colourful face skin, or throat pouches. The *Pelagic* has a dull red face with a black forehead, the *Double Crested* has a yellow throat pouch, the *Brandts* a bright, robins-egg-blue throat pouch with a buff patch, and the *Red Faced* has as one might expect, a red face and red forehead.

Another self-contained and quiet visitor to marinas is the *Eared Grebe* and one of the most appealing as they paddle under counters or pop up in an empty berth. They have black necks, golden ear tufts and a crested black head; their sterns seem to ride higher in the water than those of other grebes of which there are six species on the coast.

The *Auk* family is the northern counterpart of the penguins; they are roughly penguin-shaped and swim and dive expertly, but unlike penguins they also fly like buzz bombs. They nest, for the most part, in crowded colonies and feed on crustaceans, molluscs, algae. There are 16 species in the West, some of them with peculiar and enchanting names. A few examples: the *Rhinoseros Auklet* who grows himself, in late winter, a pair of white R.A.F. moustaches and a white plume behind his eye. The *Tufted Puffin,* a classic childrens' book bird with his large, triangular, orange-red bill, white face, and long curved ivory coloured ear tufts nests in burrows like rabbit warrens and can somehow manage to catch more fish while still carrying some in his enormous bill. The *Ancient Murrelet* whose name seems to echo a thought of Coleridge's, are small neckless looking seabirds, dark above and pale below with a black throat patch and white stipe over the eye. "It is an Ancient Murrelet. And he stoppest one of Three . . .''

17

The bird of the coast Indians is the *Raven*, woven deep into their legends and folklore as the father of the nations. The *Raven* is the largest of the passerine birds. In adult birds the blackness of their plumage is overlain by a rich irridescence. His size, rounded tail, Roman-nosed beak, and cravat of shaggy feathers distinguishes him from the *Northwestern Crow*. He has a vast vocabulary of belling notes, croaks, whispers and other more strangled noises, but never, no matter what else he might say, would he cry "Caw".

Of the birds of prey along the coast there are four which a yachtsman should see in a year's sailing. They are the *Bald Eagle, Osprey, Peregrine Falcon*, and the *Turkey Vulture*.

Although one of the biggest birds on the Coast, the *Turkey Vulture* is the least known, a contradiction it would seem. Very few people are aware of their presence here, in spite of their noble 6-foot wingspan and magnificent powers of flight. They drift up from California and return with their young in the fall before the cold weather makes it difficult for them to spend the eight hours on the wing that they need to find their carrion food. The birds will eat grasshoppers and readily gorge on fish if it is available, but a particular delicacy is snake, and one of the best places to see them is over a field just after it has been mowed, for they will come for miles to clean up small mammals and snakes killed by the cutting. They nest on the bald hills of the Gulf Islands in cracks between the rocks, caves, or hollow trees, and they have an enchanting family life, for the young are very affectionate and love to be touched. When fledged their heads are covered in a pale beige, velvet-like down which changes in the adult male to scarlet skin. They express their pleasure by a low hiss and displeasure by a more forcible hiss. The young remain on the nest for about ten weeks until they are able to fly. Once in the air the vulture is transformed from a rather ungainly bird into a graceful, kite-like flyer; a adjusting its wings to the wind, it sails for miles with never a wingbeat. The shallow, upward-turning 'V' made by its wings with widely separated flight feathers distinguishes it from an eagle in silhouette.

The *Bald Eagle* is another bird with a 6-foot wingspan who builds an unmistakable nest in the tops of usually enormous trees, they have to be big because the nest is used and added to year after year and can come to weigh as much as two tons! The plumage of the adult bird is familiar to everyone, but the young birds start life being, when first fledged, brown all over with dark eyes, a black beak, speckled breast, and yellow feet; only the feet remain the same. Gradually over a period of four to six years the speckled breast becomes a solid brown, the dark eyes change to yellow and the black beak to gold, the brown head and tail become white. *Bald Eagles* indulge in one of the most spectacular nuptial displays to be seen, for when courting, or renewing their vows (they mate for life) the two birds will soar higher and higher circling into the blue and then come cartwheeling down holding each other's feet, wings outspread, to separate just above the sea. One of the most amusing sights one may see in the late summer

Canadian River Otter

is a pair of young eagles fully feathered, and able to fly waiting bolt upright, fatly complacent, like Emperor's children for their parents to return with supper.

Ospreys with sharply angled wings stoop feet first for fish, gallant swashbucklers hunting above the sea; they are frequently tormented by eagles into dropping their catch for the lazy whiteheaded birds to eat. Like eagles they nest in trees, but their choice is generally different, being a taller, slenderer type, usually dead, or standing separate from its fellows. The nest is similar in shape but much smaller, although it is also added to each year the pair occupy it. Often the first inkling one has of an occupied nest is the sound of excited mewing ringing down at the sight of a parent bird returning with a fish. When threatened by discovery the young birds will crouch down in the nest so that it looks empty, when they are very young the adults brood them to protect them from the weather both day and night. As their wings begin to fledge out, the young become more active jumping and dancing on the bed of the nest or clutching its lip with pale bluish-yellow feet and flapping joyously, shouting like mad, bleating 'tseep-tseep-tseep-whick-whick-whick-ick-ick-ick'.

In India the *Peregrine Falcon* is called the Shahin which means 'this one is King' because of its beauty of shape, and flight, and colour, and because of its courage. Its size is much the same as that of a crow but the outline is totally different. The head is blunt, the body

Pod of killer whales rests on sea surface

broadchested with sharply pointed, graceful wings and slender tail. His full, bold, peat-dark eyes are set in a small distinctive black head with heavy moustachial stripes on either side of a notched slate-blue beak, the upperparts of body and wings are slate-blue barred with dark brown, the primaries dark brown and the tail barred like the back and tipped in light sepia, throat and entire underparts white to sienna-orange narrowly striped on chest and barred on flanks and belly. The males are one-third smaller than the female which is why they are called tiercels. The peregrine kills mainly by the impact of its strike, for the speed at which they stoop can be greater than 200 mph, although they do also break the necks of their prey once they have circled back and grasped it. The peregrine is primarily a bird eater and on the Coast its numbers are tied to those of the smaller seabirds, for they breed and lay eggs only if there is a ready availability of food for their young; they are also, because they are at the top of a food chain, very much affected by the presence of pesticides. On the Charlottes, and a part of the way down the coast, there lives a very dark race of *Peregrine Falcon*, called the *Peal's Falcon* which is unique to this part of the world.

The *Gulls* , I seem to have left out and overlooked because they are so common, comprising 43 species in the world and 17 on the coast with five more occasionally or accidentally occurring here. Of them all, my favourite is the *Bonapartes Gull.* It is the smallest and the prettiest; almost tern-like in size and habits, it has a small black bill and scarlet legs, in the winter it has a round black spot behind its eye, the adult breeding plumage gives it a blackish head, and the immature birds have the winter plumage. They are fairly tame and can be approached quite closely while they ride in the still waters of a kelp bed. They eat anything: marine life, plant and animal food, refuse, and carrion.

I have spent more time on the birds because a sailor is more likely to see them. Mammals require time and stealth from the watcher, the endless time of a child on a summer's afternoon who can sit and watch a beetle walk up a stalk of grass. From a boat there are some easily seen mammals, if one is in their vicinity, these are the whales, the dolphins, and the seals.

There are four species of toothed whale reported from the coasts of B.C., but the most commonly seen whale is not one at all, it is from the family *Delphinidae*, which includes porposes, dolphins, and blackfish; it is the *Pacific Killer Whale, orca* or *'Blackfish.'*

The *Killer Whale* is large, the overall length of the male reaching 26-feet or more, the females 20-feet. They travel in family groups or pods, and there are a number of resident pods here on the coast as well as young individuals who have not yet established a territory. Because of their prevalence in these coastal waters, the Biological Research Station at Nanaimo has become a worldwide authority on these spectacular animals. In spite of the fact that all the *Blackfish* taken for Zoos and Aquaris come from the pods resident here, with the corresponding distress and loss of life (of the *Blackfish*) occasioned by their capture, there have been no proven instances of attack by killer whales on man or his small boats.

Killer whales are unmistakable; they are black overall with a trident shaped area of white on the anal region; the abdomen, throat and chest are white, with a white or saffron yellow spot behind the dorsal fin and over the eye; the males are easily distinguished from the females by the difference in the height of their respective dorsal fins, up to 6 feet in males and 2 feet 6 inches in females. They are the wolves of the sea and, like wolves, they do not kill cleanly when tackling something far bigger than themselves, such as the larger whales. However, they more commonly eat fish, squid, sea birds, porpoise and seals, sealions.

Porpoises are much a part of the myths that haunt sailors, such as Pelorus Jack, the pilot porpoise accredited, I've been told, by Lloyds, so certain were they that he would never guide a ship on to a reef. The Argonauts play their lyres to the porpoises as they like the Argosy cleaved the wine dark sea, the tales go on and on. The *Porpoise* found here is called the Harbour porpoise and you will seldom see more than four together, never a big school of them; they are only about 6 feet long, dark grey to almost black on top and pale below with a dark line running round the lower lip. After mating in July to October and a gestation period of 183 days they produce single young of about 2 feet in length. Their food is largely soft-spined fishes and squid and they fall prey to th Orcas.

Another of the prey species of the *Killer whale* is the *northern Sea-lion*, tawny in colour, vast in size (males weighing up to 2,200 lb.) with large doleful brown eyes perpetually tearful, and fine Victorian whiskers. His small ears are a distinguishing mark separating him from the "earless" seals whose ears are internal, like the harbour seal. In hot weather when the tide is low the rocks at the entrance of Tsehum harbour look covered with stubby tilted lengths of pale-bleached driftwood. Only when one approaches does the driftwood move and quietly flop into the sea, to pop up in one's wake like large-eyed coconuts, leaving a strong fishy smell in the air. It is the *Harbour* or *Hair Seal*. Because they use only their back flippers while swimming, they are as graceful as an otter in the water, so unlike the sea lion who uses his front flippers and progresses in a series of broaches and plunges like a Victorian Duchess doing the breast stoke. This makes them easy to distinguish one from the other while they are in the sea.

A lively and beautiful inhabitant of the reefs, inlets and islands of the coast is the *Canadian River Otter*. He is often confused with his large cousin the *Sea Otter* whose range once stretched from Russia to California, until it was decimated by the fur trade and then rebuilt again by enlightened protection laws. However, though they have been reintroduced to this coast and have in part successfully established themselves, one is unlikely to encounter them as they are extremely shy and go on land only to have their young. Much more common, very brash and entertaining, the *River Otter* makes the sea its home and makes use of people's cottages to have its young in. I have just recently seen a series of charming photographs taken by a shipwright in his boatshed of a family of otter who regularly come out of the water just to play in the shavings his business causes him to have; they play with the broom he uses to sweep his shed with too, but not to any useful purpose. In Vancouver Harbour and along the Gorge in Victoria they are the most numerous aquatic mammal. They establish a holt in early March and their young, one to five, but mostly three, are born mid-March to the end of April after a gestation of usually two months, although the climatic conditions and availability of seclusion (as with all mustilidae) can affect the length of gestation. In fresh water their food mainly consists of fish, which they catch easily in underwater pursuit; however, fish are harder to obtain at sea so they eat a higher proportion of crustaceans; occasionally birds and mammals are taken but mostly crabs.

One of the most prolific of the animals of the coast is the *White Footed* or *Deer Mouse*. Because of the isolation afforded by each island, the deermice have developed into many different sub-species, many of which have not yet been described and catalogued. They are beautiful little things, with large nocturnal eyes, in most cases with white tummies, tails and feet, and rich brown top parts. They are almost omnivorous feeding on a wide variety of plant foods, seeds, berries, grass stems, insects, small shore animals such as crabs (the tiny ones) and limpets. They build cup-shaped nests of fine woven grasses in sheltered situations such as tree holes, abandoned birds nests or under logs, in which they raise litters of two to four greycoated young once or twice a year depending upon the availability of forage.

To wrap up this extremely idiosyncratic selection of some of the birds and mammals of the coast I'll put forward one of the best reasons I know for sailing up to Desolation Sound in mid-winter when it's snowing, because then one can see the *Mountain Goat* on the sea shore. *Mountain Goats* are really not goats at all but antelope, with very little kinship with goats. They inhabit the roughest and most inhospitable terrain generally above the timberline, but in the winter the snow may force the goat down to sea level for it is not fitted to survive in deep snow. Their coats are white and thick with a stiff mane running along their high shoulders which exaggerates the shape of them; they are dark eyed with sharp, black horns rising in a smooth backward curve. Their food is variable including a great variety of alpine grasses, and almost all tree and shrub species save spruce; it is one of the very few herbivores who will eat western hemlock and buffalo-berry. They make great use of alkaline earthlicks and will travel a distance to use them, mainly in July and August. The females and young are gregarious, the males more solitary except in the breeding season; though little is known of their breeding habits, the rut takes place in November with a gestation period of six months.

VILLAGE OF THE FRIENDLY INDIANS AT THE ENTRANCE OF BUTE'S CANAL

It was noon on the 30th (July, 1792) before we reached that part of the western shore, which had appeared broken, and on which the fires of the natives had been observed on entering this canal; which I distinguished by the name of "Bute's Canal". Here was found an Indian village, situated on the face of a steep rock, containing about one hundred and fifty of the natives, some few of whom had visited our party in their way up the canal, and now many came off in the most civil and friendly manner, with a plentiful supply of fresh herrings and other fish, which they bartered in a fair and honest way for nails.

— George Vancouver, *A Voyage of Discovery to the North Pacific Ocean
in the years 1790-5*, London, 1798

HISTORY

When the first European (Spanish and British) explorers navigated their way through the Strait of Georgia in 1792, they encountered many native people who greeted them with a considerable degree of civility and friendship. The summer and winter villages of these Salish people are indicated on the map and described elsewhere by H. G. Barnett (*The Coast Salish of B.C.*, 1955) and Charles Hill-Tout (*The Salish People*, Talonbooks, 1978).

Although their countries were on the brink of war, the Spanish and British explorers co-operated closely after a chance encounter near Point Grey. An extremely amicable friendship grew between the Captains Vancouver, Galiano and Valdes as they pursued their surveys through the Strait of Georgia and into Desolation Sound over a three week period in the summer of 1792. It is interesting to compare the British and Spanish charts with each other and with the present day chart. Vancouver included a few Spanish place names on his chart and many of the other place names used by the Spaniards were later incorporated on our charts by the nineteenth century

hydrographers. The Spaniards seemed to be better copiers than the British as they closely followed Vancouver's surveys of Howe Sound and Jervis Inlet (mistakes and all); while Vancouver's draughtsman was less accurate with areas the Spaniards had covered — Lasqueti, the west coast of Texada and the Vancouver Island coast south of Cape Lazo.

Around the middle of the last century the Lekwiltok (Euclatah) group of Kwakiutl pushed the Comox group of Salish from Discovery Passage to their present location south of Cape Lazo (Wilson Duff, *The Indian History of B.C.*, 1964). The Coast Salish and Southern Kwakiutl, although warlike among themselves, were remarkably friendly toward the first white settlers along the southwestern British Columbia coast, due largely to the stature of many of the first traders who moved into this area after the departure of the European explorers. These were men of the Hudson's Bay Company from Quebec and other parts of eastern Canada, Scotland and England; the fathers of the first settlers — loggers, fishermen, miners and farmers. The Akriggs (*British Columbia Chronicle*

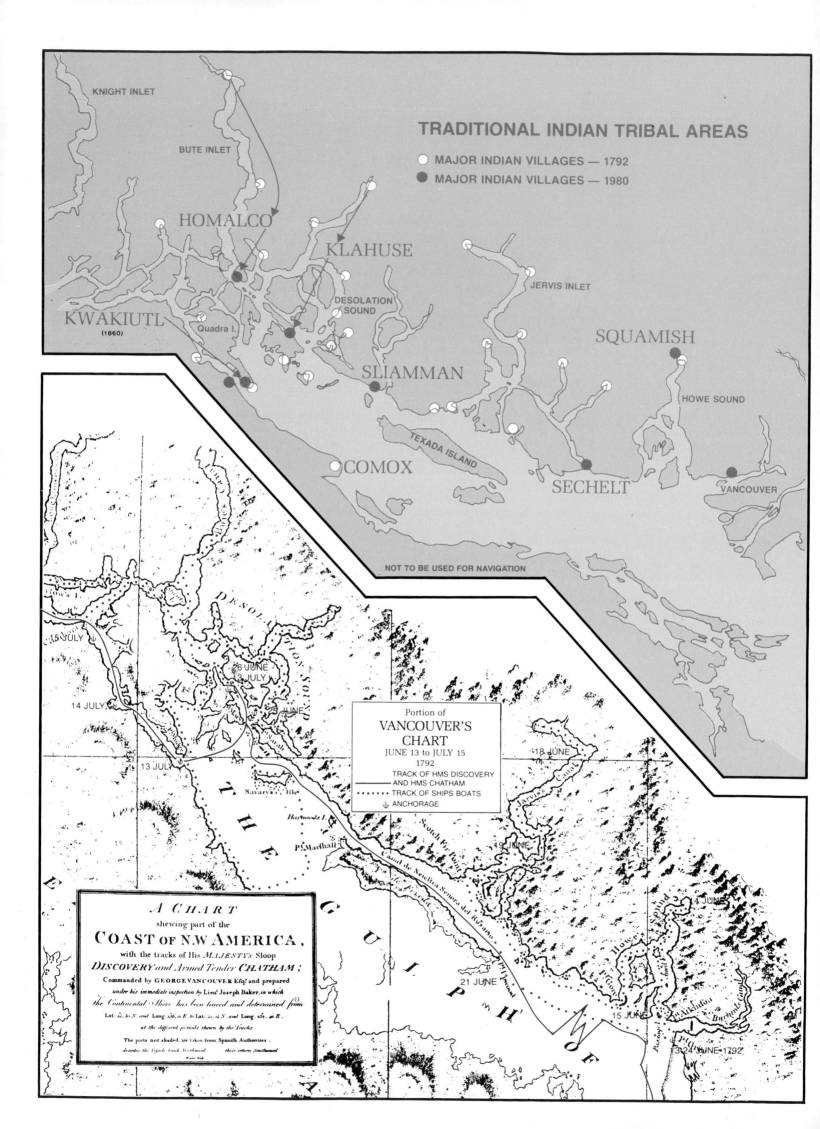

TRADITIONAL INDIAN TRIBAL AREAS

○ MAJOR INDIAN VILLAGES — 1792
● MAJOR INDIAN VILLAGES — 1980

KNIGHT INLET

BUTE INLET

HOMALCO

KLAHUSE

JERVIS INLET

DESOLATION
SOUND

KWAKIUTL
(1860)

Quadra I.

SQUAMISH

SLIAMMAN

HOWE SOUND

TEXADA ISLAND

COMOX

SECHELT

VANCOUVER

NOT TO BE USED FOR NAVIGATION

Portion of
VANCOUVER'S CHART
JUNE 13 to JULY 15
1792
—— TRACK OF HMS DISCOVERY
AND HMS CHATHAM
••••• TRACK OF SHIPS BOATS
⚓ ANCHORAGE

15 JULY

26 JUNE
13 JULY

14 JULY

13 JULY

18 JUNE

DESOLATION SOUND

Savary's Isle

Hartwoods I.

Pt. Marshall

THE

19 JUNE

Scotch Fir Point

Jervis Canal

Canal de Nuestra Senora del Rosario

21 JUNE

4 JUNE

G

U

I

P

15 JUNE

H

Howe Sound

Pt. Atkinson

Burrard's

13-24 JUNE 1792

E

A

A CHART
shewing part of the
COAST OF N.W AMERICA,
with the tracks of His *MAJESTY's* Sloop
DISCOVERY and Armed Tender CHATHAM;
Commanded by GEORGE VANCOUVER Esqr and prepared
under his immediate inspection by Lieu^t. Joseph Baker, in which
the Continental Shore has been traced and determined from
Lat: 45. 30. N. and Long. 236. 12 E. to Lat: 52. 15 N. and Long. 231. 40 E .
at the different periods shewn by the Tracks
The parts not shaded are taken from Spanish Authorities .
denotes the Vessels track Northward   their return Southward

CARTA ESFERICA
DE LOS RECONOCIMIENTOS HECHOS
EN LA COSTA NO. DE AMERICA
desde la parte en que empiezan á angostar
LOS CANALES DE LA ENTRADA
DE JUAN DE FUCA
hasta la salida de las Goletas
SUTIL Y MEXICANA.
AÑO DE 1795.
(from Carta reducida, 1793)

Enlarged portion of GALIANO
and VALDES preliminary chart
showing passage through
Desolation Sound, Arran Rapids,
Dent Rapids and Cordero
Channel.

1778-1846, Discovery Press, 1975) note:

"By and large, examining the record of the HBC, it is impossible not to be impressed by the fairness and equity, and at times the kindness and understanding, with which the HBC dealt with the Indians. And the HBC men reaped their reward. Whereas the American trading ships by their outrageous tactics had filled the Indians with hatred for the "Boston men", every Indian knew that, though the Boston men were bad, the "King George men" were good. Visitors to British Columbia, right through to the latter part of the nineteenth century, were impressed by how consistently and relentlessly the Indians held by that distinction. No doubt the Royal Navy, the Royal Engineers and the early colonial administrators did a fair bit to support this article of faith, but it was the HBC to which the main credit must be given. Anachronistically the Indians still called the British and the Canadians "King George men" far into the reign of Queen Victoria. A principal reason why the

nineteenth century passed without any wars between the Indians and the whites in the British territories was "... the nameless awe in which Indians held sacred the persons of those whom they knew to be King George's Tyhees (i.e. persons in authority)". When the Americans launched their wars against the Indians in Washington Territory, no HBC man was ever attacked by the embattled Indians. In consequence, terrified American settlers presented themselves at the HBC posts seeking to purchase as safe disguises the capots which were, in effect, the uniform of the HBC engagés. No episode could bear more eloquent testimony to what the HBC had achieved by fairness and firmness."

Unfortunately for the Indians, what the Americans could not accomplish with firearms or "outrageous tactics" was achieved by other means. Only a few short years after the 1858 gold rush brought tens of thousands of American gold seekers into B.C., the Indian population was almost annilhilated by introduced diseases — smallpox, tuberculosis and alcohol — which could not be controlled by the HBC. Those Indians who survived this onslaught were robbed of much of what was left of their cultural heritage by museum "expeditions" and by misconceived government policies which banned the potlatch and consolidated villages. Many Indians moved to urban areas as the villages were abandoned. In recent years, however, native populations have returned to pre-1858 levels and there is an increased awareness of traditional values, native pride and an effort to reoccupy ancestral homelands.

SETTLEMENT AND INDUSTRIES

Around the end of the nineteenth century, white settlement along the coast increased dramatically. The protected waterways provided relatively safe access for all manner of rowboats, sailing skiffs and steamboats to the richly abundant fish and timber resources. This was the era of individual enterprise; handloggers and handliners flourished. In a few places — minerals (Shoal Bay) and small patches of agricultural land (Southern Quadra, Cortes, Read and other islands) attracted miners and homesteaders.

Many settlers became proficient in all aspects of coastal survival — at various times they logged, fished, prospected and tended farms or gardens; but it was a very hard life as detailed in the fascinating coastal novels of Maud Emery (The Seagulls Cry), M. A. Grainger (Woodsmen of the West) and B. Sinclair (The Hidden Places).

In the early part of this century, the extraction of resources became more organized and consolidated with the establishment of regular steamship stops, canneries (Redonda Bay and Quathiaski Cove) and larger logging camps built on shore as well as on the traditional log raft. The "permanent" population reached a zenith in the 1920s, but dropped off sharply due to prolonged hardships of isolation, the depression, and the higher cost of transport beyond the areas with road access. Many of the descendants of these early pioneers have moved into the larger towns which mark the "edge" of civilization — Powell River and Campbell River — but many can still be found in isolated bays and coves of the Channels and Inlets and among the Discovery Islands which border Desolation Sound.

Powell River and Campbell River serve as the major service centres for the northern Strait of Georgia population and in addition, are the locations for two large pulp mills — McMillan-Bloedel at Powell River and Crown Zellerbach at Duncan Bay. The population of these two towns now comprises over 26,000 people (1976 census) — 90% of the total number of people living between Texada Island and Johnstone Strait. Powell River and Campbell River also have the highest percentage of boat-owning households in Canada — over 40% for Campbell River, and 45% for Powell River. This helps to explain why there is a relative abundance of marine facilities — parks, moorage and fueling docks available for the use of cruising yachtsmen.

The permanent population of the Discovery Islands is relatively sparse — Texada - 1002, Quadra - 521, Cortes - 407, Stuart - 52, Read - 34, West Redonda (Refuge Cove) - 23, Savary - 21, Sonora - 7, Maurelle - 2 (1976 census); but these numbers swell by as much as ten times (for the smaller islands) during the summer months.

SETTLEMENT, ROADS, MARINAS AND PARKS

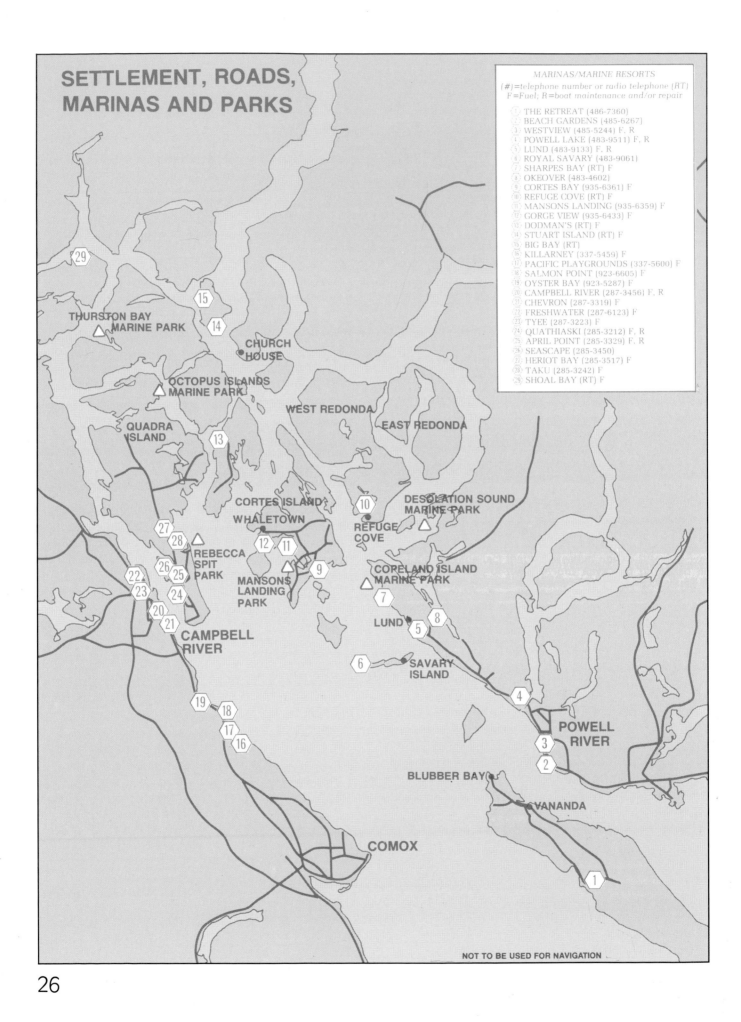

MARINAS/MARINE RESORTS
(#)=telephone number or radio telephone (RT)
F=Fuel; R=boat maintenance and/or repair

1. THE RETREAT (486-7360)
2. BEACH GARDENS (485-6267)
3. WESTVIEW (485-5244) F, R
4. POWELL LAKE (483-9511) F, R
5. LUND (483-9133) F. R
6. ROYAL SAVARY (483-9061)
7. SHARPES BAY (RT) F
8. OKEOVER (483-4602)
9. CORTES BAY (935-6361) F
10. REFUGE COVE (RT) F
11. MANSONS LANDING (935-6359) F
12. GORGE VIEW (935-6433) F
13. DODMAN'S (RT) F
14. STUART ISLAND (RT) F
15. BIG BAY (RT)
16. KILLARNEY (337-5459) F
17. PACIFIC PLAYGROUNDS (337-5600) F
18. SALMON POINT (923-6605) F
19. OYSTER BAY (923-5287) F
20. CAMPBELL RIVER (287-3456) F, R
21. CHEVRON (287-3319) F
22. FRESHWATER (287-6123) F
23. TYEE (287-3223) F
24. QUATHIASKI (285-3212) F, R
25. APRIL POINT (285-3329) F, R
26. SEASCAPE (285-3450)
27. HERIOT BAY (285-3517) F
28. TAKU (285-3242) F
29. SHOAL BAY (RT) F

THURSTON BAY MARINE PARK

CHURCH HOUSE

OCTOPUS ISLANDS MARINE PARK

QUADRA ISLAND

WEST REDONDA

EAST REDONDA

CORTES ISLAND
WHALETOWN

DESOLATION SOUND MARINE PARK

REFUGE COVE

REBECCA SPIT PARK

MANSONS LANDING PARK

COPELAND ISLAND MARINE PARK

CAMPBELL RIVER

LUND

SAVARY ISLAND

POWELL RIVER

BLUBBER BAY

VANANDA

COMOX

NOT TO BE USED FOR NAVIGATION

Land and Air Transportation

The major car ferry route linking the lower mainland with Desolation Sound is via the Sunshine Coast (Earls Cove to Saltery Bay - 5 miles east of Thunder Bay). From Vancouver Island there are ferry routes from Little River, north of Comox, to Powell River and from Campbell River to Quathiaski Cove on Quadra Island and then from Heriot Bay (Quadra Island) to Whaletown on Cortes Island. There is also ferry access from Powell River to Blubber Bay on Texada Island. Small boats which can be transported by car can use these access routes to launching sites in protected harbours at the terminus of road access.

Scheduled floatplane service is also available from Vancouver to Campbell River and to many of the small communities within Desolation Sound and the Discovery Islands.

Parks

Between Texada Island, Comox and Johnstone Strait there are over forty parks or park reserves. Most of these serve as small community recreation areas, but there is one major park with facilities for camping and a nature house (Miracle Beach) and five designated marine parks for cruising yachts and other small boats. The largest marine park (Desolation Sound) comprises a total area larger than all the other marine parks in the province combined and serves also as the largest park of any kind on the mainland coast of British Columbia.

Marinas

Major marinas and resorts are indicated on the accompanying map. More details of these and other marine facilities are included in Part II of this guide. Up-to-date information on marine services and facilities and resort accommodation can be obtained from Appendices I, II and III of the *Small Craft Guides* and from the annual *Accommodation Directory* for B.C.

Emergency telephone numbers and other contacts in the major settlements (RCMP, Ambulance, Fire, Medical facilities, etc.) are listed in Appendices IV and V of the *Small Craft Guides*.

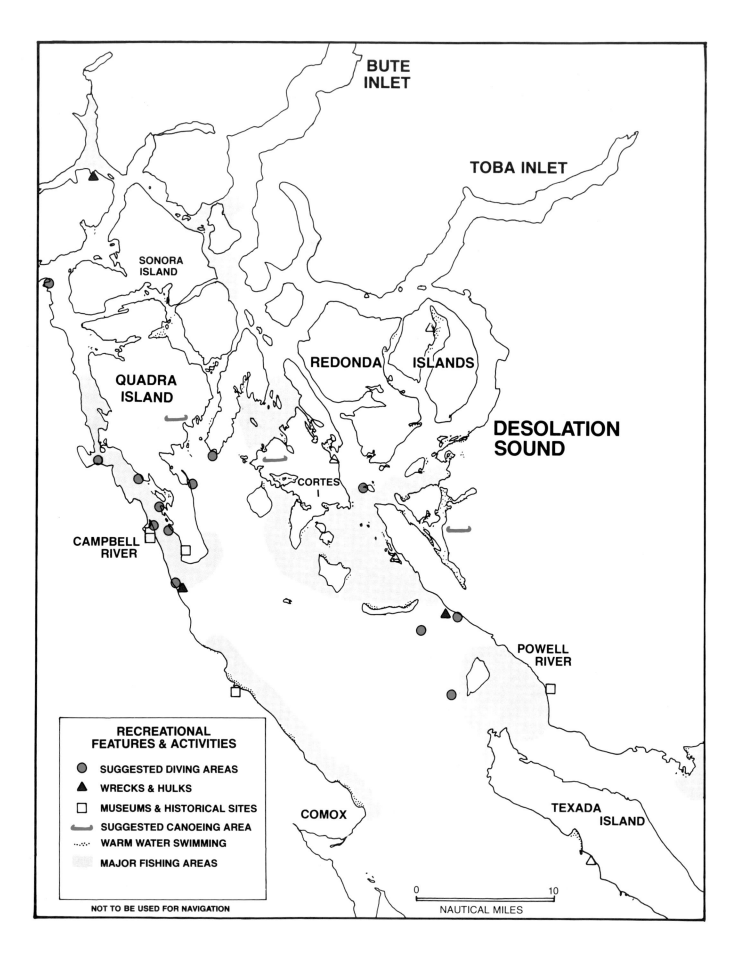

BUTE
INLET

TOBA INLET

SONORA
ISLAND

REDONDA   ISLANDS

QUADRA
ISLAND

DESOLATION
SOUND

CORTES

CAMPBELL
RIVER

POWELL
RIVER

RECREATIONAL
FEATURES & ACTIVITIES

● SUGGESTED DIVING AREAS

▲ WRECKS & HULKS

□ MUSEUMS & HISTORICAL SITES

⌐ SUGGESTED CANOEING AREA

∵ WARM WATER SWIMMING

▒ MAJOR FISHING AREAS

COMOX

TEXADA
ISLAND

0   10

NOT TO BE USED FOR NAVIGATION

NAUTICAL MILES

Exploring on Land, Beachcombing

The shorelines of the northern Strait of Georgia and the southernmost of the Discovery Islands are ideal for beachcombing. Where there are long sandy beaches (see Geology map, page 13) one can walk for miles at low tide. Crown foreshore (all land between high and low tide) is open to public access in Canada, but one should respect the privacy of upland property residents.

Many old logging roads abound throughout this area. Where these roads have been abandoned, they may be thickly overgrown and almost impassable, but in some areas they provide an excellent opportunity for inland exploration — bypassing logging camp ruins, discarded rusting machinery, deserted homesteads and orchards, warm fresh water lakes and rocky outcrops with splendid views over the surrounding waterways. A few of these old roads and trails as well as the paved and unpaved secondary roads are shown on the maps described in Part II of this guide and on pages 12 and 26.

Features and Activities

Opportunities for swimming in unusually warm (65 to 75°F) saltwater can be found close to the junction line of the major tidal streams as depicted on the map on page 10. Particularly warm waters (up to 80°F) can occasionally be found within Pendrell Sound and in various secluded bays with little tidal exchange in Desolation Sound. Colder waters are often warmed where they flow over sunbaked tidal sands, particularly on Savary and Hernando Islands and off Miracle Beach on Vancouver Island.

Fishing for salmon and cod is a popular pastime throughout this area and oysters and clams are still relatively abundant in Desolation Sound. Care should be exercised in taking only as many as one really needs and in heeding red tide and other pollution warnings.

The map opposite also indicates a few popular underwater exploration areas (as described by Betty Pratt-Johnson in *141 Dives*) and some prominent wrecks or hulks (some described by Fred Rogers in *Shipwrecks of B.C.*). Canoeing and other small boat (kayaks, rowboats) exploring is possible in much of the Discovery Island-Desolation Sound area, but tidal passes and open coasts should be avoided by small craft operators inexperienced in dealing with rough water conditions. Three protected areas, which are readily accessible by road for easy launching, include — the Village Lakes chain on Quadra Island (Chapter 11), Cortes Island lakes, lagoons (Chapters 9 and 10), and Okeover Inlet to Desolation Sound (Chapters 3 and 6).

Part Two

Cruising Guide to
DESOLATION SOUND
and the Discovery Islands

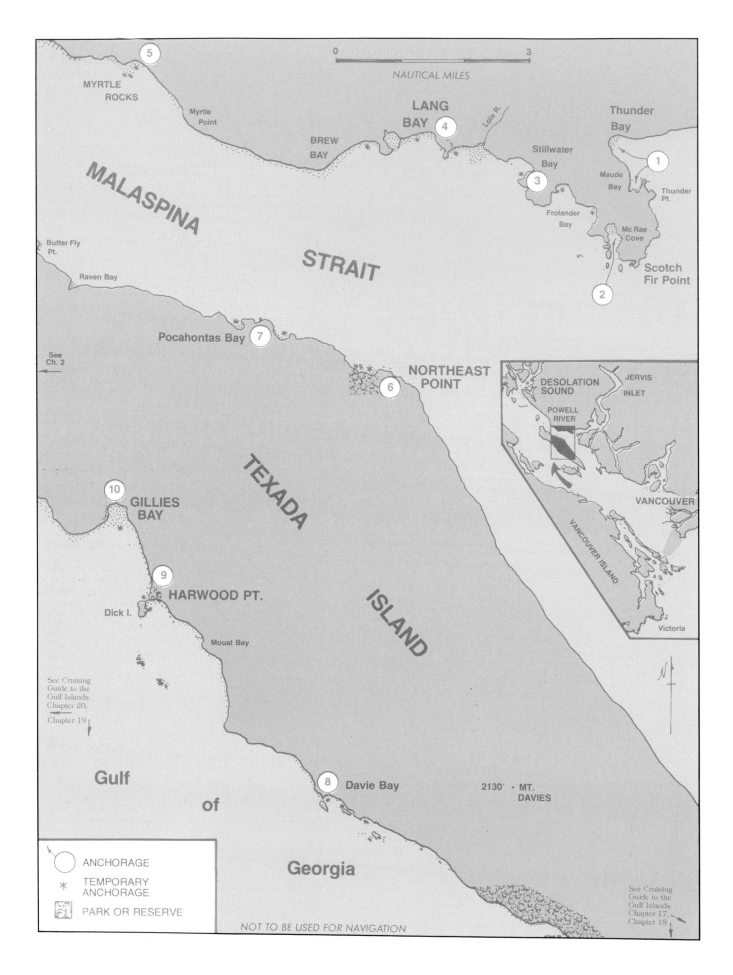

NAUTICAL MILES

MYRTLE
ROCKS

Myrtle
Point

BREW
BAY

LANG
BAY ④

Lois R.

Thunder
Bay

Stillwater
Bay

Maude
Bay

Thunder
Pt.

③

Frolander
Bay

Mc Rae
Cove

Scotch
Fir Point

MALASPINA

Butter Fly
Pt.

Raven Bay

STRAIT

②

See
Ch. 2

Pocahontas Bay ⑦

NORTHEAST
POINT

⑥

TEXADA

⑩
GILLIES
BAY

ISLAND

⑨
HARWOOD PT.

Dick I.

Mouat Bay

See Cruising
Guide to the
Gulf Islands
Chapter 20,
Chapter 19

DESOLATION
SOUND

JERVIS
INLET

POWELL
RIVER

VANCOUVER

VANCOUVER ISLAND

Victoria

N

Gulf

⑧ Davie Bay

2130′ · MT.
DAVIES

of

Georgia

ANCHORAGE

TEMPORARY
ANCHORAGE

PARK OR RESERVE

See Cruising
Guide to the
Gulf Islands
Chapter 17,
Chapter 18

NOT TO BE USED FOR NAVIGATION

CHAPTER ONE

Texada Island

Northern Malaspina Strait, Thunder Bay and Gillies Bay

Malaspina Strait, along the eastern shore of Texada Island, serves as the main route for cruising boats and other small craft voyaging north to Desolation Sound from Vancouver or from Nanaimo on the Vancouver Island side of Georgia Strait. Fewer boats cruise north along the Vancouver Island shore, but for those that do, information on that route is included in Chapters 16 and 20 of *Pacific Yachting's Cruising Guide to the Gulf Islands,* and in Chapters 13 to 16 of this Guide.

The northern tip of Texada Island, across Malaspina Strait from the large community of Powell River, is the most densely populated part of the island where most of the remaining population of 1,200 live. Almost a century ago, the population of Texada was greater than that of any comparable area in the northern Gulf.

Proceeding out of Jervis Inlet, the mainland shore north of Scotch Fir Point offers a few possibilities for reasonably protected anchorage when winds are from the west or northwest. With southeast winds, more protection is afforded on the Texada Island side of Malaspina Strait. The most protection from either northwest or southeast winds can be found within Jervis Inlet at Thunder Bay.

1 Thunder Bay

Thunder Bay and two smaller bays ½-mile to the south are well protected from most summer winds. The *Small Craft Guide* notes that Thunder Bay is "one of the few places in the inlet (Jervis) where anchorage can be obtained", meaning that it is ideal for large boats which normally anchor in depths from 15 to 20 fathoms with excellent holding ground over a sand bottom. There is a wide boulder studded beach which shallows quickly around the head of the bay and is surrounded by portions of open land and private homes.

The small bay immediately to the south is known locally as Maude Bay and is more enclosed and surrounded by woods with a few small cottages. Pasture land can be glimpsed through the trees at the head of the cove which is divided by a small peninsula. Although there are boulders on the beach all around the shoreline of Thunder Bay down to a rock in Maude Bay charted as drying 7 feet, the rest of the Maude Bay foreshore is relatively boulder-free and composed of soft sand making it possible to anchor closer to shore with a rising tide, despite the shallow depths. Warm waters provide excellent opportunities for swimming. The peninsula which separates Maude Bay from the next bay north of Thunder Point has deceptive spits stretching out from both sides of its head. Another beautiful white sand and gravel beach is located at the head of the small ¾-fathom cove northwest of Scotch Fir Point.

Northern Malaspina Strait

2 McRae Cove

This cove is seldom used as an anchorage due to its exposure to any winds blowing up Malaspina Strait and to the number of rocks and drying passages scattered between the islets which guard the entrance. The chart also indicates that tide rips and overfalls develop off Scotch Fir Point where diverging tidal streams meet contrary winds blowing in or out of

CHARTS
3590 — BALLENAS ISLANDS to CAPE LAZO
        (for southern Texada Island) (1:77,000)
3591 — CAPE LAZO to DISCOVERY PASSAGE
        (for northern Malaspina Strait)
        (1:76,400)
3508 — Plan of STILL WATER BAY (1:12,000)

Maude Bay, with Malaspina Strait in the background.

Jervis Inlet. McRae Cove is shallow but well protected from west or northwest winds. With a strong southeast wind blowing, swells entering the cove might steepen and break as the bottom shallows, making this anchorage uncomfortable. There is a private float

McRae Cove is shallow, with rocks and drying passages between the islets along the entrance, but is well protected from westerlies.

moored permanently in the centre of the cove. The head of the cove dries out completely and there is a long string of boom sticks stretching out over the mudflats. Pastoral farmland stretches beyond an old farmhouse — the home of the McRae family who have farmed here since the 1890s.

Frolander Bay is only moderately protected from northwest or southerly winds but temporary anchorage is possible here or in the more settled cove to the north. This latter cove is particularly well protected from the westerly wind and a small rocky peninsula jutting out from the western shore might provide limited protection from southeasterlies.

3   Stillwater Bay

Stillwater Bay offers more protection from southeasterlies than any of the other bays or coves on the mainland side of northern Malaspina Strait. Logs are boomed at the head of the bay and along the southern shoreline where one can tie alongside temporarily. The bay is open to westerly winds. A water tank surge tower rises 490 feet above sea level behind a small power plant and serves as a conspicuous landmark for vessels navigating through Malaspina Strait. The power plant is supplied with water from Lois Lake, 2 miles to the north. This lake was formerly known as

34

Gordon Pasha Lake after General Gordon of Khartoum fame but was renamed after it was dammed and the water level raised.

4 Lang Bay

The delta of the Lois River protrudes out into Malaspina Inlet for almost half a mile but temporary anchorage is possible between the delta and a rocky peninsula which provides protection from westerly winds. This anchorage is very shallow and the bottom is hard sand which grades into gravel at the top of the beach below a driftwood covered berm. The beaches here, at Lang Bay itself and in Brew Bay, are all composed largely of fine white clean sand — perfect for swimming and sunbathing when the weather is fair. There is a small 8-acre community park here which was formerly known as Palm Beach Park; but for the most part, the entire shoreline from here north to Powell River is private and moderately settled.

On the other side of the rocky peninsula (east end of Lang Bay proper), there is an old government wharf which now serves as a fuel oil distribution dock for large vessels. The Seabreeze Cabins and campsite provides accommodation ashore, hot showers, toilets and opportunities for swimming and fishing in Lang Bay. There is a large breakwater protected log dumping and booming basin at the west end of Lang Bay which dries out completely at low tide. The basin is not as actively used as formerly and could potentially serve to shelter small boats if partially dredged or as a community park as much of the surrounding land has not been developed.

5 Myrtle Rocks

Temporary anchorage with reasonable protection from westerly seas at low tide is possible behind the Myrtle Rocks. The rocks and surrounding foreshore are designated as a regional park primarily to protect bird nests on the rocks. The coast highway runs just above the beach east of Myrtle Rocks. Aside from the noise of traffic and lack of seclusion from surrounding homes, there is a fair beach for swimming, sunbathing and beachcombing.

The Myrtle Creek valley behind the beach and mainland hillsides up to Cranberry Lake, behind Powell River were burned over in an immense forest fire after the First World War. The forests were not considered of much value then and many homesteaders moved in to establish farms on the new "agricultural land" created by the removal of the forest cover. Attempts were made to raise sheep — a precarious pastime on the edge of the wilderness — and much time was spent in hunting and trapping predatory wolves and cougars. There was also a great abundance of salmon, trout, grouse and wild berries. The joys and hardships of these early settlers are recounted in "Pioneers in Paradise", the last story in *Raincoast Chronicles First Five* (Harbour Publishing, 1976.)

View south over Lang Bay down Malaspina Strait.

Texada Island

The extreme southern tip of Texada Island is described in the *Cruising Guide to the Gulf Islands* (Chapter 17), so this concerns the northern portion. Texada Island was first named by the Spanish explorer Jose Maria Narvaez in 1791. In 1792, Captain George Vancouver referred to the island as "Favada", possibly a misreading of the charts carried by Galiano and Valdes. Vancouver also appears to have misinterpreted the Spanish charts when he named Malaspina Strait the "Canal del Neustra Signora del Rosario" — the name given by the Spaniards to the whole of Vancouver's "Gulf of Georgia". Although Captain Malaspina's name appears several times in the Gulf (on the easternmost point of Gabriola Island, and on the Peninsula and Inlet north of Lund) there is no evidence that this "most romantic figure among the navigators of the north Pacific" (Walbran) ever sailed here. Malaspina Strait itself was named in 1859 by Captain Richards, H.M. surveying vessel *Plumper*.

Texada Island, the largest in the Gulf of Georgia proper, has been variously referred to as "Treasure

Temporary shelter from westerlies is possible at low tide behind Myrtle Rocks.

Pocahontas Bay is near the former site of one of the biggest whiskey stills on the coast.

Island'' due to its mineral wealth or as the ''jewel of the Gulf'' on account of the extremely equable climate with less than 34-in. of rain annually and an average summer temperature of over 21°C. Texada is unique in that there are no native Indian place names (other than Pocahontas, an eastern North American name) on the island. Apparently, an old legend prophesies that the island will sink beneath the sea just as suddenly as it originally came out of the sea. It has in fact risen 424 feet since the last glacial period, 10,000 years ago. The huge limestone quarries south of Vananda may be assisting in the fulfillment of this prophecy, albeit more gradually than might have been anticipated by the Indians.

The entire coast of Texada is devoid of completely protected safe anchorage until one reaches Vananda, near the northern tip. Although the steeply abrupt and visually monotonous coastline discourages any interest in close exploration for over 25 miles of its 30 mile length, temporary shelter from southeasterlies is available in a few indentations west of Northeast Point.

Log boom basin in Lang Bay and Brew Bay on right.

6   Northeast Point

Half a mile northwest of Northeast Point there is a small bight which could provide temporary anchorage or shelter, particularly when a strong southeaster is blowing. A 42-acre recreational reserve covers the upland behind this bight and a small 1.5-acre islet about 150 yards offshore. There is sufficient flat land behind a large gravel and stone delta and other small beaches to set up a tent. Some protection from westerly winds is also possible behind the small islet, but care should be taken to avoid rocks which extend southeast of this islet toward the Texada shore.

7   Pocahontas Bay

This bay and a small nook and larger bight to the southeast could also provide shelter from southeasterlies. The eastern corner of Pocahontas Bay has been used as a log dump and booming area and there is a road from here which connects with the main road system on the island. It is near here that one of the largest whiskey stills on the B.C. coast provided huge quantites of booze for U.S. drinkers during Prohibition.

Raven Bay is shallow and while it may appear that both this bay and the bight inside Butterfly Point to the north might offer some protection from westerlies, such is not the case.

West Shore of Texada Island

The western shore of Texada Island is seldom explored by cruising yachtsmen due to its more open exposure but it does offer a more interesting coastline than the eastern side of Texada with several tiny islets close offshore. Almost all of the bays and indentations are open to the southeast but several offer varying degrees of protection from west or northwest winds. The western corner of Cook Bay and two indentations south of Partington Point (not shown on the map) offer moderate shelter from westerlies. A 450-acre recreational reserve covers three miles of pea-gravel beach shoreline from Cook Bay north towards Davie Bay.

8   Davie Bay

Davie Bay includes several islets and rocks, some of which are connected by tombolo spits to Texada Island. The most protection from westerlies is afforded behind the largest island which is connected at its northern end to Texada by a low sandy spit which just uncovers at low water. At high tide westerly seas could enter the bay over the spit. In southeasterly weather, some protection might be afforded in a small nook behind an islet connected to the southern end of Davie Bay. There is an old logging road from here which connects up with the island road system behind Harwood Point.

Mouat Bay and the Mouat Islets are named after Captain William Alexander Mouat who served in the

Hudson Bay Company on this coast between 1845 and 1871. He died in Knight Inlet while on a canoe journey to Fort Rupert. Much of Mouat Bay is open to all winds. The charted "hulk" marks a breakwater protected log dump and booming ground which dries out at low tide.

9   Harwood Point

The most protection from westerlies on this side of Texada Island is just inside Dick Island south of Harwood Point (formerly known as Shelter Island and Point). Harwood Point is named after Admiral Harwood, R.N. in command of H.M. cruisers *Ajax*, *Exeter* and *Achilles* in the battle of the River Plate against the German battleship *Graf Spee*, December, 1939. Dick Island is joined to Texada by a classic tombolo spit, the apex of which covers with water at about 10 feet of tide. The height of the spit connection with Dick Island will change from year to year depending on the amount of erosion and deposition resulting from winter storms. In southeast weather, shelter from seas is provided on the north side of the spit. There are pilings from an old wharf here, the outermost of which is in sufficiently deep water to tie to.

The upper part of the beaches from Harwood Point around to Gillies Bay is shingle type gravel and at low tide fine sand is exposed. There is a 40-acre regional park here with grass fields and picnic tables, campsites, toilets and changing rooms. Frieda Van der Ree in her book *Exploring the Coast by Boat* enthusiastically describes the wonders of this part of Texada Island with miles of pebble beach and opportunities for beachcombing and rockhounding in search of the "flower rock", a black porphyry with bursts of white crystal blossoms. Nearby is "The Retreat" a summer resort with rental boats, fishing tackle and housekeeping units providing a panoramic view of the beach and Strait of Georgia.

Harwood Point was formerly known as Shelter Point, is now site of 40-acre regional park.

There are many logging roads for hiking which continue inland and down the coast from the terminus of the main Texada road behind Harwood Point.

10   Gillies Bay

Gillies Bay boasts one of the largest south-facing sandy beaches in the Gulf of Georgia. Although marked as an anchorage on the chart, it is not particularly suitable for medium to small sized boats, except in calm weather. Smaller boats can be hauled ashore if the wind gets up or, at high tide with winds from the northwest, can find more shelter at the head of Gillies Bay.

Although Texada Mines, a huge open pit and underground copper and iron mine 3 miles up the coast from Gillies Bay closed down in 1977 after more than 24 years of operation, the community of Gillies Bay continues to survive. At the head of the bay there is a general store, cafe and service station and further inland are a bank and liquor store. There is a thin, ¼-mile long, 25-foot wide strip of recreational reserve just above the western shoreline of the bay.

Gillies Bay has one of the largest south-facing beaches in the Gulf.

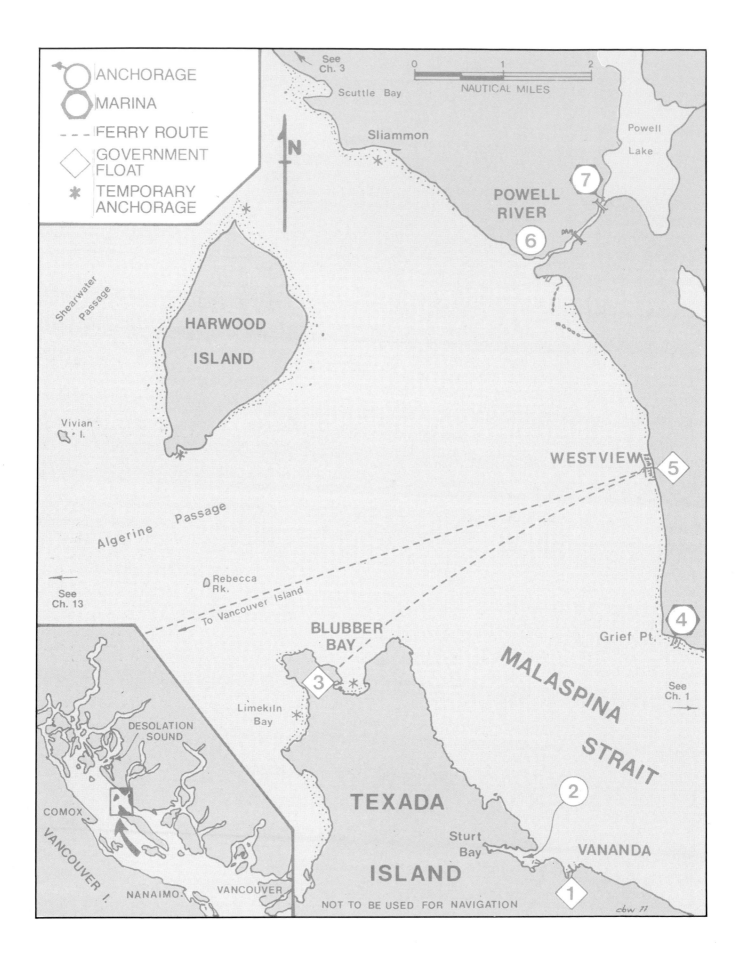

ANCHORAGE
MARINA
FERRY ROUTE
GOVERNMENT FLOAT
TEMPORARY ANCHORAGE

N

See Ch. 3

Scuttle Bay

NAUTICAL MILES

Sliammon

Powell Lake

POWELL RIVER

7

6

DAM

Shearwater Passage

HARWOOD ISLAND

WESTVIEW

5

Vivian I.

Algerine Passage

See Ch. 13

Rebecca Rk.

To Vancouver Island

4

Grief Pt.

MALASPINA

BLUBBER BAY

3

See Ch. 1

Limekiln Bay

DESOLATION SOUND

STRAIT

TEXADA

2

COMOX

Sturt Bay

VANANDA

VANCOUVER I.

ISLAND

1

NANAIMO

VANCOUVER

NOT TO BE USED FOR NAVIGATION

cbw 71

CHAPTER TWO

Powell River and Northern Texada Island

Vananda, Blubber Bay, Westview

The end of Malaspina Strait comes none to soon for many yachtsmen voyaging north to Desolation Sound. You feel you are almost there, as the enclosing shores of the mainland and Texada Island melt away to reveal the open vistas and low lying islands of the northern Gulf. In the distance, the peaks of the Coast Mountains seem to loom nearer, beckoning one onwards.

This feeling of expectation may be accentuated by a distinct change in the weather, such as a break in the cloud cover or an abrupt shift in the wind direction or alteration in wind speed. The winds of Malaspina Strait do not seem to be affected as much by diurnal trends as do other, more open parts of the Gulf. Winds tend to be channelled by the topography to a much greater extent, blowing either up or down the Strait. If one has been assisted by a southeasterly while voyaging north, a change in wind direction may be welcome if it brings sunny skies even if it means a stiff beat for the last stretch into Desolation Sound. Quite often, a northwest wind which has been blowing strongly down Malaspina Strait will decrease in strength and back slightly to the west, once one has passed Grief Point.

Although a voyage north may bring weather which is at times either fierce or depressing, this is better than having the unchangeable calm of stable condi-tions. For as Daniel Boorstin has said: "when one risks so little or experiences so little on the voyage, the experience of being there somehow becomes emptier and more trivial. When getting there was more troublesome, being there was more vivid."

Desolation Sound — the mecca of many yachtsmen — may sometimes be best remembered in these terms by those who have been there. For many, to travel hopefully is better than arriving. Especially if one is unlucky enough to experience a three week downpour in the middle of summer.

For these conditions, Desolation Sound is a most appropriate name, but there is always the hope that next year may be better. Desolation Sound in sunshine is not easily forgotten.

CHARTS
3508 — **Plan of POWELL RIVER (1:12,000)**
    (discontinued)
3591 — **CAPE LAZO to DISCOVERY PASSAGE**
    (1:76,400)
3536 — **(Metric) — Plan of POWELL RIVER and**
    WESTVIEW (1:10,000)
    Plan of STURT BAY and VANANDA
    COVE (1:8,000)
BRITISH ADMIRALTY CHART 585
    — **Sturt Bay and Vananda Cove (1:7,330)**
    — **Blubber Bay (1:24,410)**

Government wharf in Vananda Cove is exposed to seas from most prevailing winds. Good anchorage can be found in Sturt Bay (top).

Northern Texada Island

1 Vananda

The government wharf in Vananda Cove has a tiny float for small craft attached to the inside (eastern) end of the wharf. This is a very exposed location and is seldom used except by occasional vessels loading or unloading supplies. The weather here is sometimes so fierce as to sink vessels only a short distance

Blubber Bay

from the wharf. In 1913 the Union Steamship *Cheslakee* sank off the wharf with the loss of six lives. The most ferocious seas experienced in the Gulf by the writer occurred at the end of May 1970 with a 40 to 45 mph northwester against a spring flood tide. We managed to scoot into Sturt Bay with a ripped mainsail and a thorough drenching.

Iron ore, gold, copper, pink marble and limestone have at one time or another brought men and women to Texada Island. In 1880 gold was found near here and the town of Vananda was born. Within 20 years, seven mines operated around the town which had three hotels, a saloon, hospital, stores, jail, an opera house and over 3,000 inhabitants. Today the gold is gone, but limestone is still quarried at several locations around the north end of the island and the tranquil atmosphere of island life continues to hold a permanent population of 1,200 people. Vananda now includes a store, machine shop, hotel and restaurant.

2 Sturt Bay

Good anchorage is available in Sturt Bay to the west of Vananda Cove. Although the Bay appears to be open to the east, safe anchorage is possible in settled weather north of the limestone diggings or immediately adjacent to the diggings in a small nook known as Marble Bay or Ceaser Cove. This nook contains floats and a marine ways. Until construction of the Westview government harbour, Marble Bay provided the only complete shelter for small craft in over 30 miles of coast. High quality marble from this location was used in the construction of the old Hotel Vancouver as well as many other Vancouver and Victoria buildings.

Just inside the entrance to Sturt Bay behind a stone breakwater on the south shore are the floats of the Texada Boating Club. When space permits, moorage is available for visiting boats at a nominal charge. From here one can explore the inland community of Vananda or the Sturt Bay shoreline looking for evidence of past settlement and mining activity. At high tide the many islets and tiny coves in the upper reaches of Sturt Bay are accessible by dinghy.

3 Blubber Bay

Although suitable as a temporary anchorage, this bay is subject to westerly swells and is completely open to any winds with a northerly component. There is a tiny government float located between the wharf and the ferry landing on the west side of the bay. The Blubber Bay Boat Club has small private floats at the head of the bay with one float for visiting boats. A large gravel quarry and barge loading operation occupies the west end of the bay.

Blubber Bay owes its name to its being used as a location for the rendering down of blubber from whales caught in the Gulf of Georgia in the 1870s. Harry Trim, the first permanent resident on Texada Island, was an astute fisherman who lived here at this time. While fishing the west coast of Texada one day, he noticed some brilliant red-orange rock on the hillside. Samples of this rock were given to the then premier of B.C., Amor de Cosmos (alias William Smith) who in true free enterprise fashion lined up some of his political colleagues with several entrepreneurs to look into the possibility of promoting the prospect. The subsequent scandal was followed by a Royal Commission which, although exonerating de Cosmos, led to his eventual downfall. Despite this early setback, the mining industry eventually established itself on Texada and although most of the economically recoverable iron ore and gold is now exhausted, limestone continues to be quarried.

Temporary anchorage is possible in Limekiln Bay. If the weather affords the opportunity, one can row ashore and explore the brick remains of the old kilns directly beneath a conspicuous slag pile. The limestone shoreline here is weirdly eroded — similar to sandstone but much more sharp and irregular. There is a very nice sand beach a few hundred feet south of the kilns.

4 Beach Gardens Marina

Just south of Grief Point, a stone-breakwater-protected boat basin provides moorage for patrons and guests of the Beach Gardens Resort Hotel. The new Grief Point weather station which submits regular reports for rebroadcast on local radio stations is also located here. Approximately 2,000 feet of moorage space is available for boats under 60 feet. In bad weather, caution should be exercised in entering the boat basin as small boats may be maneouvring out of sight behind the breakwater. Charter boats with special rates and facilities for scuba divers are provided. Beach Gardens is known as the "Diving Capital of Canada" for the colourful and varied marine life in the clear nearby waters. The resort itself includes tennis courts, jogging trail, indoor pool and sauna, restaurant, lounge and pub as well as accommodation. There is a small grocery store one block away and the marina provides a free bus into Westview.

The shoreline between Grief Point and Westview provides shelter from southeasterly seas and is often used for the temporary storage of log booms.

Moorage is available in private marina for guests of Beach Gardens Resort, the "Diving Capital of Canada."

Marble Bay, looking across Sturt Bay Floats toward Westview.

Powell River

5 Westview

Temporary moorage for visiting boats is available in the commercial fishing boat harbour (south basin), south of the Westview ferry dock. A fuel barge is located in this south basin and there are facilities for marine repairs. Ferries from Blubber Bay on Texada Island and Little River on Vancouver Island dock at the wharf between the south basin and the north basin. The north basin is used primarily for resident boat moorage.

The town of Westview is the main suburb of Powell River and is situated to avoid the effluent from the Powell River mill. The Powell River area, including Westview, has a population of over 20,000. In Westview there is an excellent book store, marine chandlers, laundromats, pubs and almost all other large town facilities within easy walking distance of the boat basin. The nearest liquor store and shopping centre are located a few blocks up the hill north of Joyce Avenue.

Willingdon Beach Municipal Park is located half a mile north of the boat basin adjacent to picnic grounds and campsites with hot showers and a laun-

Ferrocement Liberty ships form a breakwater at Powell River mill.

dromat. There is a nature trail from here which parallels Willingdon Creek for about a mile. Directly across Marine Avenue from the Park is the Powell River Historical Museum which is noted for its display of pioneer and logging tools, Indian and local history, and an excellent archival section.

6 Powell River

Powell River is named after Dr. Israel Wood Powell who came to British Columbia from Ontario in 1862. Of Loyalist background, he fought to include B.C. in Confederation and was instrumental in choosing the location for the City of Vancouver. Powell River is the site of one of the world's largest single-unit newsprint mills, and the town is easily identifiable by the tall chimneys dispensing plumes of effluent into the atmosphere. Strangely enough, Powell River is noted for its very low incidence of fog and claims to have more hours of sunshine than Hawaii.

An encircling breakwater of floating hulks protects a large log storage basin. These hulks present a dramatic aspect to the Powell River shoreline and have a varied history. The oldest hulls, some of which have been replaced, include the former U.S. cruisers *Charleston* and *Huron* built prior to World War I and the *Malaspina,* one time pride of the Canadian Fisheries Patrol and the scourge of rum runners in the prohibition era. During the first World War she assisted in the navy patrol of B.C. waters. There is the old sailing vessel *Island Carrier* built in 1892 and the proud tanker *Albertolite* which carried oil across the Atlantic in World War I and from Ecuador to Ioco, B.C. in World War II. There are also several ferrocement ships built over the last 60 years for wartime service. Most of the hulks have had their superstructures removed and grass grows thick on their decks, but the outline of gun turrets and what appear to be bullet pock-marks (seagull droppings?) are apparent. Although many are listing noticeably, most are said to be completely watertight below the waterline as the cement improves by curing with age.

There are no facilities for small craft moorage at Powell River itself, but visitors can walk the two or

Smoke from paper mill at Powell River can be seen for miles.

Government Wharf at Westview. Visiting yachts must use southern (lower) section only, as northern floats are reserved for residents.

Remains of limekilns — intriguing relics in Limekiln Bay.

three miles from Westview or take a taxi. Visitors may also tour the McMillan Bloedel pulp and paper mill every weekday at 10 a.m. or 2 p.m. between May and August.

Powell Lake is located behind the mill, less than a mile from the sea. Powell River itself is less than ½-mile long, even shorter than it was originally, before it was dammed in 1910 to provide power for the mill. The dam raised the level of Powell Lake which extends behind Powell River for more than 30 miles and provides excellent fresh water boating, fishing and camping in an area seldom seen by anyone other than Powell River residents.

7   Powell Lake Marina

This marina provides fuel, moorage, boat and motor repairs and rentals, boat launching ramp and coffee shop. A government wharf nearby is used primarily by float planes.

Harwood Island

Harwood Island, an uninhabited Indian Reserve 3 miles west of Powell River, is composed entirely (except for the southern tip) of glacial drift deposits and is ringed with boulder-studded sand and gravel beaches. Temporary anchorage close to shore is possible in a small cove at the southern end with fairly good protection from westerly seas, or off the spit at the northern tip of the island in good weather.

The island was named by Vancouver on June 25, 1792, after Edward Harwood, the classical scholar and biblical critic who served as a surgeon in the navy, notably under Captain William "Bread Fruit"

Bligh of H.M.S. *Bounty* fame. Vancouver was not too impressed with the local scenery as he noted in his journal:

> on the coast of the mainland, opposite this island is a small brook probably of fresh water (Powell River), from whence as we advanced the shores put on a very dreary aspect, chiefly composed of rugged rocks thinly wooded with small dwarf pine trees.

Although Walbran states that this description is "as applicable now (1906) as it was 114 years ago", it is interesting to note how the Spaniards, Galiano and Valdes, described the general area in their journal on June 25, 1792 as they sailed by in company with Vancouver:

> It would certainly be impossible to find a more delightful view than that which is here presented by the diversity of trees and shrubs, by the loveliness of the flowers and the beauty of the fruit, by the variety of animals and birds. When to this is added the pleasure of listening to the song of birds, the observer is afforded many occasions for admiring the works of nature and for delighting his senses as he contemplates the majestic outlines of the mountains, covered with pines and capped with snow, when he sees the most glorious cascades falling from them and reaching the ground below with awe-inspiring rapidity, breaking the silence of these lonely districts, and by their united waters forming powerful rivers which serve to give life to the plants on their banks, and in which a large number of salmon are bred. When any men are met, although they are of a different appearance and colour, it is clear that they are of the same species from the similarity of their ideas, and the observer will see that, denied those advantages which are believed to be indispensable for life, these men are yet very intelligent, strong and cheerful, and that, without the aid which is supplied by the study and perfection of the arts, they still know how to provide themselves with the necessary sustenance, to supply their wants and to defend themselves against their enemies. (From *A Spanish Voyage to Vancouver and the North-West Coast of America*, translated by Cecil Jane, 1930).

Harwood Island was named I. de Concha by the Spaniards according to their 1795 map.

The Indian village of Sliammon is typical of many villages on the B.C. coast with its row of colourful shorefront homes clustered around a conspicuous white church. There is a small boat basin just south of the outlet of Sliammon Creek which dries at low water.

Scuttle Bay is suitable only for temporary anchorage by shallow draught boats at high tide in southeasterly weather. The bay possibly derives its name from its use by Commander Hodgson when he beached his exploratory ships here in order to scrape off barnacles. The Indian name is Klakewanum.

Three miles offshore and due west of Scuttle Bay, lies Mystery Reef. At high water nothing but a solitary black buoy marks the spot. But at midtide the vicious teeth of the reef begin to reveal themselves and at lowtide a particularly gruesome spectacle of jagged boulders half a mile in extent is exposed. Mystery Reef, including the shallows north to Savary Island, is the most significant reef area of the open Strait of Georgia. Large forests of kelp with associated plants and animals and both sandy and rocky bottom ecological systems make this a superb diving area.

Two miles southwest of Mystery Reef (about 4 miles west of Harwood Island) is another extensive reef patch known as Grant Reefs. These reef patches are probably the drowned remnants of terminal moraines left behind when the Bute and Toba Inlet glaciers retreated from the Strait of Georgia over 10,000 years ago. The reef patches are hazardous not only because of the numerous drying boulders, but as the *Small Craft Guide*, (Vol. 2) points out, because of the very rough seas resulting whenever a strong wind opposes a strong tide over shallow water. In periods of stable weather, with flat calm conditions prevailing, these reefs and tiny islets such as Rebecca Rock and Vivian Islands are very popular for diving.

Rebecca Rock in Algerine Passage, midway between Texada and Harwood Island, is noted for its nudibranchs and sponges. The currents here are deceptive. Although most charts show the flood tide moving westward or northwestward and the ebb eastward, this is sometimes reversed depending on local weather and pressure patterns. Currents in Algerine Passage run at rates up to 3 knots. Vivian Island in Shearwater Passage is celebrated for its wide variety of colourful sponges and the wreck of the *Shamrock*, a 61-ton tug which ran aground and sank along the southeast face of the island in 1926. Details on diving these areas are available in Betty Pratt-Johnson's book: *141 Dives* (1976). Vivian Island is also important as a sea bird colony where over 278 pairs of pelagic cormorants, glaucous-winged gulls and pigeon guillemots nest and breed.

North of Scuttle Bay the mainland shoreline continues low and featureless, dotted here and there with cottages and shorefront homes, giving little indication of the abrupt change in scenery which takes place only a few miles to the north.

Sturt Bay

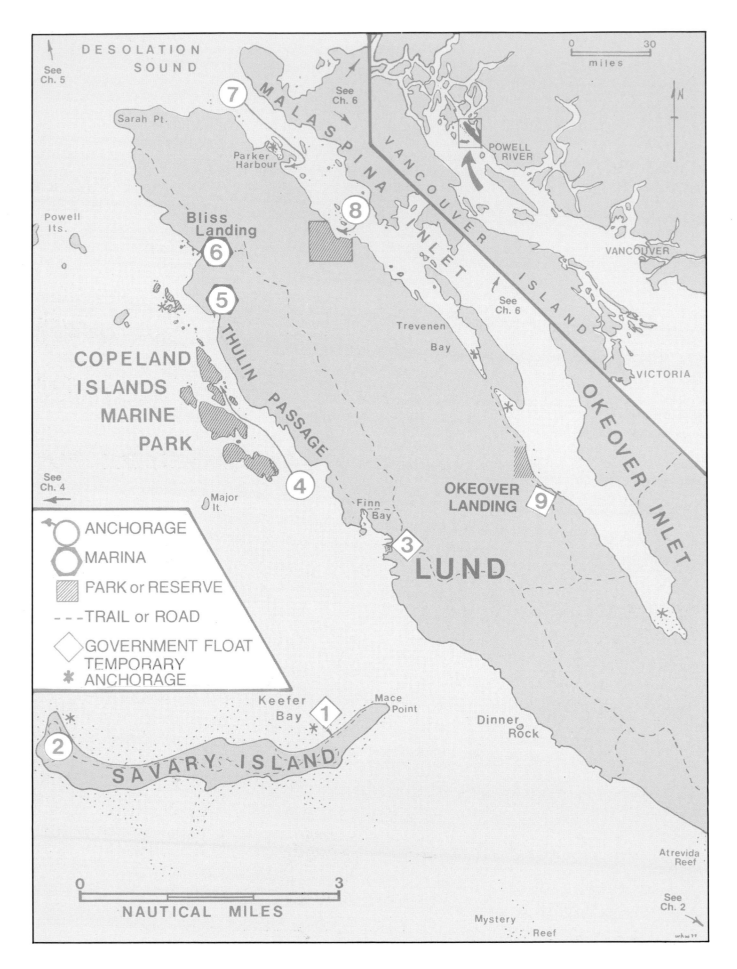

DESOLATION SOUND

See Ch. 5

Sarah Pt.

MALASPINA

See Ch. 6

Parker Harbour

Powell Its.

Bliss Landing

COPELAND ISLANDS MARINE PARK

Thulin Passage

See Ch. 4

Major It.

Finn Bay

ANCHORAGE

MARINA

PARK or RESERVE

- - - TRAIL or ROAD

GOVERNMENT FLOAT

TEMPORARY ANCHORAGE

Keefer Bay

Mace Point

SAVARY ISLAND

VANCOUVER INLET

POWELL RIVER

VANCOUVER ISLAND

OKEOVER INLET

VANCOUVER

Trevenen Bay

See Ch. 6

VICTORIA

OKEOVER LANDING

LUND

Dinner Rock

Atrevida Reef

See Ch. 2

Mystery Reef

0   30
miles

N

0   3
NAUTICAL MILES

46

CHAPTER THREE

Savary Island to Okeover Inlet

Lund, Copeland Islands, Malaspina Inlet

Proceeding north from Powell River towards Desolation Sound, the passage narrows between Mystery Reef, south of Savary Island, and the mainland shore. Atrevida Reef was named by Walbran in 1902 after the Spanish corvette *Atrevida*, (i.e. Audacious) under Captain Jose Bustamente. The *Atrevida* was one of the two vessels forming the exploring expedition of Commodore Alexandro Malaspina, whose corvette was named the *Descubierta* (i.e. Discovery). With these vessels, Malaspina made an examination of the northwest coast of America in 1791.

Two miles further north is Dinner Rock, an isolated, steep-sided, grassy-topped islet which appears to melt into the mainland shore as the sun goes down. If the sun is still shining, a small white cross atop the rock is plainly visible. On a dark night the rock is almost invisible, as it must have been on the night of October 11, 1947, when the 137-foot passenger ferry *Gulf Stream* hit dead centre at 14 knots. The force of the impact drove the stern underwater, flooding the rear passenger lounge, trapping and drowning five people including three children. The cross atop the rock was placed there by the father of the youngest victim — an 18-month-old daughter. Despite a heavy southeaster, 36 passengers and crew scrambled off the ship and onto the rock to await rescue. Today, the *Gulf Stream*, resting 120 feet below the water, is often visited by divers who marvel at the eerie lack of marine life around the virtually unscathed remains.

Savary Island

To some people, this island means more than any other place in the world. For others, it is just wonderfully unusual. It seems almost foreign, or even tropical — a misplaced "South Sea island" with all the notions of romance that implies. Partly because of its curious, Shangri-la-like qualities some visitors may find themselves succumbing to idyllic flights of fancy or to a sense of reality that may never be experienced elsewhere. It is an island that is often remembered with great affection.

What is it about Savary Island that contributes to

CHARTS
3591 — CAPE LAZO to DISCOVERY PASSAGE
(1:76,400)
3562 — REDONDA ISLANDS (1:37,500)
3573 — MALASPINA INLET (1:12,600)
(discontinued)
3559 — MALASPINA INLET, OKEOVER INLET
and LANCELOT INLET (1:12,000)
(Metric)

Glacial deposits which form basis of Savary Island have left beautiful sand beaches. Small government wharf in Keefer Bay can be seen facing north.

this aura? Possibly the island itself, but also, what surrounds it.

In contrast to the "dreary" mainland shore north of Powell River, Captain George Vancouver noted in his journal of June 25, 1792:

> The islands, however, which appeared before us, were of a moderate height, and presented a scene more pleasing and fertile. About five in the evening we passed between the main and an island lying in an east and west direction, which I named Savary's Island, about two leagues long, and about half a league broad: its N.E. point . . . forms a passage with the continental shore, along which, in a N.W. direction, we continued at a distance from half a mile to half a league. On the south side of Savary's Island were numberless sunken rocks, nearly half a league from its shores, visible I believe only at low water.

Vancouver was anxious to find a safe anchorage for the night and did not have enough time to sample the delights of Savary's Island, but five days later he sent a party to explore the area more thoroughly. Archibald Menzies, surgeon and botanist on Vancouver's ship noted in his journal:

> About noon on the 5th of July Lt. Puget & Mr. Whidbey returned to the Ship with their Boats & Party and from the Report of the former Gentlemen I am enabled to give the following short account of their excursion.
>
> After their departure on the 1st of July they proceeded agreable to orders along the Continental shore to the South East ward but were not able to go far on new ground when they stopped for the evening on one of the Islands (Savary) & pitchd their Tents in a delightful plain with a fine smooth beach before it for the Boats, that

rendered the situation both desirable & pleasant & such as they of late seldom enjoyd. Next day they continued ranging along shore to the South Eastward with fair wind & pleasant weather till about noon when having obtaind a satisfactory view of the unbroken continuation of the Continental shore & the termination of the group of Islands which here occupied a space of about four leagues in a SSE & NNW direction, they returnd back among these Islands which are low & in general thickly coverd with streight Pines, they also produce the wild fruits of the Country such as Raspberries Gooseberries Red Whortle berries &c together with abundance of wild Onions, & the sandy Beaches abounded with fine Clams easily procurd & well flavord — they also afford places of resort to Gulls Shags & other Oceanic Birds besides a great number of Seals. Thus fertilized with Fruits & Game, renderd them a desirable situation for Inhabitants, accordingly they were visited from one of these Islands by a small party of Natives who made off to the Boats over a long flat with pieces of porpus or Seals flesh in their hands which they offerd to our people in the most open & friendly manner, & though these presents were not accepted, yet their generosity & good intentions were rewarded by some little presents in return that highly pleasd them & establishd at once a mutual confidence on both sides. As their number was but small & they had no women with them some of the Gentlemen expressd their wish to be conducted to their habitations but after repeated solicitations they found them so unwilling to comply with their request, that rather than offend them they suppressed their curiosity & gave the business up, & after purchasing from them some Bows Arrows & other little articles of curiosity they parted with them on the best terms, as in these little dealings they appeard to conduct themselves with the strictest honesty & friendship. Two of them has been sent off to their Village for Fish but they were so dilatory that our party did not wait their return.

In 1859, the explorer W. Downie wrote to Governor

James Douglas: "Savary Island has all the appearance of a farm under cultivation, from the abundance of grass on it".

Today, yachtsmen approaching Savary from the south are usually confronted by high white cliffs which bloom golden yellow in the spring. The natural meadows above some of the cliffs have largely given way to broom (introduced in 1912) and second growth forest. This "back end" of Savary is seldom approached closely due to the extensive Mystery and Stradiotti Reef patches and the open southeasterly exposure.

1 Keefer Bay

The tiny (70 feet of berthage space) government float in Keefer Bay provides temporary moorage for those wanting quick access to the island. But since the float is regularly used by the Lund-Savary water taxi, mooring for longer than a few minutes is discouraged by the local wharfinger. Temporary anchorage is also possible near the wharf with good protection from southeasterlies but a moderate exposure to night-time westerlies which are frequent in the summer. Care must be taken to avoid going aground on the wide expanse of tidal sand flats either side of the wharf as the bottom shallows abruptly.

Mace Point is the only part of the island composed of hard (granitic) rock and will probably be the only part of the island remaining long after the sands and gravels underlying the rest of the island have been eroded away. Mace Point was originally known as Green's Point after John Green, an early resident and farmer who operated a trading post at this end of the island. He and a companion, Tom Taylor, were murdered in October of 1893 during an armed robbery at the trading post. It was supposed that Green was a wealthy man and his valuables were reputed to be buried somewhere on the island by the murderer and never recovered.

The majority of the island's more established summer residents are located at this end of the island. Some delightful descriptions are included in a recent book by Zoe Landale — *Harvest of Salmon — Adven-*

Royal Savary Lodge has been visitors' mecca since 1928.

Beautiful trails criss-cross the island.

Beaches on Savary are usually uncrowded.

Summer flowers in a Savary meadow.

49

Government floats at Lund; Finn Bay, right; and Copeland Islands Marine Park, top right.

tures in Fishing the B.C. Coast: "And there like a jewel lay Savary, the jade of the trees edged with white shore and reflected in the still water, infinitely peaceful and beckoning".

A maze of roads twines through the woods behind Keefer Bay. In the middle of the island the main road passes by a sand air-strip and continues westward to the other end of the island.

2 The Royal Savary Lodge

Just inside Indian Point is a reasonably safe area for temporary anchorage at the edge of the tidal flat. Savary Island offers some protection from southeasterlies and Hernando Island, 2 miles to the west, provides a moderate degree of protection from westerlies. With a rising tide one can anchor (for a short period of time) closer into the Royal Savary Lodge. If the sun has been hot and there has been an exceptionally low tide that day, the water may be as warm as soup — temperatures up to 78°F (25°C) have been recorded here.

The rustic simplicity and warm informal atmosphere of the Royal Savary Lodge (formerly "Hotel") has made this venerable institution a beloved mecca for hundreds of annual visitors since 1928. Among the many services and attractions provided by the hotel are scuba diving, barbeques, sail and row boats, lounge and dining room. One can wander for miles along the white sand beaches or hike the narrow winding island roads to the south end of the island. The sandy, well-drained soil has given rise to a varied ecology unlike much of the mainland coast and the

more typical Gulf Islands. In the springtime there is an incredible profusion of wild flowers including lily of the valley, pink orchid (sea blush), rattlesnake plantain and false mitrewort, with assorted berries and wild fruits later in the summer. The forests include stands of red alder, sitka willow, maple, cherry, dogwood, cascara, yew as well as the ubiquitous fir, hemlock, oak and arbutus. One of these arbutus trees is reputed to be the largest in North America.

There are several natural meadows along the southern shoreline and in a few places the wind has blown sand back from the cliffs to form dunes and "deserts". The once extensive "Sahara" and "Kalahari Deserts" are slowly losing way to the encroaching broom, dune grass and surrounding forest. This is a magnificent place to be in a southeast gale as huge breakers pound against the shore sending salt spray and sand up and over the 200-foot lip of the cliff.

3 Lund

The coastal highway north from Vancouver officially terminates here in the historic community of Lund. In 1889 brothers Fred and Charles Thulin came to settle in the bay and named it after the university city of Lund, near where they were born in Sweden. In 1891 they built the first hotel (soon destroyed by fire), and in 1905 they built the second (and present) hotel — a distinctive white building with green trim now known as the Lund Breakwater Inn. The hotel pub (the first licence issued north of Vancouver) is an ideal spot to relax and meet the local inhabitants. The hotel includes a dining lounge, cafe, expanded accommodation, general store (reasonably well stocked), showers, post office, laundromat as well as

50

the pub. For landward visitors there are water taxis for transit to Savary or wherever and a land taxi for those yachtsmen who would prefer to nip down to Powell River by car rather than by boat.

Approaching Lund from seaward may be confusing for the uninitiated. The largest scale chart available (3591) does not clearly show the entrances around either end of the floating breakwater which protects the government floats from westerly winds (but is not so effective against westerly seas). A fuel float extends out from the wharf head directly below the hotel at the north entrance to the harbour. Inside the harbour, the government float space (1,358 feet) is usually crammed with an extremely wide variety of craft — commercial fishermen, charter boats, gooeyduckers, oysterboats, houseboats, tugs, sailboats, motorboats, powerboats, etc. constructed in assorted shapes from plastic, tin, aluminum, wood, concrete and other more unusual materials. Usually yachtsmen try to lie alongside one of their own kind but in a place like this one must be prepared to meet some new neighbours (including the wharfinger) at any time of the day or night. There is a launching ramp here and a few hundred yards to the north of the hotel there are floats with full facilities for emergency repairs, including haulouts to 65 feet, 80 tons.

Finn Bay, ½ mile north of Lund, can provide temporary anchorage or moorage with good protection from the westerly which often blows up in this area in early evening, sometimes lasting for several days. There is a detached government float with no connection to shore used mainly by commercial fishboats and at the head of the bay are floats used by the forest service and local residents.

4 Copeland Islands Marine Park

After passing "Savary's Island" prior to entering Desolation Sound, Captain George Vancouver appeared to become disoriented. He noted in his log:

> We seemed now to have forsaken the main direction of the gulf, being on every side encompassed by islands and small rocky islets; some lying along the continental

Detached government float, with no ramp to shore, is near entrance to Finn Bay. Forest Service and private residents use floats in foreground.

shore, others confusedly scattered, of different forms and dimensions. South-westward of these islands, the main arm of the gulf extended in a north west direction, apparently three or four leagues wide, bounded by high though distant land. Through this very unpleasant navigation we sailed, still keeping close to the continental shore, which was compact. About dark we entered a spacious sound stretching to the eastward. Here I was very desirous of remaining until day-light; but soundings could not be gained though close to the shore.

> The night was dark and rainy, and the winds so light and variable, that by the influence of the tides we were driven about as it were blindfolded in this labyrinth, until towards midnight, when we were happily con-

Thulin Passage through the Copeland Islands is the main thoroughfare for boats travelling from the south into Desolation Sound.

Tiny anchorage on the west side of Copeland Islands.

ducted to the north side of an island in this supposed sound, where we anchored in company with the *Chatham* and the Spanish vessels, in 32 fathoms water, rocky bottom.

It is not absolutely clear from this description whether Vancouver used Thulin Passage, the main waterway used by present day mariners voyaging northward. The islands which perplexed Vancouver now provide a fascinating variety of coves and passages for small boat exploration. Four of the islands

Bliss Landing in Turner Bay is connected to Lund by four-wheel drive "road."

and 14 islets which protect Thulin Passage have now been designated a Marine Park. Temporary anchorage (depending mainly on boat size) is available in several nooks throughout the islands. The best anchorage is located halfway through Thulin Passage behind three islets which provide a surprising amount of protection from the wash and drone of other vessels powering through the Passage. An interesting little one-boat-sized niche is found between two of the northern islets, but is best visited in settled weather in the morning as it is somewhat open to the west. Chart 3562 (twice the scale of 3591) provides better coverage from here northwards.

Huge cement pylons, used for tying up log booms, line the Malaspina Peninsula side of Thulin Passage. Halfway through the Passage there is an Indian pictograph. This pictograph was described by Lester Peterson *(Pacific Yachting,* June 1976) as being: "just over 2 miles north of Lund. Unfortunately, it can be found by locating the word ACTIVE in black paint, on the mainland shore. A "killer whale" appears under the E, which obliterates the other symbols. It is literally the only vandalized pictograph on the coast."

5   Sharpes Bay Enterprises

Boats using Thulin Passage are advised to please reduce speed when approaching this marine station

as the wash creates considerable damage. Full fueling facilities are provided. This operation is also known as the Ragged Islands Marina after the former name for the Copeland Islands.

6 Bliss Landing

Bliss Landing Marina in Turner Bay provides moorage, laundromat, showers and a tennis court. The landing is accessible by four-wheel drive "road" from Lund and is named after Joe Blissto, an early hand-logger.

Yachtsmen rounding the northern tip of Malaspina Peninsula are sometimes astounded by the view. In marked contrast to the harsh, burned and logged off barrenness of Sarah Point, one is confronted with a startling prospect of incredibly steep mountains, the multivariate hues of purple and blue of receding headlands and hill slopes and the glistening far off whiteness of perpetual snowfields around a solitary cone-shaped peak — Mount Denman. The steep nature of the funnel-shaped channel leading towards the peak seems to draw one inwards and into Desolation Sound.

7 Malaspina Inlet

Some yachtsmen avoid this inlet because it appears at first sight to be encumbered with a massive jumble of dangerous rocks and reefs. Careful use of the larger scale charts (3562) or, better still (3573) or metric chart (3559) should bring one through safely (refer to Malaspina Inlet, Chapter 6). Although the tide runs through the inlet at rates of as much as 2 knots, the actual exchange of waters is very small and the warmer water temperatures in Okeover Inlet are the main reason for this area's importance as one of the prime oyster producing areas in B.C.

There are over 20 private oyster leases comprising

Navigating through the numerous rocks and islets in Malaspina Inlet is much easier than it first appears, as long as large scale chart is used.

over 140 acres located primarily in Trevenen Bay, Penrose Bay and towards the head of Okeover Inlet. The future potential of this area for intensive aquaculture is very high.

Temporary anchorage is available in Parker Harbour behind Beulah Island. This anchorage is somewhat exposed to northwest winds and seas and the west side of the harbour (where the greatest protection is) is rocky and shallow. The upland is private. Better, more protected anchorage is possible on the other side of the peninsula at the south end of Parker Harbour with Thorp Island providing some protection from the southeast.

The eastern shore of Malaspina Inlet including Grace Harbour and Desolation Sound Marine Park are described in Chapter 6.

8 Cochrane Islands

Good anchorage is available behind the Cochrane Islands. The upland here is part of Desolation Sound Marine Park and was originally intended to be the terminus for an access road from Lund. Future development of the park will probably be limited to hiking trails and wilderness campsites, as it is unlikely that highway expansion north of Lund will occur in the foreseeable future. Nevertheless the Malaspina Peninsula may have to be tightly controlled as unrestricted developments here might lead to degradation of the very high recreational qualities as well as the prime oyster growing potential. Water quality is of paramount importance to both these activities and in this inlet only a small amount of pollution could have serious consequences because of the warmer waters and low rate of flushing.

It is somewhat saddening to think that only 50 years

The upland around the Cochrane Island anchorage is part of Desolation Sound marine park.

ago this Inlet was moderately populated with over 20 families who lived a relatively simple but active life, subsisting on the produce of the land and sea with very little long term adverse impact on their surroundings. Such a way of life may have been hard and demanding, but who can say it was not happy and satisfying?

There was a school in the Inlet for the many children. Farms and orchards appeared wherever there was a tiny bit of flat land and suitable soil. The remains of this early colonization can be found everywhere — even the little steep-sided islet southwest of the Isbister Islets was cultivated. Today only two of three families reside in this manner in the Inlet. It seems that today's affluent lifestyles develop strong needs for modern conveniences, motorized transport and massive mechanized extraction of resources which override the opportunities for a simpler, less damaging way of life.

Trevenen Bay is suitable as a temporary anchorage especially in southeasterly weather. The isthmus connecting Coode Peninsula to the mainland is the site of one of the few remaining early homesteads in the area and the northern terminus of road access. Informal camping for small boaters is sometimes available here by checking with the owners.

9 Okeover Landing

The government float provides 240 feet of moorage space. Although trailer boats are sometimes launched here, there is very little parking space and the landing is more suitable as a site for launching canoes or kayaks. The landing provides an ideal starting point for exploration of the protected waters leading into and beyond Desolation Sound.

There is a recreational reserve north of the government float, and the foreshore below the reserve is open to the public for recreational harvesting of oysters (subject to the legal limits). In the future, this reserve may be upgraded to a provincial park with campsites.

Although oyster growth is prolific in the Inlet, it is considerate to take only as many as needed. South of the float is Okeover Resort with an excellent seafood restaurant and bar (reservations recommended). Rental canoes and bait are also available here.

Directly across the Inlet from the government float is an Indian pictograph described by Lester Peterson: "The small panels show what would appear to be prisoners, walking in a line, joined from neck to neck by some sort of bond — a most unusual tableau."

The slow interchange of inlet waters leads to very stable conditions and in winter the waters of Freke Anchorage often freeze over for a considerable distance up the Inlet.

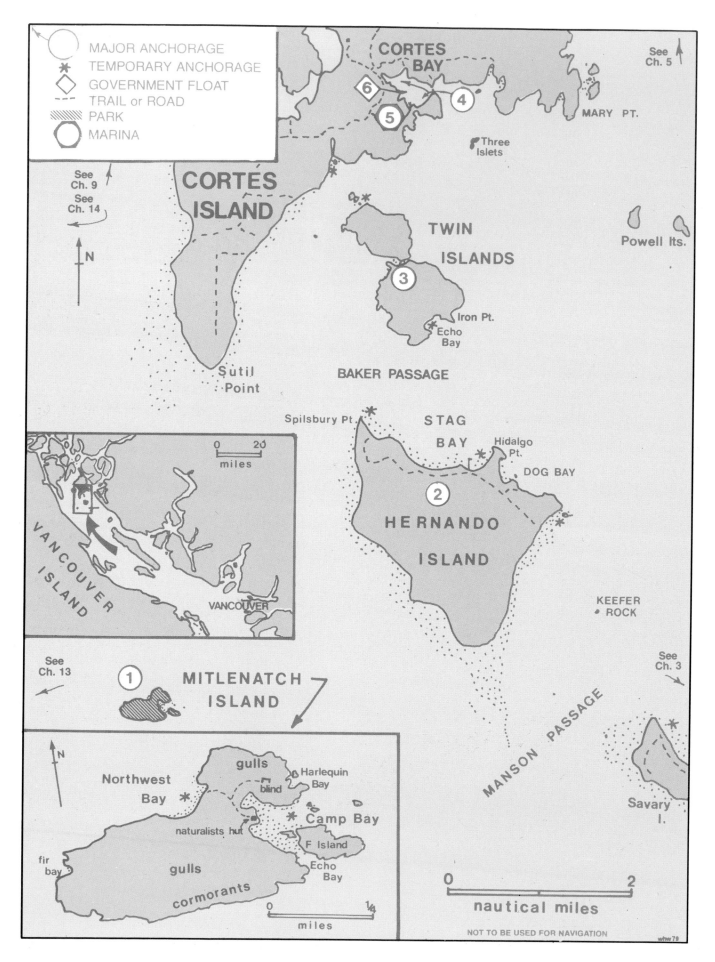

MAJOR ANCHORAGE
TEMPORARY ANCHORAGE
GOVERNMENT FLOAT
TRAIL or ROAD
PARK
MARINA

CORTES BAY

⑥

⑤

④

See Ch. 5

MARY PT.

See Ch. 9
See Ch. 14

N

CORTES ISLAND

Three Islets

TWIN ISLANDS

Powell Its.

③

Iron Pt.

Echo Bay

Sutil Point

BAKER PASSAGE

Spilsbury Pt.

STAG BAY

Hidalgo Pt.

DOG BAY

②

HERNANDO ISLAND

KEEFER ROCK

0   20
miles

VANCOUVER ISLAND

VANCOUVER

See Ch. 13

①

MITLENATCH ISLAND

See Ch. 3

MANSON PASSAGE

Savary I.

N

Northwest Bay

gulls

Harlequin Bay

blind

naturalists hut

Camp Bay

F Island

fir bay

gulls

Echo Bay

cormorants

0   ¼
miles

0   2
nautical miles

NOT TO BE USED FOR NAVIGATION

wfw 79

56

CHAPTER FOUR

Mitlenatch Island to Cortes Bay

Hernando Island, Twin Island, Southeastern Cortes Island

The southern entrance to Desolation Sound is guarded by a series of low lying islands of varying size, shape and character stretching between the mainland shore and Cortes Island. The furthest offshore of these islands is Mitlenatch.

1 Mitlenatch Island

This barren, rocky, 88-acre island, located 3½ miles south of Cortes Island, has been known by a variety of names and meanings. Indian derivations of the name "Mitlenatch" were: "where tidal waters meet" and "calm water all around" (Comox Salish). It has also been referred to as "The Sacred Island", "the stone princess" and "Bird Island" but perhaps the Kwakiutl name for the island — MAH-KWEE-LAY-LA, meaning "it looks close, but seems to move away as you approach it" gives us the most apt description of all.

Due largely to its isolation, the island is an ideal breeding and nesting site for thousands of birds as predatory mink and racoon are kept at bay by the long swimming distances from nearby islands. The island is not so remote, however, as to discourage other predators such as river otters, eagles, crows and man. In the 1890s John Manson, one of the earliest settlers on Cortes Island, attempted to raise sheep and cattle on the island but lost so many to passing fishermen that in an attempt to stop the thievery he took up full time residence on Mitlenatch in 1892. The fierce winter gales and loneliness drove him back to Cortes Island after only a year although his sheep survived on the island until the 1950s.

Mitlenatch is now the home for over 2,800 breeding pairs of Glaucous-winged Gulls, the largest concentration at any single site around Vancouver Island. Since the Strait of Georgia is the central breeding range for this species of gull, Mitlenatch is probably the most important breeding colony for this gull in the world. In addition to gulls, which have a very strong sense of territory around their saucer-shaped nests on the island's rocky knolls, there are six other bird species which are known to nest on the island and a total of 126 species have been observed since 1960. About 350 pairs of Pelagic Cormorants nest in the vertical volcanic rock cliffs along the island's south shore. One hundred pairs of Pigeon Guillemots nest under boulders and in crevices in the rocks, about 35 pairs of Crows nest on the ground and in

CHARTS
3591 — For MITLENATCH, HERNANDO and CORTES ISLANDS (1:76,400)
3594 — Covers only northern half of HERNANDO ISLAND and CORTES ISLAND (1:75,000)
3562 — For TWIN ISLANDS, CORTES BAY (1:37,000)
585 — (Admiralty Chart) Plan of BAKER PASSAGE (1:24,410)

Mitlenatch Island — important breeding area for seagulls.

shrubs and trees. A few Oystercatchers, Redwing Blackbirds and Song Sparrows also nest on the Island.

Despite over half a century of sheep-grazing, a wide variety of colourful wildflowers continue to thrive on the island. An exceptionally dry climate favours the woolly sunflower, giant mullein and the prickly pear cactus. Mitlenatch Island is one of the few places in the Strait of Georgia where the air is sufficiently dry and hot enough to allow this cactus to flower and bring forth its amazingly delicate yellow blooms. Archibald Menzies, the first botanist to set foot on the Gulf Islands (May, 1792) records in his journal that he "was not a little surprised to meet with the Cactus Opuntia (prickly pear) thus far to the northward". In some years, less than 12-in. of rain falls on Mitlenatch and although no records are kept, this island quite possibly receives more sunshine than any other area in the Strait of Georgia. In spring and early summer one can see blue hyacinths and hair bells, chocolate lilies, yellow daisies, buttercups and monkey flowers, pink fireweed and thistles, orange lilacs and tiger lilies, the wild rose, honeysuckle, violets and sea lavender (sea blush).

To protect all these natural values, the Parks Branch acquired the Island in 1960 and designated it as a nature park, the first one in British Columbia and the only one of its kind in Canada. In the summer months there is a park naturalist living in a driftwood cabin on the island who is responsible for protecting the nesting birds and helping visitors to see, understand and enjoy the island's natural life and history.

It is strongly recommended that visitors contact the park naturalist before exploring the island. Any kind of disturbance can seriously disrupt the birds' breeding habits, allow predators to raid untended nests, or cause young birds to leave their nest and be pecked to death by neighbouring birds. The naturalist will help you find the best location for observing the birds without disturbing them. There is a blind where you can watch them near the north end of the island, as shown on the map. The best time to visit Mitlenatch is in the late spring. In February the first birds arrive on the island and by the end of March they have established their own separate territories (less than 5 feet between nests). By mid-May the first eggs are laid and a month later the first eggs hatch. From mid-June until the beginning of August, when the chicks fly, is the most critical period (but also the most interesting) when disturbances must be minimized.

58

Because of Mitlenatch's open exposure, anchorage can only be temporary, subject to prevailing or expected winds. Overnight anchorage is not recommended. Northwest Bay provides good protection from the southeast and, although open to westerlies (primarily an evening or night-time wind), this bay is generally the safest daytime anchorage. The reason is that summer afternoons often bring onshore southerly winds blowing up the Strait which counteract the prevailing westerly. Camp Bay (also known as Southeast Bay), which is large enough to accommodate safely only two or three medium sized boats, is somewhat protected from light southeasterlies but a strong southeast winds send a dangerous swell into this shallow anchorage. A single mooring buoy is provided for Parks Branch and guest use. Echo Bay is not particularly recommended as an anchorage.

Manson Passage

Manson Passage, formerly known as False Passage, between Savary and Hernando Islands, is navigable for most boats except near low tide and when strong winds are blowing against a strong tidal stream. Depths in the passage average at least 3 feet below chart datum but there is a dangerous drying spit extending a mile south of Ashworth Point on Hernando Island and an isolated 2-foot drying rock almost exactly halfway between Savary and Hernando. The tidal stream flows at rates up to 2 knots through the passage. If entering from the west, one should stay south of a bearing or line between the north tip of Mitlenatch and the southernmost cliff of Savary Island until one can see the tip of Cortes Island (Mary Point) past the eastern extremity of Hernando. The shoals that extend out from Savary Island into Manson Passage are marked on their western end by a conspicuous isolated boulder which dries 15 feet and is therefore visible at most stages of the tide except near high water springs.

Eight-foot-high Keefer Rock, like a few other tiny isolated islets, is home for a few breeding seabirds. A total of seven pairs of Glaucous-winged Gulls have been observed nesting here.

2 Hernando Island

This island, and Cortes to the north, were named by Galiano and Valdes in 1792 presumably after the Spaniard Hernando Cortes, who conquered Mexico around 1520. The island, which is mainly composed of glacial drift deposits like Savary Island to the southeast, is surrounded by many beaches, some of fine sand, others of gravel, cobbles or boulders. The shallow shores of Hernando are particularly hazardous to navigate because of the many isolated and irregularly distributed boulders which are covered at high water and not all of which can be located on the relatively small scale (1:75,000) charts of the island. In only a few places are the beaches sufficiently clear of boulders to permit safe anchorage close to shore.

Visitors to Mitlenatch should contact the park naturalist before exploring the island.

Immediately south of the easternmost tip of the island there is a magnificent sand beach which becomes cobble covered at its southern end. This beach is backed by an extensive grassy meadow with bordering windswept trees similar to Tribune beach on Hornby Island. While the huge piles of driftwood and wind-distorted bushes indicate a dangerous exposure to southeast winds, in summer when westerlies prevail or only light "dry" onshore afternoon southeasterlies blow, this shore provides good temporary anchorage. The preferred anchorage is between a 10-foot drying rock and the 12-foot-high islet off the easternmost tip of the island. The islet should be given at least 100 yards clearance as there is a substantial reef extending eastwards of it which may be covered near high water.

Several years ago Hernando was rescued from foreign ownership and plans for a huge resort complex which may have been out of keeping with the surroundings. The island is now subdivided into approximately 50 lots but few appear to have been built upon as the only portions of the shoreline that show signs of habitation are in the Dog Bay - Stag Bay area. West of Hidalgo Point there is a long wharf with a

Main anchorage on Mitlenatch Island. Campbell River in background.

Primary access to Hernando Island is this private float in Stag Bay.

private float serving as the primary access to the island.

A provincial recreational reserve protects the foreshore around Spilsbury Point (formerly Tongue Point) where there is another approachable fine sand beach, similar in aspect to the one at the western tip of Savary Island, with magnificent views up through Desolation Sound to the mainland mountains. There is good temporary anchorage off this beach with reasonable protection from both the southeast and the west. Many boats retreat to this area from Desolation Sound when thick weather brings overcast skies and rain into the mountains. Partly because of the lower topography of this particular portion of the Strait of Georgia, the weather often remains sunny and dry while the channels to the north and east can be seen to be socked in with low clouds and rain.

Baker Passage

This passage between Hernando and Twin Islands may have been the route used when Vancouver took his ships the *Discovery* and *Chatham* from their anchorage in Teakerne Arm out to the Pacific via Discovery Passage and Johnstone Strait. Vancouver named the passage after one of his favourite lieutenants, Joseph Baker, who also appears to have been quite popular with the Strait of Georgia native population. It was Third Lieutenant Baker who had first spied the volcanic mountain which now bears his name and who was responsible for draughting all the charts of the expeditions surveys and discoveries. At the end of the expedition in 1795, Vancouver handed over command of the *Discovery* to Lieutenant Baker, before going up to London.

Tidal streams in Baker Passage do not always flow in the direction they are supposed to and may be different if there are abrupt changes in local wind or barometric conditions. Tides normally flood to the east at rates up to 2 knots at springs and ebb to the west. British Admiralty Chart 585 contains a plan of this passage at a scale of 1:24,410.

3 Twin Islands

The Twin Islands (now actually one island) have had an interesting history. These islands were originally named Ulloa Islands by Galiano and Valdes to commemorate the battle of San Juan de Ulloa, won by Hernando Cortes in 1519. The first owner of the islands, an Irish Anglican minister, was mysteriously murdered one night in his boat anchored between the islands. Before he died he asked that no one try to find the murderer.

At one time the passage between the Twin Islands was navigable at high water but it has now been blocked off by a causeway leaving drying lagoons on both sides of it, guarded by logbooms or rock barrier. There is also a tiny shallow private boat basin at the lagoon on the western side of the causeway.

There is a magnificent private lodge-style log cabin on the island, with an immense living room, dining room, seven bedrooms and five private bathrooms. In 1961, the island and lodge was bought by Prince Philip's sister and it is now owned by his nephew, Prince Markgraf Max von Baden who visits for one or two months every year. The rest of the time there is a caretaker on the island. During the 1971 Royal Tour, the Royal Yacht *Britannia* anchored off the island and the Queen, Prince Philip and Princess Anne spent a day ashore, barbecuing oysters and salmon, and absorbing the Desolation Sound experience.

Temporary anchorage is possible at several locations around the Island. Echo Bay in Baker Passage is open to the southeast but offers excellent protection from westerlies. The eastern shore of Twin Islands from Echo Bay (Iron Point) is quite interesting geologically. Steep reddish and orange cliffs display a much broken and contorted array of stratified rocks consisting of dark slaty argillites, quartzite and limestone. This type of rock is unique to the area (occurring with ammonite fossils, also on Hidalgo Point, Hernando Island) and is much older than the predominating granites to the northeast and the gla-

Temporary anchorage at Hernando Island.

White sand beaches extend out to Spilsbury Point on Hernando Island.

Entrance to Cortes Bay should be made to port of light in centre of channel.

cial sands and gravels to the southwest. Temporary anchorage is also possible behind a group of islets close to the northernmost tip of Twin Islands, and in various small nooks along the Cortes Island shore.

Cortes Island

The shoreline of Cortes Island north from Sutil Point is endowed with steep cliffs, boulder encrusted beaches, and two fairly extensive farms with beautiful orchards. The retreat centre of the Cold Mountain Institute — specializing in Reichian breathing, mandala drawing, rolfing massage, primal screaming, fantasy psychodrama and Jungian mask therapy (why don't they just take up sailing?) is also located along this shore. A tiny salt lagoon is located behind a debris-choked narrow inlet and a rocky islet surrounded by drying shallows. The two bays immediately south of Cortes Bay are piled high with driftwood from winter southeast gales. The Three Islets just offshore are actually one island at low tide and provide a nesting haven for one pair of Glaucous-winged Gulls and two pairs of Pigeon Guillemots.

4   Cortes Bay

The approach into Cortes Bay (formerly known as Blind Creek) is occasionally subject to what appear to be unusual wind and sea conditions. Winds which are either calm or only moderately strong within Cortes Bay or elsewhere, seem to blow with exceptional fury (from either the southeast or the west) right through the narrow harbour entrance channel. This wind effect may be compounded by any southeasterly swells rebounding back from the Cortes shoreline against incoming swells, creating especially confused seas right outside the harbour entrance. It is not unusual for boats which are moored or anchored within Cortes Bay to think that they are trapped inside by what seems to be ferocious wind and sea conditions outside, when in actual fact only moderate winds are blowing just beyond the entrance.

Some say that these "unusual" wind conditions are totally false, dreamed up by those who want to keep this beautiful and friendly bay to themselves.

To be honest, entrance into the bay is seldom, if ever, precluded by wind and sea conditions. The

Cortes Bay Marine Resort, bottom, and government floats are in southern portion of bay.

main hindrance has proven to be the rocks located to the north of the mid channel entrance beacon. Entrance into Cortes Bay should be made to the *south* (port side) of the circular light tower (a starboard hand daymark with a flashing red light) atop a rock in the middle of this narrow entrance channel. The rocks between the tower and the northern shoreline are hidden below the surface near high water.

5   Cortes Bay Marine Resort

Located at the south end of the bay, this resort provides sheltered moorage (power on floats), fuel, boat rentals, launching ramp, cottages, cabins and campsites, laundromat, showers and a store for groceries, hardware, charts, ice, bait and fishing supplies. In very strong southeasterlies, the wind whistles through the low gap behind the resort and into the bay and a swell comes through the entrance, making this southern shore of Cortes Bay the most protected. Local attractions include warm water

swimming, hiking trails, blackberry picking and birdwatching.

Poor holding ground in the centre of Cortes Bay makes anchorage here inadvisable in strong winds. With a strong north wind one should anchor in the western end of the bay, or in a strong southeasterly or southwesterly the southern shore should be favoured.

6   Cortes Bay Gov't Floats

The government floats in Cortes Bay provide 520 feet of berthage space. The road from Cortes Bay forks south around Hague Lake to Mansons Landing and north to Squirrel Cove. If one takes the road leading north and the fork which veers to the left, after 20 minutes (half a mile northwest of Cortes Bay) one comes to Gunflint Lake and the Lakeview Guest Ranch which offers fresh vegetables and milk from one of the largest farms on the Island. Gunflint Lake drains through a narrow passage into Hague Lake which empties out into Manson's Lagoon on the other side of the Sutil Peninsula of Cortes Island.

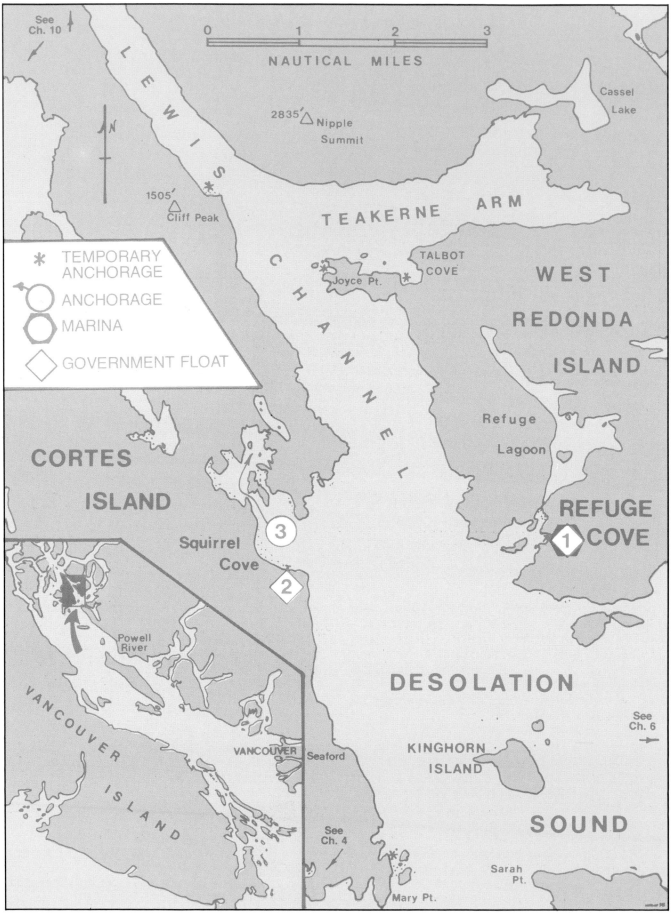

NAUTICAL MILES

0   1   2   3

See Ch. 10

N

L E W I S   C H A N N E L

2835' △ Nipple
Summit

1505' △
Cliff Peak

TEAKERNE   ARM

Cassel
Lake

TALBOT
COVE

Joyce Pt.

WEST

REDONDA

ISLAND

Refuge
Lagoon

* TEMPORARY
ANCHORAGE

◯ ANCHORAGE

⬡ MARINA

◇ GOVERNMENT FLOAT

CORTES

ISLAND

Squirrel
Cove

③

◇ ②

REFUGE
COVE

⬡ ①

DESOLATION

Powell
River

VANCOUVER

VANCOUVER

Seaford

KINGHORN
ISLAND

See
Ch. 6

I S L A N D

SOUND

See
Ch. 4

Sarah
Pt.

Mary Pt.

NOT TO BE USED FOR NAVIGATION

64

CHAPTER FIVE

Desolation Sound to Lewis Channel

Refuge Cove, Squirrel Cove and Teakerne Arm

Captain George Vancouver's entrance into Desolation Sound was not particularly auspicious. (See note under [4] Copeland Islands, Chapter 3).

> At break of day on Tuesday, the 26th of June, 1792 we found ourselves about half a mile from the shores of a high rocky island, surrounded by a detached and broken country, whose general appearance was very inhospitable. Stupendous rocky mountains rising almost perpendicularly from the sea, principally composed the north west, north and eastern quarters.

Vancouver's situation could not have been more precarious. He appears to have anchored in close proximity to Kinghorn Rocks, just north of Kinghorn Island. This island was afterwards called "Quema" by the Spaniards who appear to have anchored just south of the island.

Later that day, after sending out exploration parties in the ships' boats, the Spaniards and British were driven from their precarious anchorage by a fresh SE wind up Lewis Channel to a "more eligible anchorage, though in a situation equally dreary and unpleasant", at the entrance to Teakerne Arm.

While the ship's boats were away exploring the various channels leading out of Desolation Sound, Vancouver sailed the *Discovery's* yawl back to Kinghorn Island to make some navigational measurements and named the two points at the entrance to Desolation Sound, Sarah and Mary, apparently after his two sisters. (Walbran).

Two islets off Mary Point are joined to Cortes Island by a 12-foot drying isthmus which provides some protection from the southeast for temporary anchorage north of the isthmus and in a tiny cove on Cortes Island. Although this anchorage is open to the northeast it is not generally a dangerous exposure for winds in the summer months, but it might be open to swells at night from a strong northwest wind. Another small cove immediately to the north is the terminus for a cable crossing from Malaspina Peninsula and would therefore be unsuitable as an anchorage.

Seaford, the small community 1½ miles north of Mary Point, was once a steamer stop with a Government wharf and landing serving as the eastern terminus of a cross island road from Manson's Landing. This facility is now abandoned although the community still appears to be inhabited.

Although Vancouver spent over three weeks in this area, it is obvious from his journal that the spectacular scenery and abundant small boat anchorages which today attract thousands of yachtsmen did not appeal to him. Lester Peterson's excellent but sad article:

CHARTS
**3594 — DISCOVERY PASSAGE, TOBA INLET
 and CONNECTING PASSAGES
 (1:75,000)**
3562 — REDONDA ISLANDS (1:37,500)
**3555 — Plans of REFUGE COVE, SQUIRREL
 COVE
 (1:12,000)**

Refuge Lagoon.

British Columbia's Depopulated Coast (Raincoast Chronicles Vol. 1, No. 4) surmises that Vancouver named this area " . . . in a fit of depression brought on by his immersion in an unpeopled coast."

Vancouver was undoubtedly more contented with the lower, rolling, pastoral shorelines in the southern portions of the Gulf of Georgia and Puget Sound reminiscent of his English homeland. It is ironic today that modern man has so altered the places where he lives from what they were originally or what they could be, that he must seek out the desolate areas which still retain some degree of naturalness to regain peace of mind.

Vancouver may also have been bothered by the inconsistent tides and winds of Desolation Sound. Hydrographic charts indicate that the tidal streams flood *north* to the west of Kinghorn Island (from the Strait of Georgia) and to the *south* (from Lewis Channel) to the northeast of Kinghorn Island. It appears that this marks the boundary line between tidal streams entering Desolation Sound via Juan de Fuca Strait and via Johnstone Strait around the north end of Vancouver Island. This boundary line can move several miles in either direction depending on local wind and barometric conditions, so that while the tide may flood north only as far as Squirrel Cove in good weather, it may flood north all the way up Lewis Channel after a long spell of southeasterly winds. The currents, however, are never strong, seldom exceeding 2 knots and the actual exchange of water is very small.

Winds tend to be channelled and twisted around by the local topography and a bad weather wind may blow from almost any direction, rather than from the more usual southeast quadrant. Winds occasionally arrive unexpectedly, sometimes with considerable force and no rational explanation, making for exciting sailing. For the most part, however, winds are light, sporadic, or non-existent in the summer months.

West and East Redonda Islands were originally thought to be one island, by the British explorers. Only the Spaniards appear to have discovered the existence of Waddington Channel. Because of its generally round shape East Redonda Island was named Isla Redonda by Galiano and Valdes, and what is now West Redonda was named Isla de Cortez.

1 Refuge Cove

Refuge Cove, at the southern tip of West Redonda Island, has served as the major supply centre for yachtsmen exploring Desolation Sound, as well as for vessels passing through, for many years. The popularity of Refuge Cove is due in large part to the resourcefulness and enthusiasm of Norm and Doris Hope who built up the operation before retiring to their home at the head of the Cove. Refuge Cove is now co-operatively owned and operated by an enterprising group of families and individuals who have banded together to establish a community in relative isolation (for 10 months of the year) from the rest of civilization.

In summer the isolation ends with hundreds of boats coming in to tie up at the government floats.

Refuge Cove is the closest supply centre for the entire area between Bute and Malaspina Inlets, including Toba Inlet and Desolation Sound Marine Park. The float space available has been expanded to over 1,000 feet of berthage by the Co-op. A fuel dock is located at the northwest terminus of the floats.

The first store in Refuge Cove was started before 1920 by the Donnely family who later moved to Pender Harbour (Donnelys Landing). After the original store burned down in 1969 a barge was floated in and this is now perched high and dry behind the government wharf at the end of the cove. Aboard the barge is a general store with a wide selection of groceries and hardware, fishing tackle, post office, radiotelephone, charts, a diverse selection of books and magazines, and a liquor store. Despite the fact that everything must be brought in by boat or float plane the prices are remarkably reasonable. Just outside the barge are laundromat and shower facilities. A tiny craft shop is perched on a rock at the head of the landing and features locally made handicrafts. Regular float plane service is available to Vancouver.

For those who prefer not to tie up to floats, quieter anchorage may be possible in the northernmost part of Refuge Cove near the outlet of Refuge Lagoon, but care must be taken to avoid the rocks on the starboard side entering and the possibility of snagging one's anchor on the old logging machinery and cables which seem to litter the sea bottom here. This cove is also used occasionally as temporary moorage for homes floating on log booms and houseboats.

One of the unique features of Desolation Sound is the large number of saltwater lagoons. West Redonda Island has two of the largest — while Cortes Island has seven smaller ones. Although the bottom of Refuge Lagoon may still be salt, the surface is largely freshwater now, since the inlet for seawater has been somewhat restricted by the construction of a dam (built before 1914) and a sluice channel. This sluice channel was designed to assist the transport of logs from the Lagoon down into Refuge Cove. Although full-scale logging operations in the Refuge Lagoon watershed appear to have terminated some time ago, much evidence of this activity persists.

Nevertheless, Refuge Lagoon is a fascinating and beautifully different place to visit, especially if one has a light enough dinghy or canoe which can be lined and portaged along the outlet and into the lagoon. Chart 3594 gives a small scale indication of the number of small coves, inlets and islets in the Lagoon. A compass rose obliterates the lagoon on the larger scale Chart 3562. Over 60 years ago, a pioneering family attempted to establish a farm in the valley which runs between Refuge Lagoon and Black Lake and traces of this farm, which included an extensive dyking system, are still visible.

2 Squirrel Cove, Cortes Island

The government floats provide up to 400 feet of berthage space on either side of the terminus of a pier

Below and overleaf, Refuge Cove.

extending out from the south shore of Squirrel Cove. A short distance west of the head of the landing is the Squirrel Cove Store which includes a liquor store and post office.

From this vantage point one can look around the cove to the present Indian community with its centrally conspicuous spired church, one of the oldest on the coast, which has recently been renovated. This location has not always been occupied; the former village is said to have been situated within the inner portion of Squirrel Cove.

3   Squirrel Cove Anchorage

Safe and abundant anchorage is available in the inside northern section of Squirrel Cove. This anchorage is so popular that it is not uncommon for a hundred boats to be found in here on a summer evening. Despite the relatively large area for anchoring available, this number of boats necessitates tying alongside other anchored boats or anchoring close to shore with a stern or bow line to a convenient rock or tree. The use of anchor trips is advisable because of the sunken logs and logging cables which often snag anchors here. Those who insist on some degree of privacy might, with care, find anchorage in the rock studded passage northeast of Protection Island or at high tide in the two westernmost coves. The large scale plan on Chart 3555 is useful here. Trails from the

Squirrel Cove and Lagoon rapids.

northern tips of these two westernmost coves lead for about half a mile through some logged over patches to the head of Von Donop Inlet.

The first white men to visit Squirrel Cove were probably Archibald Menzies, surgeon-botanist aboard H.M.S. *Discovery* and William Broughton of H.M.S. *Chatham* who made a small excursion down here from the main anchorage in Teakerne Arm on one of the *Chatham's* boats. Menzies notes in his journal:

> We penetrated by a small branch a short distance into the Island on the South Side of the Channel where we lay & near its termination, seeing a large stream of water rushing down out of the Woods we landed / close by it to take some refreshment, not in the least suspecting but that it was fresh water, till we tasted it, & to our great surprize found it to be saltish. This lead us to trace its source & found it came from a Lake in the Wood which was apparently filled at high water by the impetuous force with which the Tide rushes into these narrow Inlets, but the same impelling force not acting upon its return it continued pouring out at a narrow gap a more gradual stream during the recess of the Tide which at this time had fallen from it about twelve feet perpendicular height.
>
> We here killed some large Grouse which on starting perchd in the Pine Trees, & we saw some Deer but did not get near enough to have a shoot at them; it is surprising how fond these Animals are of insulated situations to which probably they are driven by being chaced or harassed by other animals such as Wolves, Foxes &c.

The small lagoon discovered by Menzies and Broughton at the head of Squirrel Cove now provides a delightful opportunity for young (and old) to shoot the rapids by dinghy into or out of the "Lake in the

Squirrel Cove anchorage, Lewis Channel, Teakerne Arm in background.

Squirrel Cove.

Wood", depending on the state of the tide. The passage into the lagoon is straight and cleared of boulders, unlike other lagoon entrances and remarkably similar to the "canoe channels" cleared and used by early Indians on the open beaches facing the Pacific Ocean. Earlier charts of this area indicated that this lagoon might be connected with one of the Von Donop Inlet lagoons, when in fact they are separated by a mile of upland.

Visitors who are fortunate enough to enter Squirrel Cove from September to June, or on a rare summer night when all is calm and peaceful, may experience strange or "special" feelings. This "feeling" reappears in several other unique areas up the coast and has been evocatively described by M. Wylie Blanchet in *The Curve of Time:*

> There is always the same kind of peculiar silence about all these old villages — it is hard to explain unless you have felt it. I say felt, because that describes it best. Just as you have at some time sensed somebody hiding in a dark room — so these unseen presences in an old village hold their breath to watch you pass.

Teakerne Arm

There is some speculation as to the exact location where Vancouver, Galiano and Valdes anchored their vessels while in this vicinity. The most probable location is on a relatively shallow sill (20 to 30 fathoms) in Lewis Passage opposite the northern entrance to Teakerne Arm. While this is not an ideal small craft

Cassel Lake cascading into Teakerne Arm.

anchorage it appears to have provided the required degree of protection for their larger vessels.

Although Vancouver spent almost three weeks at anchor here, while his boat crews made expeditions throughout the surrounding waterways, he could find little to cheer or divert him in the surrounding countryside:

> Our situation here was on the northern side of an arm of the sound leading to the north-westward, a little more than half a mile wide, presenting as gloomy and dismal an aspect as nature could well be supposed to exhibit, had she not been a little aided by vegetation; which though dull and uninteresting, screened from our sight the dreary rocks and precipices that compose these desolate shores, especially on the northern side; as the opposite shore, though extremely rude and mountainous, possessed a small space of nearly level land, stretching from the water side, on which some different sorts of the pine tribe, arbor vitae, maple, and the oriental arbutus, seemed to grow with some vigor, and in a better soil.

The species of trees mentioned by Vancouver can still be found on this patch of what is now an abandoned homestead directly below Cliff Peak on Cortes Island. Several years ago it was reported that a cannonball was found here, but no other record of Vancouver's stay has been found. Temporary anchorage is possible with some protection from the southeast.

Vancouver's journal continues:

> The very circumscribed view that we had of the country here rendered it impossible to form the most distant idea of any circumstances relative to the situation in which we had become stationary; whether composed of islands, or of such arms of the sea as we had lately been employed in examining, or how long there was a probability of our

remaining in anxious expectation for the return of our friends. Our residence here was truly forlorn; an awful silence pervaded the gloomy forests, whilst animated nature seemed to have deserted the neighbouring country, whose soil afforded only a few small onions, some samphire, and here and there bushes bearing a scanty crop of indifferent berries. Nor was the sea more favourable to our wants, the steep rocky shores prevented the use of the seine, and not a fish at the bottom could be tempted to take the hook.

Nevertheless, the surroundings did provide a few opportunities for some pleasant diversions as the remaining crew abroad the *Discovery* "brewed some spruce beer, which was excellent" and Archibald Menzies notes in his journal:

During the absence of these Boats when the weather was any wise favourable I made frequent Botanical excursions in different directions into the Woods on both sides of the Channel as they were found here pretty thin & easily penetrated on account of being much less encumberd with Underwood than the Forests of New Georgia & those along the outer skirts of the Coast.

. . . In order to vary my excursions & search the upper regions of the Woods for Botanical acquisitions I one day ascended a hill (Nipple Summit) on the North Side of the Channel close to the Ship in company with some of the Gentlemen, & found my journey amply repaid by a number of new Plants never before discovered. As we did not know the time it might take us to reach the summit, we took with us some men to carry provision & water & landed pretty early in order to have the fatiguing part of the Journey over before the heat of the day. I also carried with me a portable Barometer to ascertain the height we might reach from the sea side, & as the day continud clear & serene without any material change of weather taking place between the observations, they will I think give the height of this Hill tolerably accurate. The first station was at the Sea Side on our landing in the Morning where the Mercury in the Barometer stood at 29.85 & the second station was on the top of the Hill in about three hours & an half after where it stood at 27.10 & where the temperature of the air by Farenheit's Thermometer was at the same time 64°. The difference between these two observations of the Barometer shew that the / Column of Mercury sunk by our ascent 2.75 which makes the perpendicular height of the Hill about 867 Yards above the level of the Sea, but it is a mere hilloc in comparison to others immediately behind it, & particularly to the great range of continental mountains which terminated our view to the Northward.

Though the day was favourable our view from the top of the Hill was very circumscribed on account of the higher mountains which every where surrounded us, those to the Southward & South West were more remote by the great Arm intervening which appeared underneath us like a large Lake checquerd over with a great number of Islands of different size & figure, many of the smaller ones were naked & rocky, but the larger ones were in general wooded with Pines of a stinted appearance, this added to the broken rugged & gloomy prospect which the Country presented on both sides made this part of the great Arm be named *Desolation Reach*.

It was probably from the top of Nipple Summit that Mr. Zachary Mudge, Vancouver's First Lieutenant, spotted Discovery Passage beyond Quadra Island and surmised that it led north to the sea via the Strait of which Mr. Johnstone was then exploring.

Vancouver later named the point at the entrance to Discovery Passage after him. (Cape Mudge).

Archibald Menzies also appears to have had a good time in Teakerne Arm:

Near the bottom of a deep Cove which obtain the name of *Cascade Cove* about a mile & a half to the North East of the Ship there was a beautifull Waterfall which issued from a Lake close behind it & precipitated a wide foaming stream into the Sea over a shelving rocky precipice of about thirty yards high, its wild romantic appearance aided by its rugged situation & the gloomy forests which surrounded it, rendered it a place of resort for small parties to visit during our stay. On the Banks of this Lake I found several species of Plants . . . & in the Lake itself we found some Bivalve Shells which were quite new to me — It appeared to be very deep & its sides were strewd with a great number of fallen Trees.

This description fits remarkably well today with the addition of a tall spar pole above the Waterfall and a large barge beneath in "Cascade Cove". This barge, provided by the Alice Lake Logging Co., has provided convenient moorage for visitors for several years. On the barge, rapidly becoming waterlogged, there is a sign which instructs those who tie alongside to pay their moorage fee at "the office". A thorough search of the woods alongside the trail leading up the cliff to Cassel Lake revealed no sign of any office in 1976. One hopes the barge will remain for many years since anchorage close to the Waterfall would be difficult because of the great depth of water. Although the area around the outlet of Cassel Lake above the waterfall is littered with discarded logging machinery and cables one can easily visualize Menzies and his colleagues enjoying the opportunity for fresh water bathing in the delightfully warm waters of the Lake. A swimming platform is located about 100 yards past the lip of the waterfall along the west shore of the Lake, below a steeply sloping rock beach.

Most of Teakerne Arm which would be shallow enough for anchorage is used for the storage of log booms, which could however be used for temporary moorage as long as one is prepared to move at a moment's notice. The easternmost arm is the centre of operations for a MacMillan Bloedel logging camp and is used for the dumping, sorting and booming of logs.

Temporary anchorage with good protection from the southeast is possible close to the southern shore of Talbot Cove or in the small cove just north of Joyce Point. Talbot Cove is open to night time northwest winds.

Despite his crew's diversions with spruce beer and Cassel Lake bathing parties, Vancouver waited "with no little impatience" the return of his remaining exploring parties as he was anxious to move on. Their situation here . . . afforded not a single prospect that was pleasing to the eye, the smallest recreation on shore (this is a surprising statement in light of Menzies' account)

. . . nor animal nor vegetable food, excepting a very scanty proportion of those eatables already described, and of which the adjacent country was soon exhausted, after our arrival. Nor did our exploring parties meet with a more abundant supply, whence the place obtained the name of Desolation Sound; where our time would have passed infinitely more heavily, had it not been relieved by the agreeable society of our Spanish friends.

It should be noted that Vancouver appears to have been thoroughly disgusted with the entire area between Johnstone and Georgia Straits as his definition of Desolation Sound encompasses all the territory reached by his exploring parties. This name is now

Archae, Tumbo *and* Pelin *in Teakerne Arm*

officially confined to the body of water south of West Redonda Island, but yachtsmen persist in referring to the larger area as Desolation Sound.

The relative distaste for this area held by the early British explorers appears to have been shared by some early settlers. Maud Emery, in her novel *A Seagull's Cry*, paints a depressing picture of logging camp life in Teakerne Arm in the early part of this century and of the hermits who often secreted themselves away in the woods, emerging only when starved for human companionship on moonlight nights. John Erikson, in his "Cruise of the Emquad" (Nor'westing) describes these surroundings in this manner:

> An awesome mist-enshrouded inlet opened up to the east flanked by incredibly steep mountains that ran up into the low overcast. A place for J. R. Tolkien. Orcs and trolls could be anywhere along the length of Teakerne Arm.

The *Discovery* and *Chatham* parted company with the *Sutil* and *Mexicana* on July 13, 1792 sailing south and out into the northern Strait of Georgia before proceeding north through Discovery Passage.

The Spaniards noted in their journal:

> We parted with many expressions of friendship and mutual confidence, and the commanders of the two expeditions mutually presented each other with copies of the explorations which had been achieved up to that point.

> As the wind was unfavourable, we delayed our departure until the tide began to come in, which was at eight in the morning, and then prepared to sail, but seeing that all our efforts to make progress were vain, we returned to the anchorage which we had left.

> On the fourteenth, after taking the sun, we set sail to avail ourselves of the favourable current, although the wind blew strongly from the north-west. We headed to the wind all the morning, making from shore to shore, being now near one, now the other, in order to escape the opposing eddies and to make use of such as were favourable. Even so however, we were able to make only about half a mile, and a great part of this we lost on our two last tacks against the contrary tide, and we anchored on the north-east coast in twenty-five fathoms, with a sandy, shelly bottom.

> Despite the fact that the weather on the fifteenth was similar to that of the previous days and promised no better results, whatever efforts we might make against it, we none the less set sail at eight in the morning and kept to the wind without any gain, until we found that we were losing ground, when we anchored at half-past two in the afternoon on the south-west coast very near the point whence we had started.

> The same unfavourable conditions prevailed on the sixteenth, except that the in-coming tide made it possible to change our course, the wind being steady in the north-west. This discovery confirmed us in the idea which we have already mentioned that there is no regularity in the tide in these channels. That which is in the same direction as the wind is strong, but that which is opposed to it, being held back by the wind, can hardly be observed. In the night we noticed that the tide from the south-east had force enough to move the ship, although the wind was not less strong. We hoped that the coming day would offer us greater promise than had the days previous, but as the tide was against us until ten in the morning we waited and at that hour set sail, continuing under canvas until two in the afternoon, when the wind which assisted us having fallen, we preferred to row very close to the shore in order to free ourselves from the force of the current.

Bedevilled by contrary winds and tides, the Spaniards took four days to leave Lewis Channel, where today a small sailing yacht might take four hours under similar conditions. Galiano and Valdes labelled Lewis Channel "La Separicion" to commemorate their parting with Vancouver.

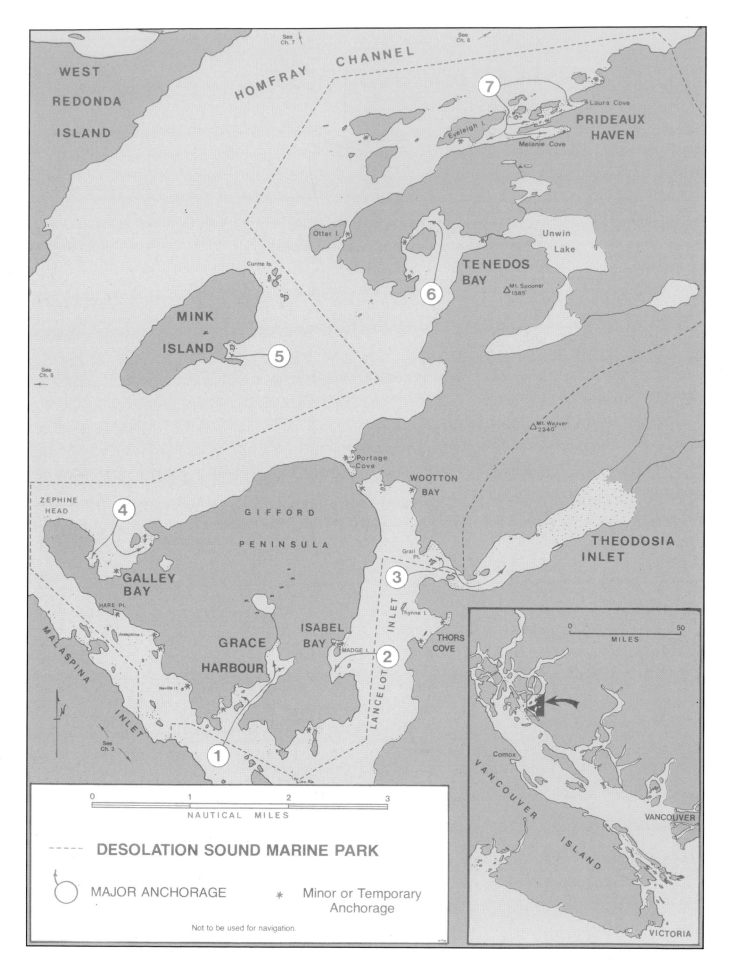

WEST

REDONDA

ISLAND

HOMFRAY CHANNEL

See Ch. 7

See Ch. 6

Laura Cove

Eveleigh I.

PRIDEAUX HAVEN

Melanie Cove

Otter I.

Unwin Lake

Curme Is.

TENEDOS BAY

Mt. Spooner 1585'

MINK ISLAND

See Ch. 5

Mt. Weaver 2340'

Portage Cove

ZEPHINE HEAD

GIFFORD

WOOTTON BAY

THEODOSIA INLET

GALLEY BAY

PENINSULA

Grail Pt.

HARE Pt.

Thynne I.

Josephine I.

ISABEL BAY

THORS COVE

MALASPINA

GRACE HARBOUR

MADGE I.

Neville It.

INLET

Lion Rk.

See Ch. 3

LANCELOT INLET

Scale

0   1   2   3

NAUTICAL MILES

- - - - **DESOLATION SOUND MARINE PARK**

◯ MAJOR ANCHORAGE   ✳ Minor or Temporary Anchorage

Not to be used for navigation.

0   50

MILES

Comox

VANCOUVER

VANCOUVER

ISLAND

VICTORIA

76

CHAPTER SIX

Desolation Sound Marine Park

Malaspina Inlet to Prideaux Haven

Many experienced yachtsmen regard the Desolation Sound area as not only the most beautiful and varied cruising area in British Columbia, but equal to, if not better than any other area in the rest of the world. This is not an idle boast. In the variety of spectacular scenery, warm summer climate and unusually warm waters (up to 26°C), abundance of shelter and anchorages, this area is a microcosm of all that is best about salt water cruising in British Columbia. The almost complete absence of development or settlement results in a high degree of isolation or "wilderness" feeling. This quality, which disturbed Captain Vancouver so much and led to his naming the area "Desolation", is a quality that many people today wish to experience. Civilization has not yet permanently branded the landscape of this part of Desolation Sound. Due in part to its location beyond the northern terminus of the coast highway, there are few shoreline cottages and no settlements, marinas or government wharves.

In order to preserve this quality, the government of British Columbia established Desolation Sound Marine Park in 1973. The park comprises over 14,000 acres of upland and 6,350 acres of foreshore and water, making it the largest marine park in British Columbia and virtually the only major park of any kind on the Pacific mainland coast of Canada. When the park was originally established, there were eleven private holdings (nine in foreign ownership) within the park. The Parks Branch policy is to acquire these holdings gradually as they become available. At present, six properties remain private. It has been re-quested that visitors to the park respect the private property rights of the remaining owners, particularly Galley Bay, Portage Cove and the south tip of the Gifford Peninsula. Parks Branch policy is for minimal development of the park to protect the wilderness qualities. In the future, a few isolated campsites, trails and toilet facilities may be constructed if increased use of the park warrants it.

The topography varies from the relatively low rolling hills of the Gifford Peninsula to the Unwin Range rising over 4,500 feet directly behind Prideaux Haven. Due to the greatly indented shoreline, there are seven major anchorage areas which provide good protection in all weather conditions. These major anchorages are themselves indented into several arms or coves. In addition, there are over 30 fairly safe temporary anchorage locations which may be used if wind and tide conditions are suitable. Only half of these temporary anchorage locations are shown on the map. Indeed, it is possible to spend over two months in this area and never anchor more than one

CHARTS
3594 — DISCOVERY PASSAGE, TOBA INLET
   and CONNECTING PASSAGES
   (1:75,000)
3562 — REDONDA ISLANDS (1:37,500)
3573 — MALASPINA INLET (1:12,600)
   (discontinued)
3559 — MALASPINA INLET, OKEOVER INLET
   and LANCELOT INLET (1:12,000)
   (Metric)
3555 — Plan of PRIDEAUX HAVEN (1:6,000)

night in the same location. All differ in character. Most are either totally or partly enclosed by low shoreline or high cliffs, islands or mountain sides, but some have spectacular open vistas up long waterways to distant mountain peaks.

A few of the smaller temporary anchorages are only safe enough for one boat at a time. In some, it is necessary to take several lines ashore to avoid swinging into the closely adjacent shoreline. It is usually difficult to find these smaller nooks by a quick perusal of the largest scale chart. Close but careful exploration of the shoreline reveals that what looks impractical or impossible on the chart is feasible in reality. It is often these smaller anchorages which prove most delightful, especially after retreating from one of the more crowded major anchorages.

Winds in this area tend to be flukey and omni-directional. The normal northwest-southeast wind pattern does not exist here. This is partly because, with the exception of Malaspina Inlet, the general trend of topography and water channels is northeast-southwest, and perpendicular to the topography which controls wind direction in the Gulf of Georgia. The southeast wind which brings bad weather to the Gulf manifests itself here as a southerly or southwesterly or even as a northerly (blowing down Homfray Channel or out of Waddington Channel), sometimes unexpectedly and often with considerable force. The good-weather northwesterly is often referred to as a

westerly and in Desolation Sound usually comes from the southwest, combining with a diurnal onshore wind to blow most consistently on summer after-noons. Characteristically, however, winds tend to be light or nonexistent.

Some people who may want to visit Desolation Sound but feel inhibited by the lack of a large enough cruising vessel to get here, should consider the possi-bility of driving to Okeover Landing (three miles south of the Park) and launching a canoe or kayak. This means of exploration is probably best suited to the quiet, protected waterways and there is an abun-dance of possible camping areas ashore, easily acces-sible from the waters edge.

Malaspina Inlet

The southwest shore of this inlet has been de-scribed earlier (Chapter 3). The northeast shore, as well as the majority of islands within the inlet are included within the boundary of Desolation Sound Marine Park. Temporary anchorage is possible in sev-eral indentations along the northeast shore with careful use of Chart 3559 or an updated version of Chart 3573 to avoid the many rocks. In particular, the cove south of Hare Point, the two coves east and

Below and at left, Grace Harbour.

Isabel Bay.

southeast of Josephine Island and the cove behind Neville Inlet. From these locations one can explore by dinghy the many islets and rocks in the inlet, noting particularly the varied intertidal life which is a product of the warmer waters and of the tidal currents keeping mainland predators at bay. Recent surveys (1977) by the Hydrographic Service have revealed a number of previously undiscovered rocks with less than six feet of water over them (below chart datum) in Malaspina Inlet. In particular — ¼ mile NW of Hare Point (previously charted as 4 fathoms), 150 yards NW of Cavendish Rock, 100 yards N of Neville Islet, 100 yards N of Lion Rock.

1   Grace Harbour

Several exploration and anchorage possibilities are found in the outer portion of Grace Harbour, particularly north of Jean Island, in that part of the Harbour which is surrounded by Indian Reserve Land. The entire north shore of Grace Harbour (on either side of the Indian Reserve) was formerly privately owned but was added to the park in 1975. The southern tip of the Gifford Peninsula from the bench mark around to Edith Island is still privately owned.

The inner part of Grace Harbour is completely protected from all winds and seas. It would be hard to find a more protected haven anywhere. A trail leads inland from the northern most arm and connects with a maze-like lattice-work of disused logging roads which cover the Gifford Peninsula. A half mile up the main trail, one comes to a delightful beaver-dammed freshwater lake where one can relax in the tepid and peaty-coloured waters. The beaver dam has caused the lake to expand and flood an extensive tract of lowland to the west and northeast of the lake. The trail winds north crossing an open wetland meadow before disappearing into the thickly wooded slopes which rise toward the east end of the peninsula.

2   Isabel Bay

Isabel Bay, in Lancelot Inlet, provides limited anchorage for a few boats in a small cove at its lower end and two tiny nooks for one or possibly two boats behind Madge Island at its northern end. The inner part of this anchorage is protected from the east by an outer reef and a tombolo like reef and islet which join Madge Island to the mainland. Chart 3573 indicates that the basin between this outer reef and the tombolo can be entered from the northeast and retains 3 feet of water at low water (chart datum).

Thors Cove

Thors Cove is outside the Park and is not an ideal anchorage. With a southeast wind blowing up

Okeover Inlet and out Malaspina, this same wind will blow up Lancelot Inlet as a southerly and almost directly into Thors Cove as a westerly. The best protection in these circumstances can be found in the extreme south end of the cove or directly behind a tiny 12-foot islet near the south end.

On the morning of June 27, 1792, Archibald Menzies and his boat crew from H.M.S. *Discovery* are reported to have had breakfast on Thynne Island after returning from an unsuccessful attempt to discover whether Theodosia Inlet led to the northwest passage.

3   Theodosia Inlet

Grail and Galahad Points, the two northern protrusions along the entrance to Theodosia were probably named by the same individual who, intrigued with Camelot, named Lancelot Inlet. Safe anchorage in front of an old homestead and orchard (formally private but now part of the Park) is possible immediately behind the conspicuous pointed Susan Islets.

The current runs quite quickly through the narrow twisting creek-like channel way which opens up inside Theodosia to a beautiful vista of subdued but

Thors Cove, Isabel Bay in background.

verdant green from the extensive grassy estuary mouth contrasting with the purple-white of distant mountains. Theodosia Inlet is almost a lagoon as the shallow entrance channel inhibits the entrance of salt water but permits easy egress for the surface fresh water outflow from the Theodosia River. Because of the predominant freshwater outflow, the direction of current in the entrance channel does not always adhere to what one might expect from the tide tables, especially in the spring when river discharge is highest. The freshwater also adds to the clarity of the entrance channel making the boulders and weeds on the bottom appear much closer than they actually are. There should always be at least 6 feet of water as long as one stays in centre channel and avoids the boulders projecting south from the point between the two islets.

These two islets, while outside the boundaries of Desolation Sound Marine Park, are protected by Park reserve. The islet at the entrance is often used as a picnic site and there are flat areas suitable for camping with a most enjoyable scenic outlook. A shallow

Looking out from entrance to Theodosia Inlet.

bay on the southeast side of the islet can be used for beaching one's canoe or kayak. The islet just inside Theodosia Inlet has a badly eroded pictograph on its south face. Good anchorage is available throughout the Inlet as well as behind this islet.

Theodosia Inlet has long been used as the base for local logging operations since the inlet waters provided an ideally sheltered location for the sorting and booming of logs. While the extensive tidal flats were once used for the storage of booms, this practice appears to have ended here. Estuaries such as these are critically important for the rearing and livelihood of many birds, marine organisms and fish, and log booming has often caused extensive damage to the natural habitat. Beyond the tidal flats and the Tokwana Indian Reserve is an extensive flat area extending back into the mountains for over 5 miles and linked by a logging road with Powell Lake. This area was originally farmed in the 1890s. One can paddle a canoe or dinghy through the tidal flats and up the northern distributary, past logged-over areas and pastoral farmland; or hike the logging road from the south shore of the Inlet.

Wootton Bay

Wootton Bay was previously named "Brazo de Bustamente" by Galiano and Valdes in 1792. Walbran *(British Columbia Coast Names)* describes Wootton as a ships officer, postmaster and harbour master in Victoria in 1862. Several temporary anchorages are possible near the head of Wootton Bay with good protection from the nightime westerly but somewhat exposed to anything from the south or southeast.

Portage Cove

On the other side of a narrow isthmus, which joins Gifford Peninsula to the mainland, is Portage Cove. This property is private and not (at present writing) part of Desolation Sound Marine Park. Unfortunately due to the attractiveness and prime location of this property, the owner has over the years been beseiged by canoeists wishing to portage the isthmus, yachtsmen and others wishing to have a look at "the other side". The low land between Portage Cove and Wooton Bay is very good agricultural land and the

Portage Cove.

Wootton Bay.

Galley Bay.

owner has tended with care a large orchard and garden. All reports are that he is not favourably disposed to casual visitors. Portage Cove itself is suitable only for temporary anchorage near high tide as it dries out almost completely at low tide.

4   Galley Bay

Another bay which is still partly private is Galley Bay. This bay has an interesting history. Known widely for many years as one of the largest communes on the B.C. coast, it attracted people from all over but mainly from Quebec and California. At times, over 100 people were settled around the bay, attempting to survive on the abundant natural foods in the area and the produce from a farm which stretches for several hundred yards behind Galley Bay towards Zephine Head. Unfortunately, few of the aspiring commune members were addicted to the hard work, cooperation and discipline necessary to keep everyone fed. In times of hardship, girls from the commune would remove all their clothes and swim out to yachts at anchor to beg for cigarettes and other edibles. This practice was greeted with much delight by the skippers, but with some degree of disdain by the skippers' mates. Zoe Landale has an interesting account of life in this commune and some of the factors which may

Galley Bay.

Mink Island anchorage.

have led to its downfall in her book; *Harvest of Salmon: Adventures in Fishing the B.C. Coast.*

Good anchorage is available in the westermost nook below the commune farm, or behind the island in the eastern part of the bay. The central part of the bay has two dangerous drying rocks and is exposed to the northwest. A small lake is located about ¼ mile south of the eastern end of the bay.

5 Mink Island

Mink Island (formerly known as Repulse Island) is outside of the park boundaries but is still one of the most popular anchorages in Desolation Sound. The outer anchorage is fairly deep and completely open to the east, although this has not proved to be a dangerous exposure in this area. Shallower, more protected anchorage is possible behind a small islet in depths of 2 fathoms near the head of the cove. Occasionally, boom sticks or other impediments block access to the head of the cove but these can usually be shifted or bypassed. A drying lagoon behind the islet is interesting to explore. Several years ago, a friendly goat was pastured on the island during the summer months, growing fat on oysters from the lagoon. Will Dawson *(Coastal Cruising)* notes that a fresh water stream pours into the cove here and a trail leads back into the woods to a strangely hushed place of drowned trees.

The Curme Islands off the eastern tip of Mink Island are also challenging to explore. Temporary anchorage (depending on the state of the tide and the size of your boat) is possible by threading your way through an extremely narrow dog-leg channel between the three northern Curme Islands. Although Chart 3562 shows this passage in a half blue tint (generally indicating depths of 3 to 6 fathoms), the channel probably dries at low tide (chart datum).

6 Tenedos Bay

When Archibald Menzies visited this bay in 1792, he described it as "the deep Bay" — the name by which it has been known locally for many years. The impression of deepness in the bay is accentuated by the steep, enclosing nature of the surrounding

Children, domestic goat and Mink Island oysters.

86

Curme Islands

Temporary anchorage at southwestern end of Tenedos Bay.

Easternmost cove in Tenedos Bay, Lake Unwin in background.

shoreline. Although the central part of the bay is over 300 feet deep, there are many small coves and crannies shallow enough for small craft to find anchorage.

The largest, most protected anchorage area is in the extreme northern end of the bay, More seclusion may be found behind the large island which is connected to the mainland by a 6-foot drying tombolo. The southern entrance to the small landlocked 3 fathom cove at the west end of this island has been charted at 9 feet but rocks immediately west of the island may dry 6 feet and the central part of the passage is reported to have a depth of only 1-foot below chart datum. The feeling of security and protection afforded by the close proximity of the surrounding bluffs may be deceptive as strong westerly winds have been known to swoop down into the gap between the island and the mainland at night.

The temporary anchorage at the southwestern end of Tenedos Bay is best entered via the passage marked 8 fathoms, as the eastern entrance while wider (at high tide), has a dangerous reef (which is not shown clearly on Chart 3562) extending south of the 10-foot islet.

Despite its partial exposure to westerly winds, the eastern most cove in Tenedos Bay is usually the busiest as this is where everyone anchors in order to visit Unwin Lake. The terminus of the stream which drains the lake is through a deserted homestead and orchard which has long been used as an informal campsite. The Lake is only five minutes by trail from the sea and halfway along the trail, it is possible to cut through the woods to the stream where some gentle rapids and deep pools provide an ideal secluded place to frolic in the very warm fresh water.

Some visitors portage their dinghies or canoes up to the Lake in order to try a little trout fishing. The Parks Branch may in future, construct trails around the lake linking Tenedos Bay and Unwin Lake with several smaller lakes between here and Prideaux Haven.

Otter Island protects an almost totally secluded anchorage, large enough for only a few boats. The passage separating Otter Island from the mainland, although extremely narrow, is deep enough for most

Landlocked 3-fathom cove, Tenedos Bay.

small craft to safely navigate. This island was named in association with other fur bearing animals honoured in Mink and Martin Islands in Desolation Sound.

7 Prideaux Haven

Undoubtedly, one of the most scenically outstanding anchorages anywhere, this well protected harbour has enough arms and interconnecting coves and passageways to safely accommodate hundreds of boats. From the main anchorage north of Melanie

Tenedos Bay.

89

Tenedos Bay.

Prideaux Haven

Point, there is a spectacular open vista up Homfray Channel toward perpetual snowfields surrounding a conspicuous mitre-shaped peak — Mt. Denman. This peak rises abruptly behind Forbes Bay to a height of 6,590 feet. Flanking this view, on either side of Homfray Channel is Mt. Addenbroke on East Redonda Island (over 5,000 feet) and Dudley Cone on the mainland (over 4,000 feet).

The entrance channel into Prideaux Haven is very narrow and shallow (8 feet of water below chart datum). Care must be taken to avoid a 3-foot drying rock close to Lucy Point on Eveleigh Island and a shelf with 2 feet of water below chart datum about 100 yards south of Lucy Point.

Prideaux Haven is a marvelous place to explore by dinghy. There are several tidal pools, miniature lagoons and marshes between the many islets and islands which surround the Haven. Some nooks and crannies might only be accessible by dinghy but some may be safely used as anchorages if tidal conditions are suitable. In particular, there is a narrow passageway between Copplestone Island and the Melanie Point Peninsula which, although it shoals rapidly towards Laura Cove, has enough water to accommodate a few boats. The tidal range for Prideaux Haven is possibly one of the largest on the lower coast — 18.4 feet for the largest tides.

At the heads of Melanie and Laura Coves are the remains of abandoned homesteads. Only traces of the old cabins, elaborate terraced rockeries and what were once thriving gardens, grape arbours and orchards are now discernible. The people who origi-nally lived here have long since gone, but two of them — Andrew "Mike" Shuttler and Phil Lavine are affectionately recalled in the *Curve of Time* by M. Wylie Blanchet.

Archibald Menzies' journal includes a fascinating description of a deserted Indian village which was estimated to have held about 300 persons:

After quitting this Bay (Tenedos) we followed the same Shore which still trended North Eastward & soon after passed by a narrow Channel on the inside of a Cluster of steep rocky Islands wooded with Pines, but did not proceed above a league when at the farther end of these Islands we came to a small Cove in the bottom of which the picturesque ruins of a deserted Village placd on the summit of an elevated projecting Rock excited our curiosity & inducd us to land close to it to view its structure.

This Rock was inaccessible on every side except a narrow pass from the Land by means of steps that admitted only one person to ascend at a time & which seemd to be well guarded in case of an attack, for right over it a large Maple Tree diffusd its spreading branches in such an advantageous manner as to afford an easy & ready access from the summit of the Rock to a conceald place amongst its branches, where a small party could watch unobservd & defend the Pass with great ease. We found the top of the Rock nearly level & wholly occupied with the skeletons of Houses — irregularly arrangd & very crouded; in some places the space was enlargd by strong scaffolds projecting over the Rock & supporting Houses apparently well securd — These also acted as a defence by increasing the natural strength of the place & rendering it still more secure & inaccessible. From the fresh appearance of every thing about this Village & the intollerable stench it would seem as if it had been very lately

Below, Melanie Cove. Overleaf, Prideaux Haven, Homfray Channel.

Prideaux Haven

occupied by the Natives. The narrow Lanes between the Houses were full of filth N nastiness & swarmd with myriads of *Fleas* which fixd themselves on our Shoes Stockings & cloths in such incredible number that the whole party was obligd to quit the rock in great precipitation, leaving the remainder of these Assailants in full possession of their Garrison without the least desire of facing again such troublesome enemy. We no sooner got to the Water side than some immediately stripped themselves quite naked & immersed their Cloth, others plungd themselves wholly into the Sea in expectation of drowning their adherents, but to little or no purpose, for after being submersd for some time they leapd about as frisky as ever; in short we towd some of the Cloths astern of the Boats, but nothing would clear them of this Vermin till in the evening we steepd them in boiling water. . . .

This Village from the disasters we met with obtaind the name of *Flea Village* & is situated about three leagues to the North East ward of the situation of the Vessels (then anchored near Kinghorn Island).

Although Menzies surmised that the original inhabitants had vacated their village on account of the Fleas, it is quite possible that this was a winter village and the Indians were away on their annual summer foraging expedition.

Many yachtsmen have searched diligently throughout Prideaux Haven for Menzies "Flea Village" but have failed to find it. It is there, *almost exactly as described* by Menzies. The large Maple tree has been replaced by several smaller ones. The steps, skeletons of Houses and scaffolds, stench and Fleas have disappeared being replaced by myriads of no-see-ums, rusty tins and ancient bottles and a thicket of small pines — the legacy of logging activity possibly 50 years ago.

Laura Cove.

Prideaux Haven is without a doubt a beautiful anchorage, but some yachtsmen mistakenly enter this anchorage in midsummer with visions of solitude, quiet and peace in their minds. Unfortunately, reality intrudes and they are greeted instead by a flottilla of boats, noisy waterskiiers and a subtle, but distinct "pong" rising from the waters. Because of the relatively shallow entrance, the large tidal range is not much help in flushing waters in and out of the Haven. From July to mid August, Prideaux Haven has the reputation of being one of the most crowded anchorages on the B.C. coast. Although many visitors enjoy swimming in the super warm water and sampling the local shellfish, it might be healthier to indulge in these pastimes before July or after August. In mid summer there are also nearby alternatives to the crowds in Prideaux Haven. Within two miles, there are at least five excellent one or two boat-size anchorages with almost perfect protection from wind and seas. One of these is so well hidden and inconspicuous on the chart that it is quite possible it never sees more than one or two boats in an entire summer. Many boats travel no further than Prideaux Haven itself, denying themselves the opportunity to experience the immensity of open space and solitude offered by Homfray Channel and Toba Inlet.

In addition, the scale of topography and amount of water space is so massive in and beyond Desolation Sound that someone used to cruising in the lower Gulf, can easily lose himself and find those qualities which make small boat exploration and cruising such a pleasure in this part of British Columbia.

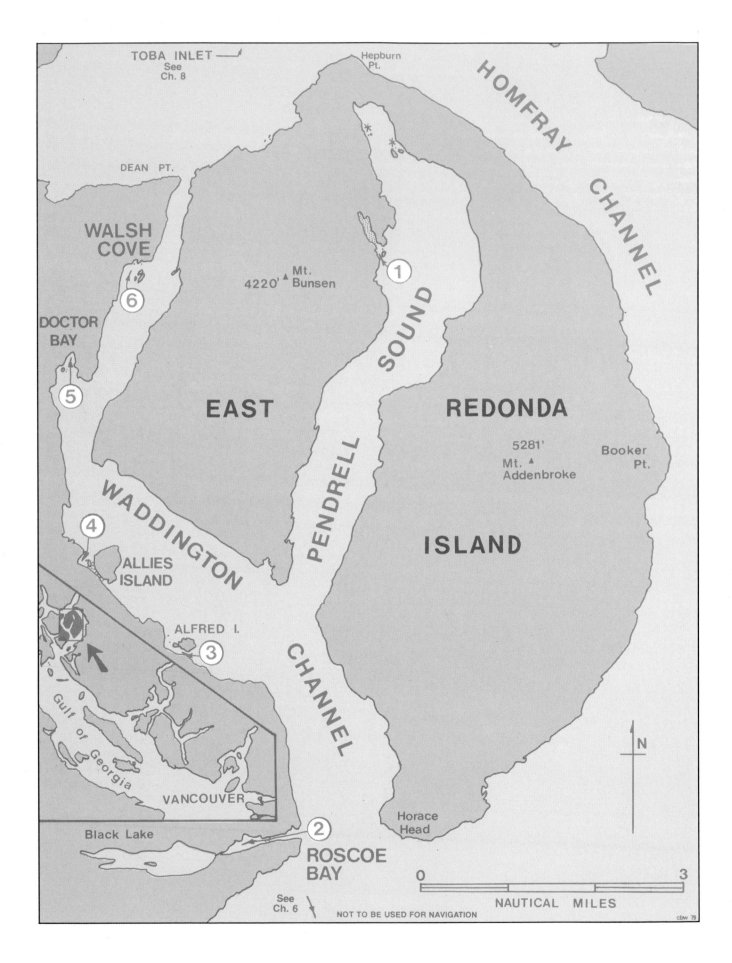

TOBA INLET
See
Ch. 8

Hepburn
Pt.

HOMFRAY CHANNEL

DEAN PT.

WALSH
COVE

⑥

4220' ▲ Mt.
Bunsen

①

DOCTOR
BAY

⑤

EAST

REDONDA

5281'
Mt. ▲
Addenbroke

Booker
Pt.

WADDINGTON

④

ALLIES
ISLAND

ISLAND

PENDRELL SOUND

Gulf of Georgia

ALFRED I.

③

CHANNEL

VANCOUVER

Black Lake

②

ROSCOE
BAY

Horace
Head

N

See
Ch. 6

NOT TO BE USED FOR NAVIGATION

0   3

NAUTICAL MILES

cbw 79

98

CHAPTER SEVEN

Waddington Channel and Pendrell Sound

Roscoe Bay, Allies Island, Walsh Cove

The waters surrounding East Redonda Island, just north of Desolation Sound Marine Park, are of considerable historic and oceanographic interest. In 1862 Captain Richards of H.M. surveying vessel *Hecate* named Waddington Channel in honour of Alfred Penderill Waddington — "an early pioneer of British Columbia, and at one time one of the wealthiest and most enterprising residents of Victoria." (Walbran).

Waddington was a truly remarkable man. Born in 1801 in London he was educated there and in France and Germany. Much of his early life was spent working in his family's mills in northern France. His brother's son was premier of France in 1879 and another nephew was a senator of France for 30 years. In 1849 he travelled to San Francisco and in 1858 at the age of 57, he came to Victoria with the first wave of adventurers attracted by the Fraser River gold rush. Over the next ten years he involved himself intensely in the life of Victoria, starting a wholesale grocery business, expanding Victoria's harbour, building new bridges and helping to establish the Fire Department, the Gas Company and the Royal Hospital. Waddington became the first Superintendent of Edu-

cation on Vancouver Island, and wrote and published the first book in western Canada (*The Fraser Mines Vindicated*). He was also elected to the Legislature and became the Leader of the Opposition. When he eventually left Victoria to pursue his Bute Inlet scheme in Ottawa (described at the end of Chapter 8) the *Victoria Daily Colonist* wrote "Mr. Waddington's career has been one of untiring industry, enterprise and zeal . . . never faltering in his belief that the Colony is destined to become one of the most important appendages of the British Crown."

It is likely that Pendrell Sound honours Waddington's middle name (originally spelled Penderill). Homfray Channel was named by Captain Pender in 1863 after the explorer Robert Homfray who was engaged by Alfred Waddington and the Hudson's Bay Company to conduct a survey of the Bute Inlet route to the Interior in the winter of 1861. The horrors of this expedition were so intense and the sufferings so se-

CHART
3562 — REDONDA ISLANDS (1:37,500)

The drying lagoon on the west side of Pendrell Sound is the most protected anchorage in the sound.

vere, that Homfray's journey has been called "one of the more remarkable on record; an epic of courage, determination and hardship which has few equals in provincial lore" (T. W. Paterson, *Victoria Colonist,* 9 March, 1975). It is interesting that Walbran *(B.C. Coast Names)* makes no mention of the connection between Waddington and Homfray. Apparently, Robert Homfray withheld publication of his journals for 30 years in deference to Waddington who, he said, "feared my descriptions of the many dangers encountered would prevent parties joining him in making the road through the Cariboo." Walbran also says of him: "He was of an eccentric disposition and for some years before his death had his tombstone erected in Ross Bay cemetery, with all particulars on it with the exception of the date of his decease, which was added after the 19 September, 1902, the day he died."

East Redonda Island

East Redonda Island is one of the largest islands in total volume of land mass for its surface area in B.C., if not the world. It towers to a height of over 5,200 feet (Mount Addenbroke) — the highest point on any of the islands lying off the mainland coast (with the exception of Vancouver Island). The great extremes in elevation for such a relatively small island have produced a unique ecosystem.

The eastern half of East Redonda Island is protected as an Ecological Reserve, the second to be established in B.C. (May 4, 1971), and the third largest in the province, comprising over 15,350 acres. The purpose of this Ecological Reserve is to preserve for scientific and educational study the four bio-geo-climatic zones which include a variety of natural life and vegetation habitats varying from the Douglas fir zone (up to about 1,500 feet elevation), western hemlock (up to 3,000 feet), mountain hemlock (up to 4,500 feet) and alpine tundra with a variety of heathers and associated high altitude wild flowers.

On the northern slopes of Mt. Addenbroke there are perpetual snowfields near the summit and the bio-geo-climatic zones all occur at lower elevations. This is possibly the only area in B.C. where widely different vegetation types can be seen over such a small area. One can also see the results of past logging activity which took place prior to establishment of the Reserve. There are three small private holdings within the Reserve, two on Homfray Channel south of Mt. Addenbroke and one west of the mountains in Pendrell Sound.

Halfway between the eastern side of Horace Head and Booker Point, directly off the mouth of Lloyd Creek on the other side of Homfray Channel, are two Indian pictographs or rock paintings (Lester Peterson). The lower painting depicts a single fish, swimming. The other painting, just a few yards up the channel portrays what could be a shoal of dogfish.

Oceanographically, the waters surrounding East Redonda Island are unique. In Homfray Channel, exactly 2 miles due east of Mount Addenbroke, is the second deepest sounding on the B.C. coast — 399 fathoms. (The deepest sounding of 418 fathoms is in Finlayson Channel on the east side of Swindle Island). Just north of Booker Point there is a huge crevice into which one could take a small boat and have a view straight up 5,000 feet to near the summit of Mt. Addenbroke. This view is now obscured by vegetation. Two miles west of Mt. Addenbroke, the waters of Pendrell Sound rise to temperatures of 78° f (26°C) in the summer months reputedly making these waters "the warmest north of the Gulf of Mexico."

Pendrell Sound

The reasons for the anomalous water temperatures of Pendrell Sound are somewhat complex. Normal water temperatures outside of Desolation Sound are considerably colder and in Johnstone Strait average less than 50°F. Apparently, heat resulting from solar radiation is not dissipated to any extent by vertical or horizontal mixing. Pendrell Sound is deep; there is no significant sill or shallow bar at the entrance, so there is very little horizontal tidal movement. Although there is no significant freshwater drainage into the Sound, a layer of water 10 to 20 feet deep with relatively low salinity is established during the early summer and acts as an insulating layer inhibiting the vertical movement of deeper cold water to the surface. There are virtually no currents or tidal exchange within the Sound and even outside currents are weak because of the depths of the channels and the close proximity of this area to the junction of tidal streams from around the ends of Vancouver Island.

Another important factor is that the high surrounding mountains act as a wind break. Because of the configuration of the Sound, a strong westerly wind will blow *up* the lower third of the Sound at the same time that it is blowing *down* the upper third of the Sound. The middle third of the Sound often re-

Looking southeast down Homfray Channel, with the head of Pendrell Sound on the right.

Walsh Cove and Gorge Islets, bottom, looking through Waddington Channel to Toba Inlet, top.

The top of Mt. Adenbroke on East Redonda Island, from Homfray Channel.

mains calm and it is not unusual for driftwood floating in the Sound in June to remain in the same general area throughout the summer months. However, the winds here can be freaky, especially in the spring or fall. In May, 1970 we enjoyed a spinnaker run all the way up Pendrell Sound with a light south wind while it was blowing a SE gale in the Strait of Georgia. Nearing the head of the Sound we prepared to down the spinnaker for the slow return beat when suddenly the wind shifted to the north for an exhilarating spinnaker run back down. By the time we reached Waddington Channel we had downed all sails and were making a comfortable 4 knots under bare poles. In July and August very strong west winds of considerable force may occur occasionally at night in the upper Sound.

The warm waters of Pendrell Sound give a beautiful, almost tropical, emerald hue to the shallower waters along the foreshore and, if conditions are right, allow oysters to breed and produce spat which is of tremendous importance to the growth of the oyster industry. Pendrell Sound is virtually the only location in B.C. where the water becomes consistently warm enough for the Pacific Oyster to produce spat on a regular basis. Over the last 30 years, Pendrell Sound has failed, on only three occasions, to produce a commercial "spatfall", (1954, 1973 and 1976). Every summer biologists from the Marine Resources Branch are stationed in the Sound to monitor water temperatures. When a spatfall is likely, they notify the oyster growers who converge on the Sound to collect the seeds (or spawn) to replenish their own stocks.

Powerboats entering Pendrell Sound are strongly urged to keep their speed below 4 knots. Large signs on shore and mounted on buoys, moored in the middle of the Sound read: "Attention: Provincial Oyster Reserve. This area is reserved for oyster seed collection. All vehicles (sic) are required to keep wash to a minimum. Violators will be prosecuted."

The reason for this caution is that the apparatus moored along the shore and used to collect the spat is often delicate and susceptible to any undue motion. The spatfall generally occurs over a three to six week period when water temperatures are at their maximum, generally starting in July.

1 Lagoon

The most protected anchorage in Pendrell Sound is in a small, 8-fathom cove behind a small islet near the outlet of a drying lagoon. The inside of the lagoon is muddy and dries about 10 to 15 feet above chart datum. In the 1920s this lagoon was apparently much deeper but recent logging may have contributed to increased erosion and silting up of the lagoon. There are wrecked barges both inside and outside the entrance to the lagoon. It is possible that these barges may have been used to collect oyster spat in past years. All along the shoreline of Pendrell Sound one can see the remains of various attempts to collect oyster spat.

There is reasonably good anchorage behind Alfred Island, across from the entrance to Pendrell Sound.

Temporary anchorage is also possible near the north end of the Sound behind clusters of islets which are connected to the shore at low tide. In the summer months this entire area is often taken up with log booms and other floating arrangements for collecting of spat. The biologists monitoring the Sound usually moor their barge behind the islets on the eastern shore near the head of the Sound.

West Redonda Island

2   Roscoe Bay

Near the southern entrance to Waddington Channel a narrow inlet known as Roscoe Bay knifes into the southeastern tip of West Redonda Island. There is a shallow bar halfway down this inlet which is awash at chart datum and which restricts access to and from the inner portion of the bay. Until quite recently, the northern shoreline of the inner anchorage was used as a log dump and booming ground. As logging in this part of West Redonda Island has diminished, the

Parks Branch is considering this anchorage as a potential park.

Black Lake which lies less than 10 feet above sea level is located approximately 100 yards west of the terminus of Roscoe Bay. When timber harvesting was occurring on Black Lake, a flume was constructed between the lake and the Bay. Remnants of this flume are still visible. There is an old logging road which leads from the Bay to some bare rocks on the north shore of Black Lake which are ideal for sunbathing or diving into the warm, fresh waters.

3   Alfred Island

There is reasonably good anchorage behind this previously unnamed island across from the entrance to Pendrell Sound. Due north of here the shoreline of East Redonda Island rises abruptly in a spectacularly sheer cliff, almost 1,800 feet from the water.

4   Allies Island

Formerly known as Prussian Island, this island was renamed in a bout of patriotic fervour following World War I. Good anchorage is available behind a small islet between Allies Island and West Redonda

Another good anchorage is behind the small islet between Allies Island and West Redonda Island.

Island. The passage between Allies Island and West Redonda dries about 10 feet and is crammed with oysters. Close to high water, this area is fascinating to explore by dinghy. A sign on shore reads: "Oyster Lease: These tidelands are Private Property. Trespassers will be prosecuted." In B.C. there is no such thing as "private tidelands", as almost all land between high and low tide is "Crown foreshore". Crown foreshore is administered by the government to ensure public access. Leases are granted to individuals or companies for limited periods to protect certain rights (such as commercial oyster harvesting) but do not convey private property rights.

5   Doctor Bay

This bay provides well protected anchorage at its head or near an islet in the western part of the bay.

There is a stream from a small lake about ½ mile west of Doctor Bay and there are a few logging roads providing the opportunity for inland exploration. A sunken booming boat lies in front of two houses on the western shore.

6   Walsh Cove

This small anchorage has long been a favourite among many Desolation Sound yachtsmen because of its compactness, location and seemingly perfect protection. Strong north winds have a tendency to funnel down into the cove however. The Gorges Islets protects one somewhat from any wash from passing powerboats in Waddington Channel. A small promontory north of the Gorges Islets (west of Butler Point) was formerly known as Kate Point. There is a 3-foot drying rock at the entrance to the small nook behind Kate Point. At Butler Point, there are two sets of Indian pictographs. These may be what Lester Peterson described as being located at Bishop Point near Doc-

Good protection from all winds is available in Doctor Bay.

tor Bay: "The head and body of a fish stand upright, as if the creature is in the act of leaping clear of the water. One sharp eye seeming to watch the observer creates a rather startling effect." In 1911, the geologist J. Austen Bancroft noted the presence of a beautiful pink granite here which was somewhat similar to the celebrated Baveno granite near Lake Maggiore, Italy, "but the shade of pink is more delicate and its general appearance more pleasing."

Because of the beauty of the surroundings and the critical location, Walsh Cove is being considered as a potential provincial marine park. Walsh Cove serves as the last protected anchorage in Waddington Channel for yachtsmen preparing to explore Toba Inlet.

Walsh Cove is a very pleasant anchorage which can be shared with a few other boats without any undue sense of crowding. However, at times other boats' activities which are not completely compatible with the surroundings can be somewhat disconcerting. Several years ago, friends reported that they were peacefully anchored here almost alone, the nearest other boat being anchored at a considerable distance to the south. Suddenly the still of the evening was broken by the sound of plopping splashes around their own craft, as if the fish were jumping in the cove. Just before casting their fishing lines over the side they noticed that an unexplained whizzing sound preceded each splash. With binoculars they looked for large birds passing overhead to no avail. Then they scanned a large vessel to the south where two gentlemen, resplendent in golfing attire were practising their golf swings on the foredeck.

Although the narrows between Dean Point, West Redonda Island and East Redonda Island at the north end of Waddington Channel are less than 200 yards wide, there is only a moderate (less than 2 knots) tidal current here, which is somewhat influenced by winds and outflow from Toba Inlet. Generally, the flood tide moves south, the ebb north. There is a small cave behind a distinctive shield rock on the shoreline just past the 8-foot high rocks midway between Dean Point and Hepburn Point on East Redonda Island.

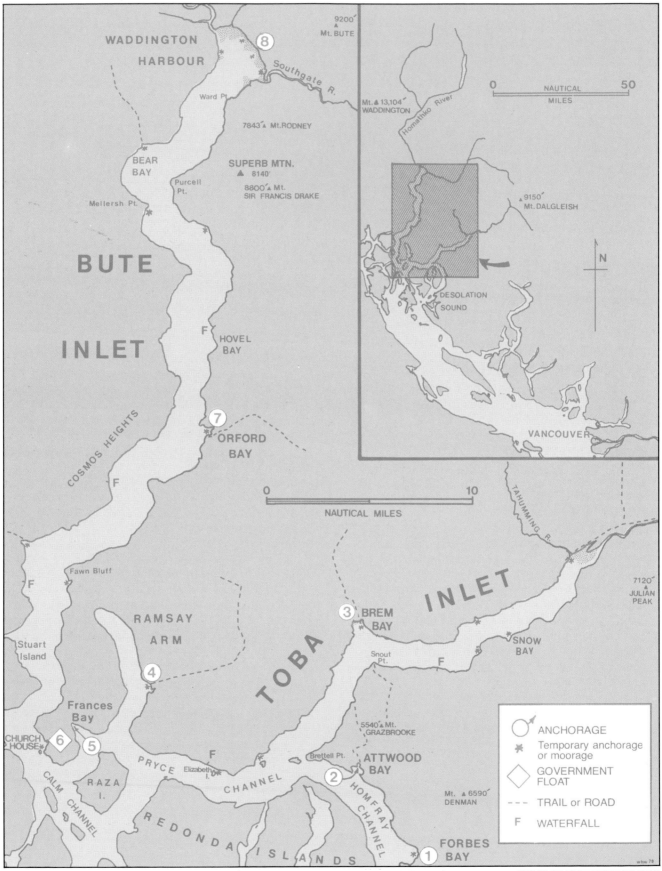

WADDINGTON HARBOUR

9200' ▲ Mt. BUTE

Southgate R.

Ward Pt.

Mt. ▲ 13,104 WADDINGTON

Homathko River

7843' ▲ Mt. RODNEY

BEAR BAY

Purcell Pt.

SUPERB MTN. ▲ 8140'

8800' ▲ Mt. SIR FRANCIS DRAKE

▲ 9150' Mt. DALGLEISH

Mellersh Pt.

0   NAUTICAL   50
MILES

BUTE

INLET

F HOVEL BAY

COSMOS HEIGHTS

F

N

DESOLATION SOUND

VANCOUVER

ORFORD BAY

F

0   NAUTICAL MILES   10

TAHUMMING R.

Fawn Bluff

F

RAMSAY ARM

TOBA   INLET

3 BREM BAY

7120' JULIAN PEAK

Stuart Island

Snout Pt.

F

SNOW BAY

4

Frances Bay

5540' ▲ Mt. GRAZBROOKE

CHURCH HOUSE 6

5

RAZA I.

PRYCE   CHANNEL

Elizabeth I.

Brettell Pt.

ATTWOOD BAY

CALM CHANNEL

REDONDA   ISLANDS

2

HOMFRAY CHANNEL

Mt. ▲ 6590 DENMAN

○⟋ ANCHORAGE

✳ Temporary anchorage or moorage

◇ GOVERNMENT FLOAT

- - - TRAIL or ROAD

F WATERFALL

1 FORBES BAY

NOT TO BE USED FOR NAVIGATION

106

CHAPTER EIGHT

Bute and Toba Inlets

Bute and Toba Inlets, penetrating deeply into the Coast Mountains north of Desolation Sound, can provide the inquisitive yachtsman with an awesome cruising experience. These lonely and remote Inlets are seldom visited because they are completely devoid of marinas, permanent settlements, parks or well-protected anchorages. Unlike other inlets further up the coast, they have no towns at their heads nor roads nor rail connections with the interior of the Province.

The mountains which surround Bute and Toba Inlets cannot be said to be truly spectacular but they have been described as immense, barren, austere and majestic. The enclosed, isolated feeling which they give to the solitary traveller may be oppressive or intimidating to some, while others may feel greatly humbled and full of wonder. J. Austen Bancroft writing in 1911 for the Geological Society of Canada described these two inlets (and Knight Inlet) in this manner:

> In the grandeur of their scenery (these) inlets surpass all the others within this area and must rival in their magnificence all examples of the fiord type in the world.

He also noted:

> the Government would do well to reserve one or two of the most picturesque fiords as parks, while they are yet in a state of almost primeval grandeur.

This has yet to happen, although some would say it is too late.

While completely protected anchorages are hard to find along the shores of these inlets, there are many nooks and crannies or tiny bays where it is possible to lay out an anchor in deep water with one ot two stern lines ashore to prevent swinging. If the water is too deep for safe anchoring and the cove is small enough, it may be possible to moor with bow and stern lines to opposite sides of the cove.

At the heads of the inlets and in larger bays where rivers discharge over broad tidal flats there is usually an area of suitable depth for temporary anchorage. Because of the opaque milkiness of glacially fed waters entering these inlets it is often impossible to determine the depth of the water by eyesight. This is a special hazard on estuarine tidal flats as depth sounder or lead line may not reveal the presence of nearby underwater obstructions such as sand bars, snags (usually root stumps or buried deadheads) and isolated boulders. If the wind should shift, the anchor could drag and pull out in deeper water over the edge of the delta or swing the boat onto a sandbar or underwater obstruction. For these reasons, and because of the openness to occasionally violent winds, anchorages in inlet estuaries are described as "indifferent" (B.C. Pilot) and boats should not be left untended for long unless securely moored fore and aft. At several locations along these inlets there may be private or logging company floats which could be used in an emergency or for temporary moorage with the owner's permission.

In summer, winds tend to blow up the inlets during the day, being particularly strong in the afternoon and down the inlets at night and in the early morning. This is a general rule, as it is not unusual to have calm winds or completely different winds blowing in the inlet at the same time.

CHARTS
3594 — for TOBA INLET and approaches to
      BUTE INLET (1:75,000)
3562 — for HOMFRAY and PRYCE CHANNELS
      (1:37,500)
3563 — for RAMSAY ARM (1:37,500)
3524 — for BUTE INLET (1:75,000)

Mountain enshrouded in clouds and mist, trees dripping, water falling off cliffs to the sea. Mood of Pryce Channel in late August is dark and sombre.

Winds may even blow in different directions on opposite sides of the same reach, or come gusting down a steep valley as a "williwaw" hitting the water violently before shooting perpendicularly across the inlet. In winter, both inlets are subject to occasionally fierce down-inlet winds whenever there is an outbreak of cold polar air from a high pressure area on the Interior Plateau. The "Bute wind" is notorious for being one of the most ferocious winter winds on the B.C. Coast. It often begins unexpectedly and can blow down the inlet at speeds gusting over 100 mph for several days.

Although tidal ranges in the inlets are substantial (17.9 feet at springs), normal tidal currents are minimal because of the great depths of the inlets and the absence of any substantial sills at their mouths. There is often a prevailing outward surface current caused by the flow of fresh water in a layer over the salt water. This current flows at 1 to 2 knots being strongest after prolonged rainfall or after hot weather in early summer has caused rapid melting of snow and glaciers in the mountains. Spring ebb tides may increase this current to 3 knots while the flood may reduce it by a knot or so. A strong down-inlet wind may also increase this surface current and a strong up-inlet wind of long duration may eliminate the current altogether.

The surface current tends to be strongest along the western or northern shores of the inlets. It is therefore best to keep to starboard when travelling in these inlets — along the eastern or southern shores to avoid the current when travelling up the inlet, and along the west or northern shores to gain full advantage when coming down the inlet.

Since their first discovery by European explorers these inlets have had tragic histories as both have been touted at one time or another to become the Pacific terminus of trans-continental railways or roads. These speculations led to various explorations, surveys, road construction efforts and settlement attempts which often ended disastrously after incredible suffering and hardships.

Homfray Channel

Of the three possible approach channels to Toba Inlet, the easternmost — Homfray Channel — is probably the least used due to its circuitous course around the bulging bulk of East Redonda Island. Two small coves in front of homesteads on the mainland side of Homfray Channel between Lloyd Creek and Forbes Bay could be used as temporary anchorages although both are somewhat exposed to the southwest.

1   Forbes Bay

More protected temporary anchorage is available in Forbes Bay, either in a small 2-fathom nook along the southern shore or close to the delta shallows of Forbes Creek. Until a few years ago the remnants of a logging company float provided temporary moorage and access to the shore here. Some abandoned logging camp buildings were restored to serve as the home for a venerable retired logger, living in peaceful solitude directly beneath one of the most spectacular peaks on the B.C. coast — mt. Denman.

2 Attwood Bay

Safe anchorage is available in Attwood Bay but the prime anchorage location, in a small cove at the head of the bay, is presently being used for the booming of logs. Because the centre of Attwood Bay is so deep it is preferable to anchor close to shore with a stern line ashore to a tree or rock. A logging road trail from Attwood Bay crosses above Brettell Point and down into a small bay in Toba Inlet.

The upper reaches of Homfray Channel and Pryce Channel to the west are greatly affected by the milky-grey glacial fresh water outflow from Toba Inlet, transmitting a beautiful translucent turquoise hue to the water as it becomes diluted into the salt water.

Toba Inlet

Toba Inlet was first examined by Don Valdes in the launch of the *Mexicana* on June 27, 1792. He named it "Tabla" because "on the coast to the east he had seen on the shore a kind of wooden plank, on which were drawn various geographical figures". Although some historians surmised that "Toba" was a mis-spelling of "Tabla", it is possible that Galiano and Valdes may have decided to change the name on their later 1795 map, to honour Antonio Toba Arredondo, one of the officers of the Malaspina expedition. The next day on his way out of the Inlet, Valdes met one of Vancouver's boats entering the Inlet and although he told them there was no need to proceed further as the inlet terminated several miles inland, "the English officer (Peter Puget) continued to go to explore it himself." This apparent obstinacy was more on account of their orders from Vancouver to personally examine every navigable opening on the mainland shore than their own innate curiosity. However, they were amply rewarded with magnificent scenery; Archibald Menzies notes: "On each side were high steep mountains covered towards their summits with snow which was now dissolving and producing a number of wild torrents and beautiful cascades."

The surroundings of Toba Inlet must have created a slightly different impression on a later explorer, Mr. W. Downie, who reported to Governor James Douglas in a letter dated 19 March, 1859: (speaking of the Klahous Indians at the head of Toba Inlet) " . . . we got a few potatoes from them so there must be something else besides rocks in Desolation Sound."

View from Homfray Channel up a valley drained by Homfray creek.

The only islet, unnamed, in Toba Inlet.

3   Brem Bay

Brem Bay (formerly known as Salmon Bay) is located in an indentation where the Inlet makes an abrupt turn to the east and a wide U-shaped valley enters from the north. Reasonably safe temporary anchorage is possible close to the edge of the estuary delta. The preferred locations are in the western end of the Bay or in the northeastern corner near an old log dump marked by an A-frame on sheer legs. An old stone breakwater structure extending across tidal flats was probably formerly used as a pier for log dumping in deep water or to protect the booming area. This breakwater does not provide much protection for small craft from winds coming up the Inlet. The log dump leads past the extensive remains of an abandoned logging camp and continues for several miles up the Brem River valley.

On the east side of Snout Point, across the Inlet from Brem Bay, is a logging company float and a logging road winds up the hillside towards Mt. Grazebrooke. The most beautiful waterfall in the Inlet is directly below an extensively logged over patch on the south shore of the Inlet, just over 3 miles past Snout Point. Bancroft and Menzies might turn in their graves if they could see it now.

Just past this waterfall and the logging company floats and booming area the Inlet bends to the north-east. Temporary anchorage is possible just behind a small islet (the only one inside either Bute or Toba Inlets) joined to the mainland by a rocky isthmus at low tide. Due north of this islet on the opposite side of the inlet is a small cove, formerly known as Stapleton's Bay, which might prove safe as a temporary anchorage. Several years ago this bay housed a fish buying station and general store. Just over a mile past the islet on the south side is Snow Bay where boats are sometimes able to pick up chunks of ice or snow for their ice boxes in mid-summer. After particularly cold and humid winters snow may accumulate to a depth of 200 feet here.

The head of the Inlet has impressed many with its beautiful sense of tranquility. As Vancouver's boats approached the estuary, Menzies noted in his journal: "we rounded out in very shallow water, extending so far from shore that we could not land tho' allured by the prospect of a pleasant Valley with a considerable track of marshy Meadows backed by a forest of Pines & high snowy Mountains from which a number of foaming torrents fell into the Valley & formed a considerable winding Stream that glided gently through it."

In 1911, Peter Champion visited this valley, returned to Vancouver and enticed over 30 families to move up the coast and settle in what he considered the most beautiful and potentially productive valley he had ever seen — a homesteaders paradise. There was also the possibility that Toba Inlet might serve as

the terminus for another trans-continental railway. However, the isolation, loneliness and lack of nearby markets gradually defeated the homesteaders. Today, a wanderer in this deserted valley may find old wheels, cooking pots and stoves and a tall cottonwood tree growing through the centre of an old Model T Ford (M. Emery).

While anchorage is possible close to the estuary delta, the majority of boats stopping at the head of the Inlet prefer to tie up on log booms located near the end of a log dump and small float at the terminus of a road on the northwestern shore. This road bridges the estuary of the Tahumming River before continuing for several miles up the Toba Valley. On the south shore of the Tahumming River Estuary is an Indian cemetery, burial ground of the Klahous Indians. Directly across the inlet from this cemetery is Julian Peak (7,120 feet) which honours an old Toba Indian Chief. The majority of Klahous Indians relocated their village several years ago to Squirrel Cove, Cortes Island.

It is possible for a small, shallow draught (less than 1 foot) boat to navigate up the Toba River for over 25 miles almost to the foot of Mt. Dalgleish (9,150 feet) where the Toba glacier, source of the river, can be seen. It is best to travel up river with a flooding tide, taking care to avoid the sand bars and many sunken snags especially at the entrance to the river along the eastern shore of the inlet.

On the Pryce Channel side of the mouth of Toba Inlet is a possible temporary anchorage behind Dou-

In April, snows come down almost to sea level. When weather warms up, specatular waterfalls drain the snowfields into Bute Inlet.

ble Island. Temporary anchorage is also possible in depths of 10 fathoms between Elizabeth Island and the mainland. A beautiful waterfall drains some lakes behind a mountain which looms 3,800 feet directly above Elizabeth Island. The northern shore of West Redonda Island appears even steeper with castellated rampart-like cliffs rising directly above the channel. Sailing close to such steep shorelines can be a terrifying experience. Huge boulders occasionally dislodge themselves and come hurtling downward, jolting the other boulders and debris into motion. The rumble and thump of such rock avalanches can often be heard echoing across the channel.

The northern tip of West Redonda Island was named "Connis" after the Skye terrier dog which accompanied Captain Pender in his survey along this coast in the *Beaver*, circa 1864. (Walbran).

4 Ramsay Arm

This miniature inlet containing many cliffs and sheer bluffs is also the home base for active logging operations, the Quatam River estuary serving as the base camp complete with air strip. A log dump and floats are located at the north end of the estuary.

111

Logs boomed at the head of Bute Inlet.

5 Frances Bay

Frances Bay, formerly known as Fanny Bay, provides well protected anchorage in 5 fathoms at its head. Raza Island provides protection from the south and, while the bay is completely open to the southeast, winds from this exposure are uncommon in this area. The unobstructed view down Pryce Channel provides magnificent vistas of distant mountains.

6 Church House

Temporary anchorage in Calm Channel is possible close to the mainland side behind Bartlett Islet which is almost joined to the mainland by a shallow submerged tombolo. When Vancouver visited the mouth of Bute Inlet in 1791 he referred to it as "The District of the Friendly Indians" for the willing assistance provided by the Indians in helping his boats pass through the Arran rapids and because they brought the explorers "a plentiful supply of fresh herring and other fish, which they bartered in a fair and honest way for nails". These same Indians were probably of the Eucletah tribe which were described by later explorers as being fierce and warlike. Descendants of these Indians may have been decimated by the smallpox epidemic of 1862. The Indians now residing at Church House are Homalco Indians, originally from the head of Bute Inlet, who have somehow sur-

vived the onslaught of white civilization. A priest who once served in Church House remarked: "leave them to themselves, they must work out their own salvation". Other people who have known Church House have added also "leave to them the things which were originally theirs: the trees, the hills, the salmon and herring".

Bute Inlet

Bute Inlet has intrigued me for a long time. Its very immensity with mountain tops almost always hidden by clouds and distant headlands often shrouded in mist give the Inlet an aura of mystery and fascination. It is not the longest inlet on the B.C. coast, being 20 miles shorter than Knight Inlet, but it can be claimed the consistently widest and deepest inlet, as well as being flanked by the highest mountains. Another unique facet of this inlet is the obscure waxy substance of unknown origin which occasionally accumulates just below the surface of the water in very cold weather and congeals on shore in huge masses weighing several tons after particularly strong down-inlet winds. It has been speculated that this substance, which occurs nowhere else on the coast, may be derived from the pollen of lodgepole pine. In warm temperatures, the wax becomes oily and melts, disappearing beneath the waters of the inlet.

For several years I have waited to explore Bute Inlet in good weather in order to have unobstructed views of the surrounding mountains, but have been consistently foiled. One summer evening, after hiking across Stuart Island, I stood on the beach and looked up the Inlet. With a thick overcast down to about a thousand feet above sea level, Bute had looked particularly ominous until the clouds suddenly parted for a brief moment, permitting a thin sunbeam to spotlight a solitary sailboat rounding Fawn Bluff, 4 miles to the north. There was not another soul or sign of civilization to be seen or heard anywhere as the yacht slowly tacked down the Inlet beneath the bleak and barren cliffsides in the gathering gloom.

We decided not to go up the inlet that summer, but in April 1978 it appeared that there might be good weather so I managed to convince some friends to accompany me on an exploratory trip up Bute Inlet and the Homathko River in an inflatable dinghy. This dinghy, a 13-foot Zodiac, was kindly provided to us by Zodiac Marine on Wharf Street in Victoria, and proved to be a most suitable craft for the voyage, with shallow draught ideal for river travel and enough speed to get us from the nearest road access and back in the limited time we had available. It also proved very seaworthy considering the questionable weather we eventually experienced.

Temporary Anchorages

In spring the inlet is particularly beautiful as it is filled with numerous waterfalls as melting snow cascades down the sheer cliffsides. While the open exposures and deep soundings close to shore along the inlet discourage safe anchorage for large vessels, there are a few tiny coves or short, protected lengths of shoreline where it is possible to beach a small boat or find temporary shelter or anchorage with a line ashore to prevent swinging.

Below Fawn Bluff there is a tiny cove with a small stream draining Leask Lake, less than ½ mile inland. Across the Inlet there is a slightly larger cove. A trail from here leads through a shallow pass in the mountains to the head of Estero basin 1½ miles to the west.

Mountain goats can sometimes be seen on the steep cliffsides and rocky ledges between the snowfields on Cosmos Heights. Orford Bay, (7) halfway up the Inlet, provides protected anchorage in the north end of the bay or temporary moorage at the logging company floats along the south shore.

Hovel Bay, 4 miles north of Orford Bay, is named after a Norwegian sailor and logger, Johnny Hovel, who at age 70 retired in this remote location in the 1930s on a log float house tied to the cliffside. He met a tragic end one winter while tending his trapline 5 miles up the Inlet. Some circumstance, possibly a strong wind or unexpectedly high tide, tore his rowboat from its moorings, leaving him marooned with no alternative to a long, cold swim but to climb up the

Homalco Indian community of Church House in Calm Channel, at the entrance to Bute Inlet.

Milky waters of Bute Inlet are fed by glaciers in mountains high above.

cliffs and over the mountains back down to Hovel Bay. His bones were found several months later on top of a cliff directly above his float home.

Temporary anchorage is possible off a beach where there is a homestead marked by three deserted cabins, in the bight below Purcell Point. South of Mellersh Point is another homestead with a log boom protected float. The estuary of the Bear River which empties into Bear Bay has been homesteaded by a retired logger who has lived there since 1946. Temporary moorage is possible on log boom floats to the west of the estuary. Superb Mountain (8,140 feet), between Mounts Rodney and Sir Francis Drake, is named after H.M.S. *Superb*, commanded by Captain Keats in the battle of San Domingo, 1806. Walbran notes that:

> As the action began with the band on the poop playing "God save the King", and "Nelson of the Nile", Captain Keats brought out a portrait of Nelson which he hung on the mizzenstay, where it remained throughout the battle untouched by the enemy's shot, though dashed with the blood and brains of a seaman who was killed close beside it.

Approaching the head of Bute Inlet, one is overpowered with the sheer immensity of the surrounding mountains and spectacular overhanging glaciers and snowfields. Last April, after a particularly bumpy trip around Ward Point, we tied up at the Southgate logging dock with the intention of exploring ashore. Suddenly we noticed a deep roar and a cloud of dust approaching us as a big yellow beaten-up logging truck came tearing down the gravel road embankment over the tidal flats toward us. A tall, thin logger wearing filthy long jeans and tattered wool trousers, with a face that looked as though it had survived a hundred bunkhouse fights, jumped out of the truck and bellowed: "How the bloody *$!X?$!? hell did you get here?"

I proudly pointed to our faithful Zodiac tied up at the float and the logger's eyes seemed to double in size while his toothless mouth gaped open.

"You bloody *$X?$! fools! Have you no respect for this *$X?$! Inlet?" he yelled as he waved his arms furiously around him while the sky darkened noticeably. I looked at my companions who appeared somewhat subdued. Their enthusiasm for continuing our exploration to the head of the inlet and up the Homathko River seemed to be rapidly waning. As the logger's conversation was becoming increasingly fascinating, I sniffed mutiny in the wind if we stayed any longer.

8   Waddington Harbour

Waddington Harbour is named after Alfred Waddington, a great promoter of British Columbia, who in the early 1860s attempted to have a road built from here to provide access to the Interior goldfields (see Chapter 7). In 1864, fourteen men out of 17 working on the road were massacred by a band of Chilcotin Indians and the scheme was abandoned, Waddington losing almost every penny he possessed. In the late 1860s, Waddington was again advocating Bute Inlet, this time as the route for a trans-continental railway. He died in Ottawa in 1872 from smallpox while pursuing this goal. His gravestone honours him as "the original promoter of the Canadian Pacific railroad", and historians have noted: "Waddington's stubborn advocacy of his Bute Inlet scheme helped to convince the British and Canadian Governments that a railway must go west through Canadian territory and thus, in spite of his apparent failure, he exerted a not inconsiderable influence on the making of B.C."

We crossed the head of the Inlet to the mouth of the Homathko River in our Zodiac. Although the head of the Inlet is called a Harbour and there are extensive patches of suitable depth for anchoring at the edge of the tidal flats, the "harbour" is completely open to up-inlet winds. Admiralty Chart 2870, surveyed in the last century and now superseded by Canadian Chart 3524, gives soundings for 2½ miles up the Homathko River (average 1 to 3 fathoms). The shallowest portion is right at the mouth where there is a sand bar with 1-2 feet of water at chart datum.

On the west shore near the outlet of the Homathko River there are some log booms and four deserted cabins ashore. The roof of the third cabin appeared to

Homathko River at head of Bute Inlet.

be slightly a-kilter and when we investigated we found that the entire main floor of this cabin had been squashed and reoccupied by an immense square shaped boulder which appeared to have fallen down the mountainside and into the cabin, leaving the roof on top only slightly damaged but flattening all the surrounding walls. We also found a pair of rubber boots sticking out from under the boulder and wondered if the occupants had had any warning.

Anticipating a break in the weather we travelled up the Homathko River in the hopes of glimpsing Mt. Waddington, 13,104 feet high, the highest mountain located totally within British Columbia. (Mt. Fairweather, 15,300 feet is shared with Alaska). This mountain, long referred to as "Mystery Mountain" due to its inaccessibility, eluded us, but it is said to be visible from 12 miles up the Homathko River (by river or logging road) and a few have claimed to be able to see it from the lower slope of Mt. Rodney above the Southgate River.

It is hard to believe that if there had been no Chilcotin massacre and if Waddington had succeeded, this barren, lonely area could conceivably have replaced Vancouver as the location for the largest city on the west coast of Canada.

A correspondent to *Pacific Yachting* (A.J.E. Child,

July 1979) noted that in good weather the scenery is spectacular:

As we made our way up the Inlet the mountains on each side appeared in folds, their giant shoulders sloping down to the water. The highest peaks, snow-covered, appear sharp-pointed against the sky behind the ranges which border the Inlet. There are four changes of course to the end of the Inlet and a breath-taking new vista is presented as the boat swings around each head-land. The ridges of mountains rise one behind the other all along both shores. Finally, around Purcell Point the end of the Inlet comes in sight. The mountainsides come almost together in a shallow V. A wide meadow-like expanse, the estuary of the Homathko River, stretches across the base of the V. Far up above the V against the sky is the gleaming white edge of the Homathko Glacier, a huge expanse of snow and ice lying atop the mountains at 10,000 ft.

The easier return trip presented a quite different view of the Inlet shores. Going up seemed to be a panorama of receding mountain slopes. In reverse, one notices the steep walls of the mountains, mostly tree-covered, coming straight down into the water. In places some giant force has cracked open the mountain wall creating vertical crevasses large enough to drive our boat into. There were several waterfalls, no doubt spectacular in early summer. We saw only one habitation in Bute Inlet and no boats of any kind.

Of all my explorations on the coast this was the most unique and spectacular. Venturing part-way into the Inlet would not be all that worthwhile, like eating only the bun of a hamburg. The great thrill is rounding the last turn and perceiving the symmetry of the mountains coming together at the head of the Inlet, and the stunning sight of the white fields of the glacier suspended high above and beyond the shimmering water of the Inlet's farthest shore.

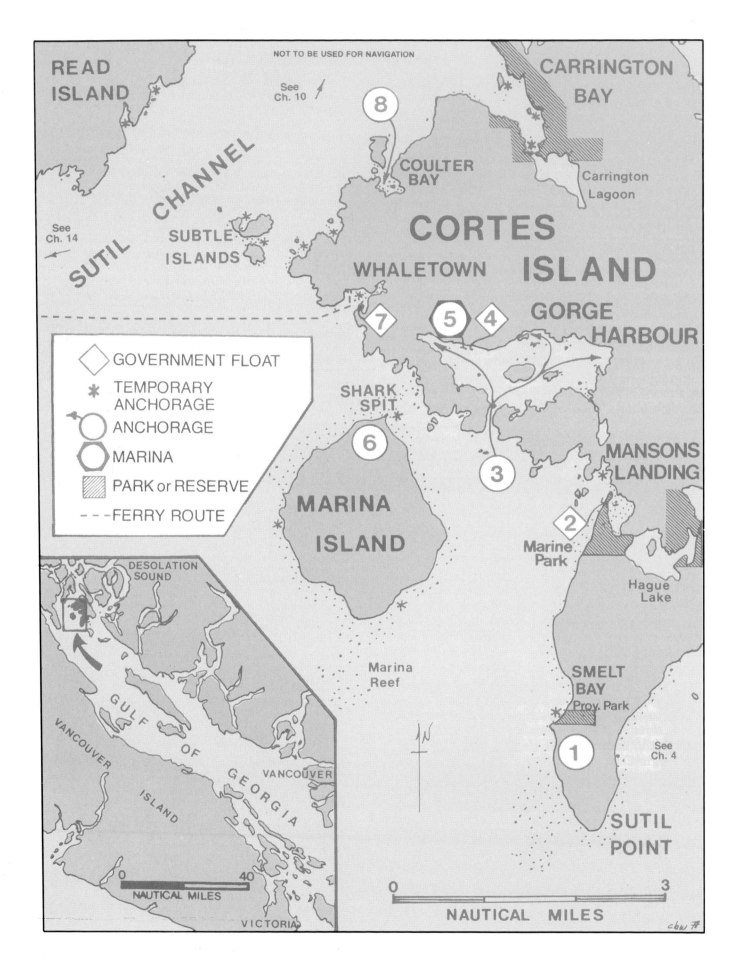

READ ISLAND

CARRINGTON BAY

Carrington Lagoon

See Ch. 10

⑧

COULTER BAY

SUTIL CHANNEL

See Ch. 14

SUBTLE ISLANDS

CORTES ISLAND

WHALETOWN

GORGE HARBOUR

⑦ ⑤ ◇④

◇ GOVERNMENT FLOAT

✳ TEMPORARY ANCHORAGE

◯ ANCHORAGE

⬡ MARINA

▨ PARK or RESERVE

--- FERRY ROUTE

SHARK SPIT

⑥

MARINA ISLAND

MANSONS LANDING

③

②◇

Marine Park

Hague Lake

DESOLATION SOUND

Marina Reef

SMELT BAY Prov. Park

GULF

VANCOUVER

ISLAND

OF

GEORGIA

VANCOUVER

N

①

See Ch. 4

0   40
NAUTICAL MILES

VICTORIA

SUTIL POINT

0   3
NAUTICAL   MILES

cbw 78

116

CHAPTER NINE

Southwestern Cortes Island

Mansons Landing, Gorge Harbour, Whaletown, Carrington Lagoon

The southwestern corner of Cortes Island exemplifies most dramatically the diversity of environments peculiar to the northern Gulf of Georgia. This diversity is based on a distinct change in geology which has a subsequent and sometimes subtle effect on landforms, scenery, climate, vegetation, settlement patterns and type of anchorage. Marina Island and that part of Cortes Island south of Manson's Landing is composed of glacial deposits resulting in a relatively flat landscape with broad, boulder-studded sand and gravel beaches. North of Manson's Landing the coastline is rocky, more precipitous and indented with numerous bays, tiny coves and enclosed harbours.

Winds

The winds in this area tend to be moderate in the summer season. An onshore diurnal southerly wind often counteracts the strength of the prevailing westerly winds which may be blowing with more strength in other areas. The diurnal (afternoon) southerly wind can be either a southwesterly or what is known locally as a "dry southeaster" to distinguish it from the "wet southeaster" which brings bad weather — strong winds, rain and heavy seas. With an open fetch of 40 miles south of Cortes Island, this area is also subject to swells resulting from heavy seas generated by a southeaster in the Gulf of Georgia.

Sutil Point, at the southern tip of Cortes Island, is named after the Spanish exploring schooner *Sutil*, (Galiano's ship) which explored this area in 1792. The point was formerly known as Reef Point due to the dangerous, boulder-encrusted shallows which extend for almost a mile southwestward from the Point, but was renamed Sutil in 1946.

Captain George Vancouver described the *Sutil* as a brig, about 45 tons burden, mounting one swivel gun and four small guns, with 18 muskets, 24 pistols and 18 cutlasses. The crew consisted of a commander, a lieutenant and 17 men. Length overall, 50 feet 3 inches; beam, 13 feet 10 inches. It is interesting to note

CHARTS
3594 — DISCOVERY PASSAGE to TOBA INLET
     (1:75,000)
3563 — SUTIL CHANNEL to STUART ISLAND
     (1:37,500)

Trenches dug by the Indians to defend against the marauding Yacultas can still be discerned behind the white beaches of Smelt Bay, now a park.

Mansons Landing public park, with lagoon to the right.

that although this vessel was only 10 feet shorter than Vancouver's consort, H.M.S. *Chatham*, she carried less than half the crew and weighed one-third as much as the *Chatham*. Vancouver, after partaking breakfast with Galiano aboard the *Sutil*, noted in his journal regarding the officers quarters:

> Their apartments just allowed room for sleeping places on each side with a table in the intermediate space, at which four persons with some difficulty could sit, and were in all other respects the most ill calculated and unfit vessels that could possibly be imagined for such an expedition; notwithstanding this, it was pleasant to observe, in point of living they possessed many more comforts than could reasonably be expected. (Walbran).

1 Smelt Bay Provincial Park

A mile north of Sutil Point one finds Smelt Bay Provincial Park (40 acres), with fairly good temporary anchorage (subject to prevailing or expected wind and tide conditions) close to shore just north of the conspicuous red-roofed barn. A beautiful white sand beach extends from the park frontage at the south end of Smelt Bay around the shoreline south of the point on which the barn is located. South of this area the beach is encumbered by many boulders and is extremely dangerous to approach by boat, although fascinating to explore on foot at low tide.

Smelt Bay is named after the capelin fish which swim ashore to spawn in the tens of thousands, usually in the middle of the night during a full moon. Long, rolling grassy hillocks extending behind the beach are said to be earthworks built by the local Indians to defend Ku'maxn (pronounced Quooman-han) from the marauding Yaculta Indians.

Facilities now provided by the Parks Branch include water supply and toilets. Campsites may be developed further inland in the future to prevent over use and erosion of the beach backshore.

An Indian petroglyph on a huge granite boulder is located on the foreshore between the old Indian village of Paukeanum, just north of Smelt Bay, and Manson's Landing. The boulder reveals the pecked outline and empty eye of a huge fish, 9 feet long.

2   Mansons Landing Marine Park

In 1886, Michael Manson, one of four brothers who had come to British Columbia from the Shetland Islands, became the first settler on Cortes Island. Michael was a romantic figure, having earlier eloped with his business partner's daughter. They escaped from Nanaimo in a dugout canoe and were married in Victoria. Of their 13 children, only half survived a diphtheria epidemic. He later became the local justice of the peace and was instrumental in apprehending various desperadoes (see Chapter 10). In 1909 he was the MLA for Comox and from 1928 until his death in 1932 he was MLA for the Mackenzie riding (mainland coast). Michael Manson and his younger brother, John, established a trading post in 1887 on the sand spit known by the Indians as Clytosin which guards the entrance of Manson's Lagoon.

The government float, which provides 360 feet of temporary moorage space, is protected from westerly seas by Cat and Sheep Islets but is exposed to southerly swells and southwest winds. The end of the float is used regularly by float planes. Good temporary anchorage is possible almost anywhere in Manson Bay with the best protection between or behind Cat and Sheep Islets or at the head of the bay in settled weather. Small shoal draught boats can venture into the Lagoon by following the narrow, twisting channel which leads to a large deep basin at the south end. Local residents sometimes moor their deep-draught vessels in this basin but access would be restricted to high water as the channel appears to dry at least 10 feet.

The 117-acre Marine Park was established in 1973 to protect the magnificent sand beaches, comprising 4,000 feet of ocean beach facing Marina Island, 3,400 feet of beach facing the Lagoon and 1,300 feet of freshwater beach on Hague Lake. The Hague Lake beach of glistening white sand has long been a popular area for yachtsmen anxious to soak some of the salt out of their system and into the crystalline clear warm water of the Lake. The Lake is used as a drinking water supply by local residents and for this reason motorboats are forbidden and bathers are requested to refrain from using soap for washing. Hague Lake can be reached by a short, ½ mile hike south from the gov-

Government floats at Mansons Landing have 360 feet of berthage. Lagoon can only be entered on spring tides.

Narrow entrance to Gorge Harbour, with Guide Islets, foreground.

Government wharf in Gorge harvour has only 106 feet, is usually crowded. Gorge View Marina, top, offers full facilities.

ernment float to the Seaford Road (first road to the left). The short trail through the woods into the Lake is located about 100 yards down the Seaford Road.

Fuel and water is provided at the government wharf and there is a post office, telephone and store at the head of the landing.

3   Gorge Harbour

The narrow, high-walled entrance to Gorge Harbour is located behind the Guide Islets and is easy to confuse with a similar topographic indentation half a mile to the west when viewed from a distance. Tides run at rates up to 4 knots through the relatively shallow (6 fathom) entrance.

The original Gorge Harbour Indians were a different tribe from the more "modern" Squirrel Cove Indians (who actually came from Toba Inlet) and were noted for their cunning defensive tactics. They once arranged a parley with invading northern Indians directly below the entrance cliffs. Before the parley, huge boulders which had been precariously balanced at the top of the cliffs were sprung loose, obliterating the unwary northerners. Before being decimated by smallpox in the 1800s, the Gorge Harbour Indians made rock paintings on flat patches of rock half way down the Gorge cliff. These paintings could only have been executed by individuals lowered by cedar ropes from the top of the cliff. On the opposite side of the entrance where the shoreline recedes more slowly, huge boulders form caverns which were used by the Indians as burial caves. Unfortunately, the relics from these caves have all been pillaged, some by tourists scavenging for local artifacts, but some are reportedly protected in the Provincial Museum in Victoria.

Gorge Harbour is a fascinating place with several islets and tiny coves to explore. Anchorage throughout the harbour is good because it is wholly enclosed and has relatively good holding ground. In strong westerly winds the preferred anchorage is along the northern shore or at the west end of the harbour. The Gorge Harbour government float (4) is usually crowded, with only 106 feet of berthage space.

Although still relatively undeveloped it is hoped that increasing pressures do not bring a crowded, noisy and dirty harbour. This is a distinct possibility that must be guarded against, since there are many lots for sale. The warm water and deep harbour basin with a shallow entrance inhibits tidal flushing and could lead to high concentrations of pollution.

5 Gorge View Marina

This marina (formerly the Hacienda Marina) offers moorage, fuel, complete marine facilities for small boats, campsites, store, cafe, laundromat and showers at a very reasonable rate.

6 Marina Island

Marina Island, protected under the western arm of Cortes Island, is said by Walbran to have been named by Galiano and Valdes in association with Cortes Island:

> after the fair and famous Marina whom Cortes in the spring of 1519, at San Juan de Ulloa, obtained with numerous other captives. Cortes made her his mistress, and out of devotion to him she acted as the interpreter, guide and counsellor of the Spaniards in their attack on Mexico, and frequently saved them from various reverses. Named by Galiano and Valdes in July, 1792. Viage p. 79.
>
> The name appeared as Mary Island on Admiralty charts from 1849 to 1906, when the Geographic Board of Canada both for the sake of historical accuracy, and to avoid duplication, replaced the original form. (Walbran)

Marina Island was once homesteaded and used for fox farming. Although the island is almost completely surrounded by boulder studded beach, making anchorage close to shore difficult, temporary anchorage is possible east of the southern tip (good protection from westerlies) off the westernmost tip (beautiful beach and huge deserted orchard) or inside Shark Spit where there is a fine grassy camping area on top of an old Indian midden.

Uganda Passage between Shark Spit and Cortes Island is not difficult to navigate as long as close attention is paid to the buoys and beacons (use Chart 3563). The tide floods north and west through the passage at a maximum rate of 2-3 knots.

Two rocks mark the entrance to Whaletown. Government floats, left, lead to general store, post office.

Uganda Passage at mid-tide, showing Shark Spit and beacon in centre channel.

Narrow, high walled entrance to Gorge Harbour has Indian petroglyphs on west side.

7 Whaletown

This town came into existence in 1867 when Governor Sir James Douglas selected the site as the location where whales caught in the Gulf of Georgia could be rendered, flensed and the products shipped to market. By 1870 the whales had been virtually eliminated in the Gulf and the Dawson Whaling Company moved on leaving nothing but the town's name.

The government float here provides fuel and 394 feet of moorage space. The float is fairly well protected from all winds but a southerly swell occasionally sets into the bay during the night, possibly the aftermath of seas generated in the Gulf by onshore afternoon winds which arrive after the usual night-time westerly wind has begun.

The terminal for the ferry from Heriot Bay on Quadra Island is located at the north end of the bay and temporary anchorage, exposed to the SW, is possible throughout the bay. It is interesting to note that the maximum tidal range for Whaletown is the largest for any of the ports in the Discovery Islands — 17.1 feet.

A general store is located at the head of the government float and nearby are a tiny post office, library and the Columbia Coast Mission Church — St. John the Baptist. The Bunkhouse Craft Shop with local and South American handicrafts and homebaked goods is located above the eastern extremity of Whaletown Bay and is accessible by dinghy at high water, by trail around the shoreline or by road.

Proceeding north around the western tip of Cortes Island, through Plunger Pass one passes the Subtle (English translation of the Spanish "Sutil") Islands. These Islands (formerly known collectively as Camp Island) are joined by a sand and gravel spit which is just barely covered at extreme high tide and is a popular place for picnics and camping. Temporary anchorage is possible in Plunger Pass between the two islands with fairly good protection from most winds, or in a beautiful tiny bay surrounded by arbutus trees facing up Sutil Channel. This bay, and two other coves on the Cortes shore between the Subtle Islands and Coulter Bay, may be exposed to nightime northerlies but are well sheltered from afternoon southerlies.

8   Coulter Bay

Good anchorage is available in Coulter Bay. Coulter Island provides fair protection from the prevailing westerly. A tombolo drying 10 feet joins Coulter Island to a small islet which is joined to the Cortes mainland by a tombolo drying 6 feet.

A trail from the head of the bay connects with the road system which winds throughout the island. The roads at the south end of the island are fairly well developed and used. Tthose covering the north part of the island are more delightful to explore being little used, meandering over hill and dale, across meadows, by farmsteads but mostly through deserted forest. Many of these roads were formerly used for logging access and most are still passable as narrow trails.

Carrington Bay

Temporary anchorage is possible behind the islets in this bay or near the outlet of Carrington Lagoon which has been blocked up by driftwood. The driftwood piled on the shores is a good indication of the open exposure to strong northwesterly winds which occasionally spring up with little warning, usually in the late afternoon. The anchorage at the head of the bay can become uncomfortable when these conditions prevail. Much of the shoreline of Carrington Bay is protected by a 130-acre provincial recreation reserve.

If the opportunity affords, Carrington Lagoon is well worth a visit. Small boats can be portaged over the outlet of the lagoon. An old deserted farmstead with overhanging grape arbours in an orchard overlooks the head of the lagoon.

Subtle Islands are connected by a sand and gravel tombolo which is barely covered at extreme high tide. A favourite spot for picnics and camping.

Carrington Bay is site of 130-acre provincial recreation reserve, but is open to northwesterlies. Carrington Lagoon in foreground.

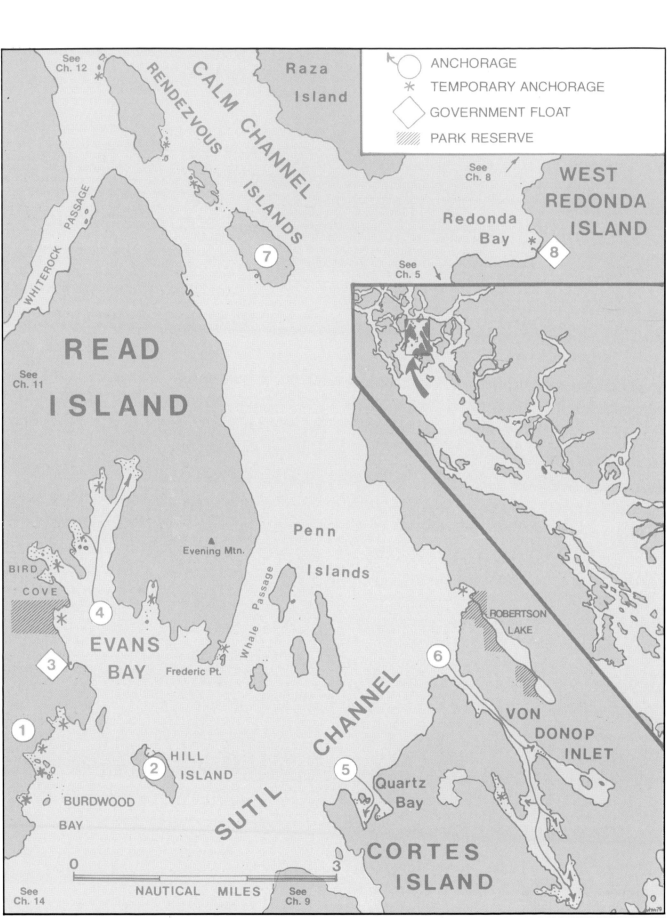

ANCHORAGE

TEMPORARY ANCHORAGE

GOVERNMENT FLOAT

PARK RESERVE

See Ch. 12

CALM CHANNEL

Raza Island

RENDEZVOUS

ISLANDS

See Ch. 8

WEST REDONDA ISLAND

Redonda Bay

See Ch. 5

WHITEROCK PASSAGE

⑦

⑧

READ ISLAND

See Ch. 11

Penn Islands

Evening Mtn.

BIRD COVE

Whale Passage

ROBERTSON LAKE

④

⑥

③

EVANS BAY

Frederic Pt.

VON DONOP INLET

①

②

HILL ISLAND

⑤

Quartz Bay

SUTIL CHANNEL

BURDWOOD BAY

CORTES ISLAND

0   3

NAUTICAL MILES

See Ch. 14

See Ch. 9

NOT TO BE USED FOR NAVIGATION

124

CHAPTER TEN

Northern Sutil Channel

Burdwood Bay, Evans Bay, Redonda Bay, Von Donop Inlet

Although northern Sutil Channel is a little off the beaten track for the majority of yachtsmen cruising Desolation Sound, it is definitely worth exploring. This is an area with generally good sailing winds, abundant anchorages and some of the most beautiful scenery on the coast. This area also has an unusually turbulent history in marked contrast to the present atmosphere of sparse settlement and tranquility.

Despite the northeast-southwest orientation of northern Sutil Channel, winds from the southeast and northwest blow frequently across the Channel, being little hindered by the relatively low surrounding topography. Although winds tend to be light in the summer months, strong westerlies often break through from Johnstone Strait, particularly on late afternoons.

Read Island

Read is unusual among the major islands in the northern Strait of Georgia, being the only one without a Spanish name. It seems to have been missed completely by the earlier explorers and it was not until 1864 that Captain Pender named it after Captain William Viner Read of the Hydrographic Office. Many other names in this area honour other officers serving in the Hydrographic Office at this time (Burdwood, Carrington, Penn, Mayes and Frederick Evans — see Walbran for details).

At one time over 150 families lived all year round on Read Island but for one reason or another this number has dropped to fewer than ten today, and the island roads pass many old homesteads, farms and orchards. In the summer months the island's popula-

tion exceeds its former permanent population and the old homestead's are reoccupied.

1   Burdwood Bay

Burdwood Bay, inside five small, encircling islets, is a very good anchorage when the wind is from the west and would probably remain reasonably comfortable in a moderate southeaster of short duration. (The western tip of Cortes Island and the Subtle Islands, 2½ miles south, do offer some degree of protection.) However, with a prolonged strong southeast or southerly wind this anchorage would likely be untenable due to its openess to seas coming up Sutil Channel from the south. In such conditions, the anchorages immediately south of Burdwood Bay or north of the five islets would be more protected while the 4-fathom cove north of Burdwood Bay remains open to southerly seas.

Burdwood Bay has had a particularly violent early history. Cecil Clark, chronicler of the early history of the B.C. Provincial Police, tells the story that in the early 1890s several new settlers arrived from Deadwood City, South Dakota. These settlers arrived under curious circumstances, changing their names in the process, and shortly thereafter there were several murders. In 1893 a whisky peddler known as Harry Myers shot a local logger through the back in a drunken brawl after the logger had insulted Myers'

CHARTS:
3563 — SUTIL CHANNEL TO STUART
ISLAND (1:37,500)
3555 — FOR PLAN OF REDONDA BAY
(1:12,000)

Burdwood Bay, which has a violent history, is a good anchorage when wind is from the west.

dog. Myers took his dog and headed up to Francis Bay near Ramsay Arm with the Provincial Police in hot pursuit. Abandoning his boat, Myers climbed over the Downie Range of mountains and down into Bute Inlet. Although heavily armed, Myers was afraid to shoot any game in case the police would hear the shot. Near starvation, he was forced to bludgeon his dog but couldn't force himself to eat the meat raw. The police spotted the smoke from his campfire and apprehended him. He was later shot while attempting to escape after being sentenced to life imprisonment in New Westminster.

A year later another logger named Benson was found dead with a smashed up face, floating down Sutil Channel in his small rowboat. No one in Burdwood Bay seemed to know what happened to him. After a lengthy investigation it was discovered that Benson had been in the habit of visiting Laura, the wife of John Smith. Smith was supposed to have been away on a hunting trip with his best friend, the Burdwood Bay hotelkeeper Edgar Wylie; but had returned home unexpectedly to find Benson and his wife Laura in *flagrante*.

After disposing of Benson with a mallet, Smith's wife and his mistress Kate Wylie, the local schoolmistress (and wife of Edgar), cleaned up the mess and set Benson's body adrift in a rowboat.

In the court case (The Queen vs. Smith, 1895), the accused was lucky to be defended by William J. Bowser whose gift of oratory was so persuasive that the jury surprisingly returned a verdict of "not guilty". Bowser eventually used his talents to become premier of B.C. Smith was so astonished at the verdict that following the custom of his homeland, he jumped up and started shaking hands with the jury. The infuriated judge bellowed "Tell that man he's not in the United States now, and get him out of this court".

Life in Burdwood Bay appears to have continued relatively peacefully from then on. The original Burdwood store, hotel and home of the Wylies is located conspicuously on the shore just north of the five islets. Half a mile inland from the drying tidal flats at the head of Burdwood Bay one passes the old cordwood trail that leads across the island to Hjorth Bay in Hoskyn Channel and a wood-surrounded abandoned oat field which bears no resemblance to its former shape. The 1946 earthquake, centred in the northern gulf, buckled and twisted the field, leaving huge fissures and gullies up to 15 feet wide and several feet deep. The earthquake also disrupted the drainage of a nearby stream, creating a small pond and a miniature waterfall. The island road continues on to the south end, bypassing beautiful Rosen (Charlie) Lake which was also altered by the 1946 earthquake.

2 Hill Island

A small cove at the north end of Hill Island is protected from northwesterly seas coming out of Evans Bay by a log boom breakwater. Entrance into the cove is made between two large barrel-shaped buoys which mark the ends of the logboom breakwater. The floats in this cove served at one time as moorage for Mitchell's Marina which provided overnight accommodation on shore as well as moorage, fuel and other facilities. The marina is now closed to the public.

3 Read Island Gov't Floats

These floats are well protected from all winds, tucked behind a large hill at the southern entrance to Evans Bay. Strong southeasterly winds occasionally send a heavy swell curling around the corner, which can make the moorage uncomfortable. There is about 100 feet of float space providing berthage for up to four boats on the float but as many as 15 boats have been accommodated here, rafted alongside. Temporary moorage is sometimes available on log booms south of the beacon-marked five-foot drying rock, just off the government floats.

There is a small store here which periodically offers fresh eggs and other produce from island farms.

4 Evans Bay

Evans Bay is actually made up of seven separate inlets or coves, each further broken up into several nooks or arms providing a variety of anchorage opportunities. All of these coves are open to the south to varying degrees, but in the summer months this is not a particularly dangerous exposure if one keeps an eye

Beautiful Read Island is laced with trails and old logging roads.

Government wharf in Evans Bay.

A drying isthmus in Whale Passage, behind Frederic Point provides a temporary anchorage in summer months.

Frederic Point.

on the barometer and expected weather conditions.

The land around the bay immediately north of the government float is protected by a provincial recreational reserve but the bay itself and the central portion of Bird Cove to the north are open to the southeast with a four mile fetch across from Cortes Island. Small boat anchorage is possible directly behind the 15-foot islet which guards the entrance to a tiny drying nook along the southeastern shore of Bird Cove. There is always at least 3 feet of water behind this 15-foot islet, while the central part of this nook would be suitable as an anchorage for shallow-draught boats at most tides — it just barely dries at extreme low water. The maximum tidal range for this area is 17 feet.

Drying rocks to be avoided in this nook are located off the northern point — charted as drying 3 feet (enter close to the 15-foot islet) and just west of the thumb of land extending from the southern shore toward the 15-foot islet. The land surrounding Bird Cove is private and a weather-beaten sign on shore warns: 'DANGER — Shooting across roads and trails may result in HOMICIDE' — possibly a reference to Read Island's troubled history.

Doris Anderson (*The Evergreen Islands*, Gray's Publishing, 1980,) notes:

> Ed Wylie (the former Burdwood Bay hotelkeeper) was buried in a crack in a huge boulder on Lot 340 on a point by Bird Cove, known locally as Healey's Point. He was a small man, but the crack failed to conceal him entirely, so cement was poured into the crevice. Before it hardened, small stones were set into the cement to spell out ED WYLIE and the date of death. The grave was seen there for many years but eventually roots of a nearby tree split the cement and the skeleton was revealed, perhaps giving rise to some of the stories of "skeletons found in shallow graves".

There is a channel through the drying flats at the head of Bird Cove which leads south of the 16-foot islet and which could be used by shallow-draught boats when the tide is not low. This almost competely landlocked portion of Bird Cove is extremely peaceful and beautiful despite the muddy shore and is well worth exploring by dinghy. The island road passes through the woods less than twenty feet from the head of the cove.

Immediately north of Bird Cove is another cove with more protection from the southeast provided by the Evening Mountain peninsula of Read Island and three small islets about 35 to 40 feet high. The anchorage behind these islets has approximately 5 feet of water below chart datum. A deserted farmstead and

View to the southeast over Bird Cove and Evans Bay; Cortes Island in background.

orchard are located behind the woods at the head of the bay.

The two arms of the inlet which extend to the north of Evans Bay also provide reasonable anchorage although the westernmost arm is more open to the south. The land adjacent to the eastern arm has recently been logged over and is not particularly attractive although it is probably the safest all-weather anchorage in Evans Bay.

At the bottom of the Evening Mountain peninsula are some interesting coves. The westernmost of these provides good temporary anchorage behind a cluster of rocks, all of which (except the 18-foot islet) are covered at highwater. The head of the bay dries almost completely and the upland is settled.

In Whale Passage there is a delightfully tiny temporary anchorage behind a 14-foot drying isthmus

Von Donop Inlet

Narrow Von Donop has many quiet anchorages like this one.

which connects a small islet to Frederic Point. This anchorage would probably be safe throughout the summer months but is exposed to winter northeasterlies. Another temporary anchorage can be found on the eastern side of the northernmost Penn Island.

Cortes Island

5   Quartz Bay

Just north of Carrington Bay on Cortes Island is a small two-armed bay which provides well sheltered

Von Donop lagoon is best explored by dinghy at high water.

anchorage. The westernmost arm is protected to a degree from westerly winds by an islet connected to Cortes by an isthmus which dries at low tide. Both arms of the bay have been settled with floats at their heads. Shelter from the westerly is available in the eastern bay between the float and a northward jutting peninsula in depths of 2 fathoms. It is possible that this bay is named after the abundant quartz veins found in this area. In 1898, mineral claims reported small quantities of molybdenite in these veins.

6   Von Donop Inlet

This long narrow inlet, averaging only a few hundred yards in width and almost three miles in length, almost cuts Cortes Island in half. It was originally named Von Donop Creek by Captain Pender around 1863 after Victor Edward John Brenton Von Donop of the Royal Navy. He arrived on this coast aboard HMS *Charybdis*, 21 guns, which had been ordered here "owing to the threatened hostilities between England and the United States, growing out of the Mason and Slidell affair". (Walbran) Mason and Slidell were two confederate agents en-route to England in a British mail steamer to enlist support for the southern states in the U.S.Civil War. They were forcibly taken from the steamer by a U.S. gunboat.

While the entrance channel of Von Donop Inlet is open to the northwest, the Inlet itself is so narrow and twisting and the surrounding topography sufficiently high, that anchorage throughout is perfectly safe no matter what strength or direction the wind is blowing outside. A rock with less than 6 feet of water over it at low tide is located in the narrowest portion of the entrance channel and is marked by kelp in the summer months. The deepest channel bypassing the rock is close along the southern shore.

Anchorage is possible in a bight along the north shore where the inlet widens and a large salt lagoon empties out. Early charts surmised that this lagoon might be connected to the Squirrel Cove lagoon thereby splitting Cortes into two islands. No surveys were made into the lagoons since they were obviously unnavigable by large ships. A dotted line joined the two lagoons together until surveys in the 1920s found that there was in fact a substantial chunk of dry land between them. The lagoon is best entered and explored by dinghy close to high water as the passage into it is difficult if not impossible to negotiate at other times due to the swift current and many boulders. Several years ago, five killer whales entered the lagoon at high water and chose to remain and die here although they had the opportunity to leave on succeeding high tides.

Less than 1 mile down the Inlet there is a small cove and a long shallow inlet on the western shore and a tiny shallow nook on the east shore which are very popular as anchorages. The most popular anchorage is however, at the very head of the inlet. There is a logged over patch extending from the eastern shore of the head of the Inlet almost as far as the westernmost indentation of Squirrel Cove, less than ½ mile to the southeast. This patch was intended to serve as an airstrip but since it could conceivably have cut communication to the north end of the island it was never developed. Several years ago, the southwestern shore of the head of the Inlet was the home of Jim Leighton, a generous man who had developed beautiful gardens of flowers and vegetables on the small islet connected to his property at low tide. His hospitality was greatly abused by tourists demanding fresh vegetables due to unwanted publicity from American boating magazines. Jim Leighton no longer lives here. His house burned down in 1976. Old logging roads and trails lead from this area to the southern parts of Cortes Island by way of several inland lakes and Carrington Lagoon.

The Provincial Parks Branch has a long standing proposal to establish Von Donop Inlet as a provincial marine park. The proposed park would include the area surrounding the Inlet to the height of land, the northern portion of Squirrel Cove (excluding the Indian Reserve) and the land surrounding Robertson and Wiley Lakes where there are already two recreational reserves. Unfortunately, the Parks Branch land acquisition budget is low and there are a number of private holdings in the Inlet which would have to be acquired before the Park could be established.

Temporary anchorage is possible in the small bay below Robertson Lake. There is a trail to the lake and along the south shore to Wiley Lake where there are two beaver lodges. Although both lakes are somewhat choked by marsh and log debris, the water is reported to be warm for swimming and there is good fishing.

7 Rendezvous Islands

When Galiano and Valdes passed these islands in 1792 they referred to them as 'The Three Marias'. In the early part of this century enough people lived in the neighbourhood to support a school on the northernmost Rendezvous Island. There was a fertilizer plant here, a post office, and the islands were a regular stop on the Union Steamship route for a number of years. In 1917 these islands were logged by the author's grandfather.

While the islands do not offer well protected anchorage, temporary anchorage is possible in a few small nooks, particularly around the northernmost island, behind islets close to the north and south ends, in a 5-fathom cove facing Whiterock Passage and in a rock infested bight (used as the primary moorage for the owners of the island) off the southeastern shoreline. The middle Rendezvous offers slightly more protection in small coves on its western shoreline and the southern Rendezvous, behind an islet in a bight at its southern end.

8 Redonda Bay

Redonda Bay (formerly "Deceit Bay") is not a particularly good anchorage because of its openness. Although the steep hills surrounding the bay provide

Boulder-strewn entrance to Von Donop Lagoon at low water.

good protection from southeast winds and may deflect northwest winds, swells from almost any wind often make the anchorage uncomfortable. The government float here, formerly providing 130 feet of berthage space, is at present not open to public use. Signs on the wharf, which have fallen into disrepair, read "No Trespassing — B.C. Forest Service".

Redonda Bay is now being used as a corrections camp. Offenders are being rehabilitated and employed by the Forest Service in replanting seedlings in the logged over patches of West Redonda Island. When the job is completed, possibly by 1981, the camp will be moved to some other location up the coast.

Redonda Bay was formerly a community of considerable significance with regular steamer stops and a large cannery. Although the cannery burned down several years ago and the bay is unoccupied with the exception of the transitory corrections camp, Redonda Bay still appears as a major community on many recent charts and maps. The dilapidated remains of homes, cannery buildings and boilers and machinery strewn along the foreshore are interesting to explore.

A provincial archives manuscript by Thomas Manson notes that in 1835 the Salish Indians had a summer village near Deceit Bay. The remains of a stone circle, a type of weir used for trapping fish, can be seen on the foreshore at the mouth of Lillian Russell Creek. Other traces of the Salish are petroglyphs on the east side of Ellis Lake (accessible by logging road — 5 miles southeast of Redonda Bay or 2 miles north of Teakerne Arm).

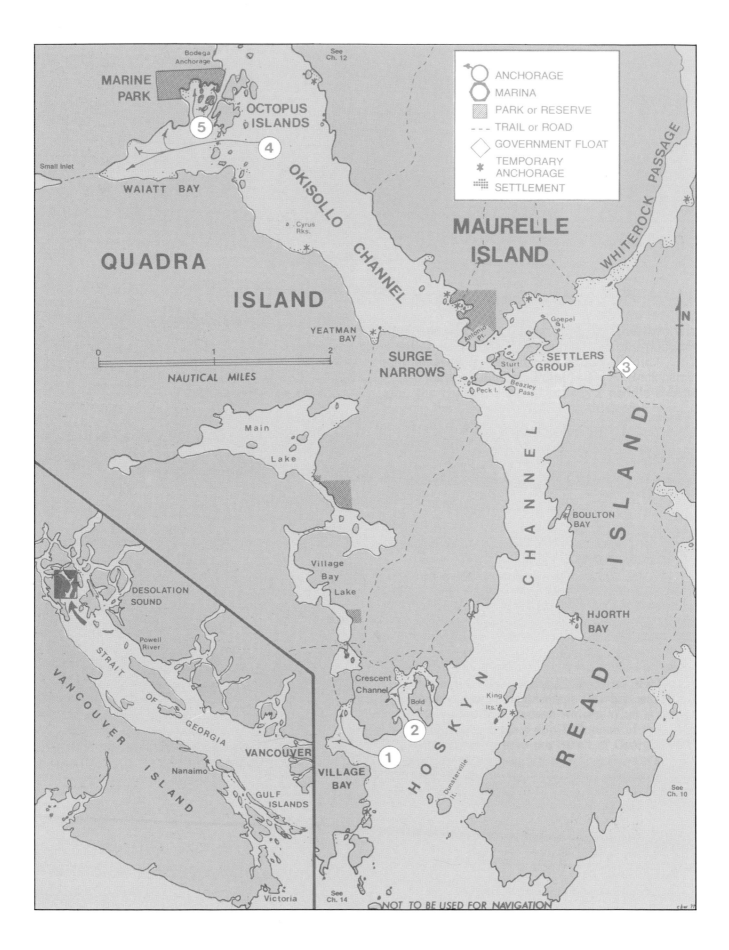

MARINE PARK

Bodega Anchorage

OCTOPUS ISLANDS

Small Inlet

WAIATT BAY

QUADRA

ISLAND

Cyrus Rks.

OKISOLLO CHANNEL

MAURELLE ISLAND

WHITEROCK PASSAGE

See Ch. 12

ANCHORAGE
MARINA
PARK or RESERVE
TRAIL or ROAD
GOVERNMENT FLOAT
TEMPORARY ANCHORAGE
SETTLEMENT

N

YEATMAN BAY

SURGE NARROWS

Antonio Pt.

Goepel I.

Sturt I.

SETTLERS GROUP

Peck I.

Beazley Pass

0   1   2

NAUTICAL MILES

Main Lake

CHANNEL

READ ISLAND

Village Bay Lake

BOULTON BAY

DESOLATION SOUND

Powell River

STRAIT

OF

GEORGIA

VANCOUVER ISLAND

Nanaimo

VANCOUVER

GULF ISLANDS

Crescent Channel

Bold I.

King Its.

HOSKYN

Dunsterville I.

HJORTH BAY

VILLAGE BAY

Victoria

See Ch. 14

See Ch. 10

NOT TO BE USED FOR NAVIGATION

ckw 7?

CHAPTER ELEVEN

Surge Narrows

Hoskyn Channel, Settlers Group, Okisollo, Octopus Islands

Quadra Island, the largest of the Discovery Islands, is separated from Read Island by Hoskyn Channel and from Maurelle Island by the lower portion of Okisollo Channel. These waterways contain over 100 small islands and islets and several bays and tiny coves providing numerous opportunities for exploration. Some of the bays provide well protected anchorages but the majority of the smaller coves are suitable only for temporary anchorage due to shallowness, open exposure to winds or seas or lack of swinging room. A few of these temporary anchorages are indicated on the accompanying map.

Neither Okisollo Channel nor Hoskyn Channel have any appreciable tidal currents (Hoskyn Channel floods south and ebbs north, contrary to what is indicated on some charts) but where the two channels meet at Surge Narrows, the current flows at maximum rates of 9 to 12 knots.

Quadra Island was named by the Geographic Board of Canada in 1903 after Juan Francisco de la Bodega y Quadra, Knight of the Order of Santiago, the Spanish naval captain who explored the British Columbia coast in the late eighteenth century. When Captain George Vancouver was sent by Britain in 1792 to restore to the Crown the Nootka colony on the west coast of Vancouver Island, Quadra was governor of the Spanish occupied settlement there. Vancouver noted in his journal, December, 1792:—

> ... The well known generosity of my other Spanish friends will, I trust, pardon the warmth of expression with which I must ever advert to the conduct of Senor Quadra; who regardless of the difference in opinion that had arisen between us in our diplomatic capacities at Nootka had uniformly maintained towards us a character infinitely beyond the reach of my powers of encomium to describe. His benevolence was not confined to the common rights of hospitality, but was extended to all occasions, and was exercised in every instance where His Majesty's service, combined with my commission, was in the least concerned.

On finally parting company with Quadra in January, 1793, Vancouver's journal again refers to Quadra's kindness, and that the prospect of never again meeting him was a "painful consideration"

CHARTS

3594 — DISCOVERY PASSAGE to TOBA INLET (1:75,000)
3565 — DISCOVERY PASSAGE (includes HOSKYN and OKISOLLO CHANNELS) (1:38,000)
3563 — SUTIL CHANNEL to STUART ISLAND (includes WHITEROCK PASSAGE, HOSKYN CHANNEL) (1:37,500)
3521 — OKISOLLO CHANNEL (includes WHITEROCK PASSAGE) (1:24,354)

Hjorth Bay provides temporary anchorage, and has old cordwood road leading across island from south end.

(Walbran). They never did meet again for Vancouver returned in 1794 to England and died four years later while Quadra died one year after their parting. Vancouver originally intended that the island now named solely after him be called the "Island of Quadra and Vancouver", but this was never used because of its awkwardness.

1 Village Bay

Village Bay, so named because it was once the site of a fairly large Indian village, offers fair anchorage in the southwest corner. Anchorage is also possible behind an islet at the north end of the Bay but this location is somewhat open to the southeast.

A trail leads from this area ¼ mile north to the southern end of Village Bay Lake. Another ½ mile to the northeast, the Lake narrows and is crossed by a road bridge. Village Bay Lake is joined to Main Lake by a tapering, marshy waterway inhabited by many kingfishers and navigable only by canoe or dinghy. Together, this interconnecting chain of lakes comprises the largest freshwater waterway within any of the Gulf or Discovery Islands.

An extract from the B.C. Land Surveyor's Report notes:
  . . . These lakes would make a delightful summer resort. They are surrounded by mountains and hills which slope gradually to the shore, and offer good inducements for canoeing, fishing and hunting. During the summer the Hastings Sawmill Company constructed a dam at the outlet, the object being to raise the level of the lakes sufficiently to overcome the shallows and allow of (sic) the towing of logs. They will also construct a flume about a quarter of a mile in length to carry these logs down from the outlet of the lakes to Village Bay. . .
  (Report by R. E. Palmer, December 31, 1894.)

The lakes have not changed much since 1894. A few people have cottages on Village Bay Lake; the Parks Branch have placed recreational reserves (indicated on the map) on some of the islets in the lakes, and in areas suitable for primitive camping. There is a fine sand beach near the eastern end of the outlet of upper Main Lake and a deserted farmstead at the end of the northernmost bay in Main Lake. Little Main Lake is accessible by a short portage over a gravel streambed from the westernmost arm of Main Lake.

The lakes are best explored by canoe, kayak, dinghy or cartop sailboat. Access by road is from southern Quadra Island and the ferry from Campbell River. Access from saltwater is possible from Village Bay or from a short trail joining the Bold Point Road just north of Crescent Channel, or from Yeatman Bay in Okisollo Channel.

2 Crescent Channel

Well protected anchorage is available in Crescent Channel and behind Bold Island but one must be wary of the many drying rocks and reefs. Logs have re-

Currents can run at 12 knots through Beazley Pass in the Settler's Group, safest passage through islands.

Passage between Peck Island in Settler Group and Quadra Island, is not recommended.

Surge Narrows government wharf has 200 ft of berthage. Dodman's store has groceries, fuel and post office.

Distinctive, sheer-sided hill marks Sheer Point at entrance to Boulton Bay.

Prettiest bay on west side of Read Island is Melibe Anchorage in Boulton Bay.

cently been boomed around the northern shoreline of Bold Island and could provide temporary moorage if they are not likely to be moved while one is alongside.

The chart shows Bold Point as the southern extremity of Bold Island but another Bold Point is found a mile to the north. The community of Bold Point included a hotel, store and post office as well as a government wharf which served as a landing place in the days when steamships made regular trips through the islands. A cement block marks the old pierhead. An orchard and what appear to be abandoned houses peer down a narrow chasm spanned by an old bridge.

The bulk of Bold Point Hill (455 feet) provides some protection from southerlies to Conville Bay. The northern tidewater terminus of the east Quadra road is found in the small bay just south of Surge Narrows.

Read Island

Temporary anchorage, somewhat exposed to westerlies, is possible in several coves along the western shore of Read Island — inside Dunsterville Islet, the King Islets and in Hjorth Bay. The northern portion of Hjorth Bay and Melibe Anchorage, another mile to the north, provide the best protection. Melibe Anchorage, also known locally as Boulton Bay, is sheltered from westerlies by a prominent, steeply sided hill rising above Sheer Point.

3   Surge Narrows

The government float here provides 200 feet of berthage space and access to Dodman's store (groceries, fuel and post office for Read Island). The store serves as the exchange for the 60-year-old telephone network which links the islands' 20 to 30 residents. In addition, many 1910 vintage artifacts and implements useful for island homesteading are stocked in the store. The road inland leads past the island schoolhouse (a quonset hut), and several beautiful farms in the centre of the island, to the eastern shore of the island (Bird Cove, Evans Bay) and then continues south to Burdwood Bay and the southern part of the island.

A boat passage at the south end of Whiterock Passage, 1 mile north of Dodman's Store, has been dredged to a depth of 5 feet below chart datum and is navigable with close attention to the leading beacons. Although the tidal stream through the Passage never exceeds 2 knots (flooding north and ebbing south), this current could be sufficient to slide one out of the very narrow channel onto the drying bank or into any one of the numerous boulders which line the passage. Coastal freighters and oil barges use the passage regularly. At high tide, it appears fairly innocuous; but low tide reveals a boulder-studded maze.

Transit into the first part of the passage is accomplished fairly easily by lining up the leading beacons (see Chart 3521) over the bow and ensuring that the two triangles continue to form a diamond shape (or at night — that the lights stay one on top of the other). Leaving the passage is made difficult by a

dog-leg turn in the middle requiring either a head which rotates easily or quickly through 180° or a mate with a pair of binoculars to keep careful watch as the leading beacons used to exit the passage are lined up (over the stern).

Whiterock Passage forms a convenient connection with Calm Channel for those wishing to avoid Surge Narrows and Hole in the Wall.

The southern end of Surge Narrows, between the southern tips of Maurelle Island and Quadra Island, is clogged by the Settlers Group of Islands. The safest passage through this group is Beazley Pass between Sturt and Peck Islands. This Pass should ideally be transited close to slack water. Currents reach up to 12 knots at springs and the presence of Tusko Rock makes it particularly dangerous especially when travelling north with an ebb tide.

Anchorage in the vicinity of the Settlers Group is not recommended due to the tidal currents and poor holding ground. Temporary anchorage, with less current, is possible in a few tiny coves north of Goepel Island. Numerous rocks make the passage between the Settlers Group and Maurelle Island a challenge to navigate with strong tidal streams bringing upwellings, small whirlpools and backeddies.

Maurelle Island

Maurelle Island is named after Francisco Antonio Maurelle, the first officer under Lieutenant Comman-

Entrance to Whiterock Passage at fairly high water looks innocuous, but at low water it is studded with boulders.

Proceed with caution when tide is low in Whiterock Passage.

The Octopus Islands Marine Park consists mainly of the uplands on Quadra Island behind the two finest bays. Hole-in-the-Wall in background.

Waiatt Bay, background, with Small Inlet, foreground, on the other side of Quadra.

der Quadra when Quadra explored along the British Columbia coast in the *Sonora* in 1775 and in the *Favorita* in 1779. Just north of Antonio Point is a provincial recreational reserve protecting two small anchorages which could be used while awaiting a favourable tide through Surge Narrows. A logging road leads from this area, which is being actively re-settled, into the central part of the island where there is an extensive flat meadow and marshy area and the remains of old farmsteads.

There are several other possible temporary anchorages in shallow or tiny coves and behind islets which cling closely to the Maurelle shore. Okisollo Channel, between the Upper Rapids and Surge Narrows, is usually less crowded than other waterways in the Discovery Islands because of the need to time passage through the rapids close to slack water, thus keeping through traffic to a minimum. On the Quadra side of Okisollo Channel good temporary anchorage can be found in Yeatman Bay or south of Cyrus Rocks where there are very nice sand beaches. A new trail leads south from Yeatman Bay about ½ mile to Main Lake.

4 Waiatt Bay

Extensive, well protected anchorage is available throughout Waiatt Bay. Entrance into the Bay can be made close to the southern shoreline, through the centre of rocks and islets which encumber the mouth of the Bay, or between the northernmost Octopus Island and Quadra Island. A blazed trail links the head of Waiatt Bay with Small Inlet on the other side of Quadra Island.

5 Octopus Islands Marine Park

The Octopus Islands Marine Park does not actually include the two largest of the Octopus Islands but comprises mainly the Quadra upland behind the two delightful bays inside the Octopus Islands. Well protected anchorage is available in these bays from which one can proceed to explore the maze of tidal waterways separating the many islets and islands. Although the two largest islands are privately owned, signs warn that they may be enjoyed as long as care is taken and no fires lit. At the northeast corner of the park on Quadra Island, an orchard is hidden almost completely from the sea. Eddies and strong tidal currents from Hole in the Wall and the Upper Rapids extend down Okisollo past the islets off Bodega Anchorage as far as the Octopus Islands. Bodega Anchorage is sometimes used by larger vessels awaiting slack water in the rapids.

Well-protected, all-weather anchorages in Octopus Islands.

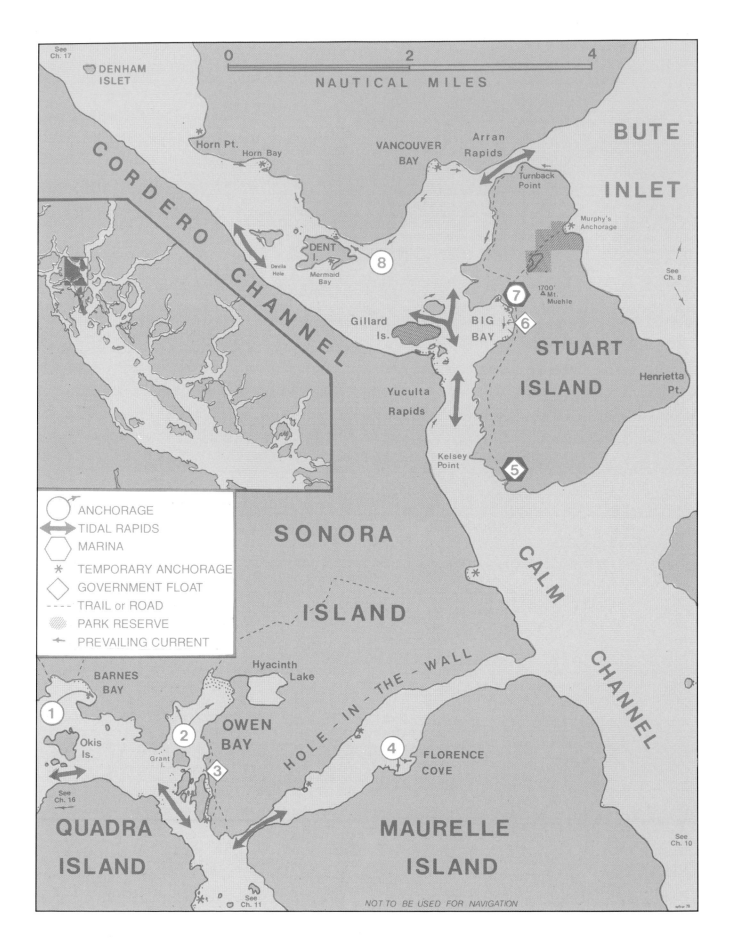

DENHAM ISLET

See Ch. 17

CORDERO CHANNEL

Horn Pt.
Horn Bay

VANCOUVER BAY

Arran Rapids

BUTE INLET

Turnback Point

Murphy's Anchorage

See Ch. 8

Devils Hole

DENT I.

Mermaid Bay

(8)

Gillard Is.

BIG BAY

(7)

1700' Mt. Muehle

(6)

STUART ISLAND

Henrietta Pt.

Yuculta Rapids

Kelsey Point

(5)

SONORA

CALM CHANNEL

ISLAND

ANCHORAGE
TIDAL RAPIDS
MARINA
* TEMPORARY ANCHORAGE
◇ GOVERNMENT FLOAT
--- TRAIL or ROAD
PARK RESERVE
← PREVAILING CURRENT

Hyacinth Lake

BARNES BAY

(1)

Okis Is.

(2)

Grant I.

OWEN BAY

(3)

HOLE - IN - THE - WALL

(4)

FLORENCE COVE

See Ch. 16

QUADRA ISLAND

See Ch. 11

MAURELLE ISLAND

See Ch. 10

NOT TO BE USED FOR NAVIGATION

0   2   4
NAUTICAL MILES

CHAPTER TWELVE

The Yucultas

Owen Bay to Cordero Channel, Hole-in-the-Wall, Stuart Island

Until the beginning of this century the large group of islands north of Campbell River at the northern end of the Strait of Georgia were all thought to be one island — commonly known as Valdes, after the Spanish explorer. It was not until the long and narrow rapid-filled passes of Okisollo Channel and Hole-in-the-Wall were discovered to be navigable, that Valdes Island was found to be in fact — three islands, which are now named Sonora, Maurelle and Quadra.

These three island names honour the Spanish explorers Maurelle and Quadra who in 1775 sailed north from Mexico in the tiny 36 foot schooner *Sonora*. Translations of the accounts of this voyage were published with some embellishments in London newspapers leading Captain Vancouver to describe their voyage as one of the most epic, heroic and tragic navigational feats ever known. According to one account, disaster had first struck when the *Sonora's* only boat was lost and seven of her crew were murdered by Indians near Port Grenville while attempting to land to replenish their water supplies. The *Sonora* continued sailing north reaching as far as 58° North latitude where they saw Mt. Edgecumbe in Alaska before turning south. Gradually, scurvy, starvation and ophthalmia, a blinding eye-disease, laid low the surviving members of the crew. By the time

they reached Dixon Entrance, north of the Queen Charlotte Islands, only Quadra and Maurelle remained on their feet, with the rest of the crew scattered throughout the ship and on the decks. Somehow, the two alone succeeded in sailing the *Sonora* through several gales back down the coast to Mexico.

The waters separating the eastern half of Sonora Island from neighbouring islands are interrupted with no fewer than six separate tidal rapids of varying ferocity. Most yachtsmen travelling beyond Desolation Sound prefer to pass north of Sonora Island, through the Yucultas, although these rapids (including the Gillard and Dent rapids) are considerably more powerful and potentially dangerous than the rapids to the south of Sonora Island. Seymour Narrows in Discovery Passage also tends to be avoided because of the higher concentration of large shipping

---

CHARTS
3521 — **for OKISOLLO CHANNEL,
  HOLE-IN-THE-WALL (1:24,354)**
3522 — **for YUCULTA RAPIDS, CORDERO
  CHANNEL (1:24,330)**
3594 — **DISCOVERY PASSAGE, TOBA INLET
  and CONNECTING CHANNELS
  (1:75,000)**

Government floats at Owen Bay were built to serve a community which moved away before they were completed.

traffic. Yachtsmen using these routes should refer to John Chappell's book *Cruising beyond Desolation* as well as the appropriate sailing directions (B.C. Coast, Vol. 1).

Despite the lower volume of water which floods and ebbs through Okisollo Channel, the Lower and Upper Rapids flow at rates up to 9 knots at spring tides and must be treated with caution and navigated as close to slack water as possible. These particular rapids are also encumbered with the added hazards of

Owen Bay log booming area. Hyacinth Lake, a quarter of a mile inland, is filled with water lillies and bordered by white hyacinths.

heavy overfalls on an ebb tide and rocky shoals which could prove embarrassing or even fatal for the unwary.

Small craft wishing to bypass the Lower Rapids generally travel north of the Okis Islands where there is considerably less current and no obstructions. If one is committed to navigating the Lower Rapids, Gypsy Shoal, midway between Okis Island and Quadra Island, should be given as wide a berth as possible.

1 Barnes Bay

Although much of the shoreline of this bay is used for the booming and storage of logs, safe anchorage is usually available in the eastern end of the bay behind a tiny 8-foot-high islet. Logging roads lead from two log dumps past small settlements and into the interior of Sonora Island where there are several lakes. There are several tiny coves on Okis Island and along the shoreline on both sides of Okisollo Channel which could provide temporary anchorage subject to the strength of the tidal streams and the bottom conditions. In areas like this, where one might expect good holding ground with mud or sand, the bottom is sometimes scoured clean by swift tidal currents, leaving bare rock.

2 Owen Bay

Entrance into Owen Bay is generally made to the north of Grant Island, taking care to avoid the rocks off Walters Point. Abundant anchorage space is available

throughout the bay with the favoured locations being in a small 5-fathom cove offering the most protection from westerly winds or close to the drying flats at the head of the bay.

Hyacinth Lake, located less than ¼ mile inland, is filled with water lilies and bordered by white hyacinths. The land between the bay and the lake is private property and should be respected as such. A tributary creek enters the lake in the northeast corner through a string of swampy meadows where wild hay and vegetables were once grown. At the north end of Owen Bay there is a log dump and road extending into the interior of Sonora Island.

3 Owen Bay Gov't Floats

The approach to the Owen Bay government floats can be made to the south of Grant Island, taking special care to pass inside the rocks located off the southwest and southeast corners of the island. The government float with 260 feet of berthage space was built in 1959 to serve a thriving local community which included a post office, store, sawmill, fuel supply outlet, mink ranch, machine shop, school and several homes and orchards. The community deserted the bay for unknown reasons only months before the wharf and floats were finished. The 1929 vintage sawmill was recently restored for local use and small groups of people through succeeding years have attempted to get the community going again. Nevertheless, an ominous feeling pervades the bay. In the Spring of 1967 the upturned dinghy of cruising sailors who had just returned from the South Pacific was found near the rapids while their unoccupied yacht remained moored in Owen Bay. It is not advisable to explore the group of islands southwest of the government floats as the tidal stream rushes between the islands with remarkable force even at neap tides although the passage through these islands is used by local residents. It is possible however to explore the narrow winding lagoon which leads south from the government floats by road or by dinghy at high tide.

Transit of the Upper Rapids is best negotiated as close to slack water as possible (55 minutes before the change at Seymour Narrows), navigating slightly east of centre channel to avoid a reef off Cooper Point on Quadra Island and Bentley Rock. The time of slack water for both Lower and Upper Rapids and for Hole-in-the-Wall is virtually identical so it is advisable, if travelling east, to be passing through either at LW slack or with enough of the last of this flood to be able to continue through the western entrance of Hole-in-the-Wall where currents reach 12 knots at springs. Within only a few minutes of slack water the current is so strong here and the passage so steep and narrow that one experiences a sense of vertigo as one is impelled along. As the flood builds up there is the very strong impression that one is travelling downhill as you proceed eastward beneath the hovering walls of rock and forest of Hole-in-the-Wall.

Currents reach 12 knots in Hole-In-The-Wall.

Upper Rapids

4 Florence Cove

The tidal stream dissipates rapidly to almost nothing where Hole-in-the-Wall begins to open out and deepen. Halfway through, on the Maurelle Island shore is Florence Cove where there is safe anchorage. Temporary anchorage is also possible behind tiny islets along the Sonora shore of Hole-in-the-Wall.

Maximum currents run at rates less than 2 knots through the deep eastern exit into Calm Channel. This area is a popular salmon and cod fishing area. Calm Channel is well named for although the orientation of the channel would seem to make it particularly susceptible to southeast winds, in fact, strong winds from this direction seldom penetrate into this area. Temporary anchorage is afforded in a small unnamed bay on Sonora Island, a mile north of Hole-in-the-Wall, and is particularly useful as a peaceful place to wait for the tide change in the Yucultas.

5 Stuart Island Resort

Stuart Island was named by Captain Vancouver most probably after the Rt. Hon. John Stuart, Earl of Bute. It is not unlikely that Stuart, who was a great friend of King George III, assisted in the outfitting of Vancouver's expedition. He died shortly after the expedition left England.

Government floats provide over 466 feet of berthage space with the first float being used primarily as a gas dock for small craft taking on fuel and for seaplanes (regular flights to Campbell River). The floats tend to be crowded especially close to slack water. There is a prevailing northward setting current along the Stuart Island shore as far north as Kelsey Point except for one hour before the turn to flood and for a period two hours after the turn to flood. There is a laundromat here, showers and a store while the resort includes cabins, lodge, coffee shop, restaurant and lounge. Half a mile north of Kelsey Point in a small bay on Stuart Island is the A. Spit Boatworks with a marine ways for hauling out boats up to 50 feet and full facilities for boat repairs. Moorage and rental boats are also provided.

Yuculta Rapids

These rapids, known far and wide as "UKE-LA-TAWS", should be navigated by those who are unfamilar with them as close to slack water as possible. It is prudent to approach the rapids an hour or so before high water slack, taking advantage of a back eddy along the Stuart Island shore until one is close to Kelsey Point, then crossing over to the Sonora Island shore where there is a prevailing northerly current. One should then have enough time to transit the Gillard and Dent Rapids before the ebb has had time to build up to full force.

Tidal Current Publication No. 23 contains useful charts of the rapids showing the location of upwellings, whirlpools and overfalls and the relative strengths and directions of the stream for each hour of

Big Bay, Stuart Island, right foreground; Gillard Pass, centre left; Dent Rapids, upper centre; Cordero Channel, background.

the tidal cycle. This publication is especially valuable to have on board if one finds oneself navigating through the rapids at times other than slack water (unadvisable even at neap tides). Selected information from this publication is summarized in the maps on pages 146-147. The general rule is to stay in centre channel and avoid the areas of broken water, upwellings and whirlpools. If caught in a whirlpool, do not attempt to fight it but maintain speed until one has enough steerage way to ease out of it. In the Dent Rapids it is best however, to stay closer to the Sonora

Island shore. If one is late for slack water and unsure of the Dent Rapids, it might be preferable to wait for the next slack water in Big Bay.

One important word of caution. Large powerboats tend to pass through these rapids at full throttle for no explicable reason (other than sheer fright?), causing considerable havoc not only for floats and herring boxes along the shore but for the many small craft frequently found fishing in these waters. Powerboat wakes when they combine with strong tidal streams often result in unnaturally heavy seas which could prove more dangerous than the actual rapids themselves. One should be especially wary of this additional hazard.

6 Big Bay

Big Bay, formerly known as Asman Bay and Yaculta Landing, is the home base for a large community of fishermen, loggers, trappers, fishing guides and resort operators. On an ebb tide there is a fairly strong clockwise backeddy current circulating in the bay. On a flood tide there tends to be a complex double backeddy (figure 8) current with the floodstream at the entrance to the bay moving *south*, a backeddy in the centre of the bay moving *north* and a counter-current along the eastern shore of the bay moving *south*. The prevailing current past the Big Bay Marina (7) and the government floats (6) therefore

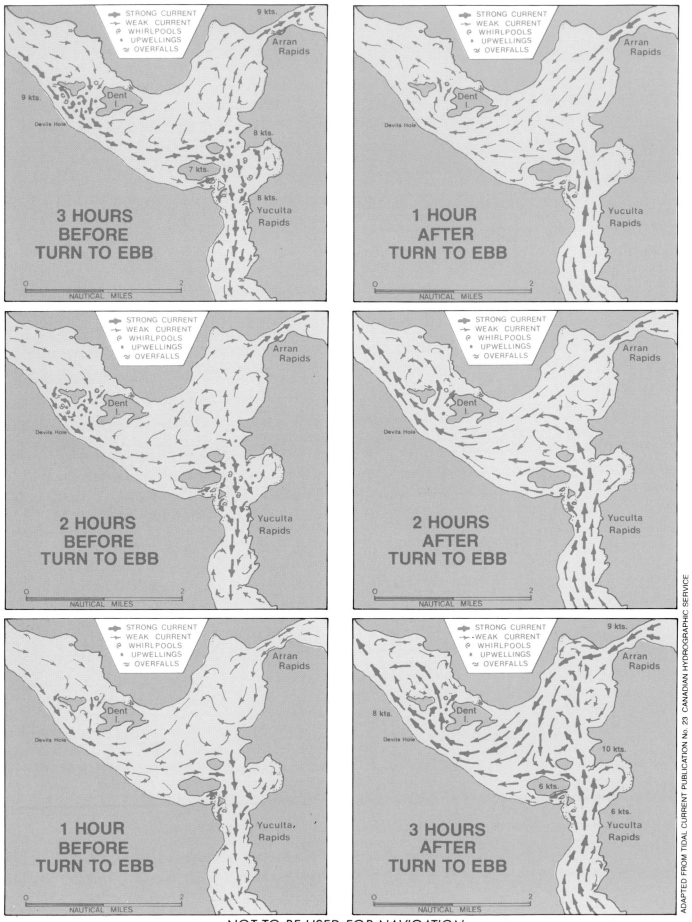

STRONG CURRENT
WEAK CURRENT
WHIRLPOOLS
UPWELLINGS
OVERFALLS

3 HOURS BEFORE TURN TO EBB

9 kts.
Arran Rapids
Dent I.
Devils Hole
9 kts.
8 kts.
7 kts.
8 kts.
Yuculta Rapids

0   2
NAUTICAL MILES

1 HOUR AFTER TURN TO EBB

Arran Rapids
Dent I.
Devils Hole
Yuculta Rapids

0   2
NAUTICAL MILES

2 HOURS BEFORE TURN TO EBB

Arran Rapids
Dent I.
Devils Hole
Yuculta Rapids

0   2
NAUTICAL MILES

2 HOURS AFTER TURN TO EBB

Arran Rapids
Dent I.
Devils Hole
Yuculta Rapids

0   2
NAUTICAL MILES

1 HOUR BEFORE TURN TO EBB

Arran Rapids
Dent I.
Devils Hole
Yuculta Rapids

0   2
NAUTICAL MILES

3 HOURS AFTER TURN TO EBB

9 kts.
Arran Rapids
8 kts.
Dent I.
Devils Hole
10 kts.
6 kts.
6 kts.
Yuculta Rapids

0   2
NAUTICAL MILES

NOT TO BE USED FOR NAVIGATION

ADAPTED FROM TIDAL CURRENT PUBLICATION No. 23 CANADIAN HYDROGRAPHIC SERVICE

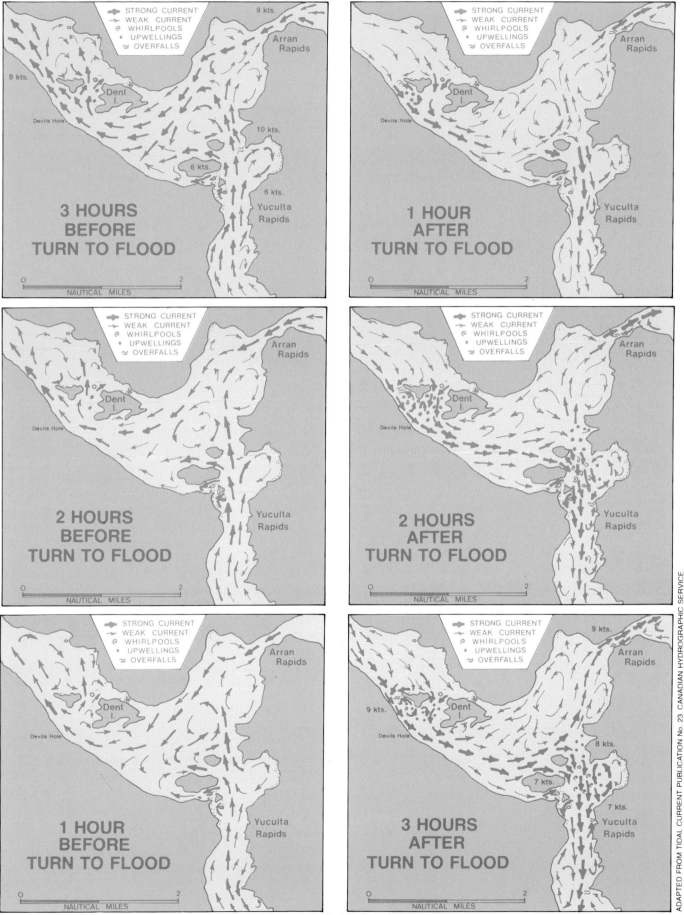

ADAPTED FROM TIDAL CURRENT PUBLICATION No. 23 CANADIAN HYDROGRAPHIC SERVICE

NOT TO BE USED FOR NAVIGATION

Heavy mist moving up Cordero Channel.

tends to be southerly no matter whether the tide is ebbing or flooding. This information is helpful in avoiding the large patch of kelp over the 2 fathom shoal in the centre of the bay, when approaching floats or when fishing in the bay.

The government floats (670 feet of berthage space) are protected by a huge log piling breakwater from both the buildup of driftwood and the occasionally fierce northerly Bute winds which whistle over Stuart Island in the winter time. A trail behind the floats links the Big Bay community with the south end of Stuart Island.

7 Big Bay Marina

This marina provides safe, secure and relatively calm moorage, fuel, well stocked store, showers and laundromat. Cabins and fishing guides are also available.

There are three interesting areas to hike to within two or three hours from Big Bay. If one is energetic, Mt. Muehle rises abruptly to 1,700 feet and provides good views over the rapids up Cordero Channel, across Sonora Island where Florence Lake lies hidden and on to Johnstone Strait. To the north, the turquoise waters of Bute Inlet snake between mountains rising to heights of over 8,000 feet. Mt. Muehle is best approached from the south side as the west and north facing slopes are steep and bare with little vegetation for hand holds. A trail leads north from behind the marina into the interior where it divides with the right fork bypassing the beaver-dammed Eagle Lake. This lake is occasionally used for warm water swimming and is the home for a colony of 30 to 40 eagles some of which can be seen perched on the drowned snags at the southeast end of the lake. A 140-acre provincial recreational reserve protects this lake and the continuation of the trail down through beautiful wooded meadows to Murphy's Anchorage. This anchorage (known locally as Bassett Bay) is well protected from the prevailing summer westerly winds, but is exposed to winter Bute winds and diurnal down-inlet winds which often blow on summer nights.

Arran Rapids

The left fork of the trail north from the marina leads to Arran Rapids. At spring tides you can stand on the shoreline here below the level of the water flooding through from Cordero Channel. This is a remarkable sight with roaring whirlpools and churning surf and an incredible concentration and variety of marine and birdlife including eagles, killer whales and sea lions feeding on the intertidal marine life and the fish which are brought to the surface by the rapids.

Across from here on the mainland shore on July 2, 1792, the English explorers discovered a "pretty considerable village of upwards of twenty houses and about 30 canoes laying before it; from which they concluded that its inhabitants could not be far short of a hundred and fifty". The sketch of this village drawn by the English explorers places the village on the hillside directly above the rapids although the description left by the Spanish explorers who were here eight days later locates the village either on Lawrence Point a few miles to the north, or in Vancouver Bay, just west of the rapids.

The English explorers welcomed the willing and friendly assistance of the Indians who helped in lining their boats along the shore through the rapids. However, once they had reached Cordero Channel, the weather changed abruptly (as it often does today) setting in "so thick and rainy" that they were forced to abandon their explorations for the moment and return to the ships, still anchored near Teakerne Arm.

After warning the Spaniards how difficult this passage was, the English took their ships out to Johnstone Strait via Discovery Passage. The Spaniards however were game to try the rapids with their ships, the Sutil and the Mexicana, which were both about 50 feet long and carried crews of 24. Approaching Arran Rapids somewhat warily, they anchored at several locations (including "Fondeadero de Murphy") before awaiting the change of tide in an anchorage they called "Concha" immediately next to Turnback Point.

The journal of their voyage (Cecil Jane's translation) notes:

The Indians, indicating the course of the sun, signed to us that the favourable moment for which we longed (slackwater) would come when the sun was near the peak of a high mountain on the continent. The time passed quickly with the entertainment afforded by watching the rush of waters, the many trees which were washed down by its violence, the continual passage of the birds, and the play of the fish which made lovely colours on the shingle where we were anchored.

The natives removed to some distance from the schooners without in any way lessening their friendly attentions; on the contrary they gave unequivocal proofs of their interest in our welfare, since in addition to pre-

Sunset from Stuart Island.

senting us with the first fresh salmon which we had seen in the strait and a great number of freshly caught sardines, they let few moments pass without making energetic signs to us of the dangers which we were about to encounter and the manner and time for overcoming them. They explained to us the method which they followed in making this navigation and the continual mishaps which they none the less encountered, ending by making signs that the size and power of resistance of our vessels could not promise us any better fate, but rather one more unfortunate than that with which they met in canoes.

As slack water approached,

The Indians came and accompanied us in their canoes, serving as pilots. We seized the opportune moment and were shortly beyond the most critical point, but the tide which had not stopped except for a moment, began to

Dent Rapids at full flow can be a fearsome obstacle. Hamburger Island and Tugboat Passage in foreground.

acquire force and reached the *Sutil*. It took away her steerage-way and began to carry her along. The *Mexicana* was somewhat farther along and succeeded in anchoring in Fabio (either Vancouver Bay, or more likely, the anchorage behind Dent Island (8)). As soon as the *Sutil* escaped from the currents she proceeded towards this place but when close to it a new eddy carried her off and into the Canal de Carbajal (Cordero Channel) which we were due to follow. Immediately the *Mexicana* weighed anchor and followed her through the canal where the currents were violent and the whirlpools frequent, and so strong that one, which the *Sutil* could not avoid (The Devil's Hole?) turned her around completely three times, at such a lively rate as to be surprising. The *Mexicana* was close to her but was more fortunate on this occasion. In spite of the danger in which the *Sutil* so unexpectedly found herself, a scene never before witnessed by any of those present, it unavoidably caused great laughter, not only among those who were in danger, but among those who were momentarily expecting to be.

(Extract from diary of Galiano and Valdez).

150

8 Dent Island

Galiano in the *Mexicana* probably anchored between Dent Island and the mainland in a backwater with virtually no current and good protection from the strong westerly winds which blow down Cordero Channel afforded by two small islets, the largest of which is known as Wee Dent. There is a small pass between Dent and Wee Dent Islet known as Canoe Pass which is only suitable for dinghies with less than 1 foot of water at low water. It is passable for larger craft at high water slack but should only be attempted in an emergency due to the large number of boulders at the western end.

On July 28, 1972, an American en route from Alaska in an outrigger canoe attempted to navigate the Arran Rapids. He did not succeed; the canoe overturned, and he was drowned. The remains of the canoe can be seen on Wee Dent Island in Canoe Pass as a memorial to his death and to the uncounted others who have met the same fate.

Mermaid Bay, at the south end of Dent Island is commonly used as an emergency tie-up for log booms and tugboats which cannot make it through the rapids till the next slack water. The bay can also provide temporary moorage in an emergency for small craft alongside the booms or temporary anchorage at the head of the bay with a mud bottom.

After passing Dent Island (which the Spaniards named "Bueltas" to commemorate the three turns of the *Sutil*), the *Sutil* and the *Mexicana* attempted to reach the mainland shore to anchor for the night but were constantly foiled by continual cross currents, backeddies and whirlpools. Finally, late at night they succeeded in anchoring in Horn Bay with stern lines ashore and with Horn Point providing some shelter from the westerly wind. Horn Bay is not a particularly good anchorage, even at the best of times, because of the large number of drying rocks and shoals found within it. They probably did not sleep too well, thinking of their narrow escape from the rapids and their journal notes:

> Much later the wind increased in strength, so that we heard it whistling through the plants above us and through the trees on the mountains. At the same time the violent flow of the waters in the channel caused a horrible roaring and a notable echo, this producing an awe-inspiring situation, so that we had so far met with nothing so terrible.

The Spaniards may also have been unconsciously

Sportfishermen play the backeddies in the Yucultas, one of the prime salmon areas on the coast.

Dangerous whirlpools along the shore in Dent Rapids.

affected by the quite noticeable change in climate and vegetation which occurs once one is through the rapids. The water temperature drops several degrees, the wind generally increases from the west and fog is prevalent. There is a noticeable dampening in the air and the arbutus tree has disappeared from the landscape. There are few deciduous trees, with the conifers growing right down to only a few inches above mean highwater. It is a shame that Vancouver did not personally visit this area for he would have been hard pressed to find a more descriptive name for this area than the one he had already given to Desolation Sound only 15 miles south, where the surroundings are almost tropical by comparison. Although for some this area has its own special charm, the Spaniards attempted to leave as soon as possible. After two frustrating days of head winds and confusing currents the *Sutil* and *Mexicana* were still in Horn Bay.

> The periodic tide which we had observed in Carvajal (Cordero) Channel began to run out at half-past six in the evening. The gusts of wind had not entirely ceased, but they were not so violent as they had been on the previous day, as we eagerly desired to continue our voyage, even at the cost of running some probable risks, we set out at seven in the evening. The *Mexicana*, which was farther

out than the *Sutil*, had first to undertake the task, and she achieved it, proceeding for a considerable distance with her oars. The *Sutil* followed her at some three cables' distance, and this short distance was sufficient to enable the *Mexicana*, although with difficulty, to make Eddy (Horn) Point, with the *Sutil* meeting with equal good fortune. The backwash increased when she was already near the point and carried her rapidly on to the shoal which is a cable east of the point, and then bore her towards the coast. In order to clear from it, it was necessary to use her oars as punt poles, and despite the energetic manner in which this resource was employed, the eddies carried her to Refuge Creek (Horn Bay). The effort was then repeated: caught by the currents and whirlpools, she was carried to Eddy (Horn) Point with such speed that it seemed to be vain to make any attempt to avoid running on the coast, but the waters themselves bore her to Refuge Creek (Horn Bay). The effort was repeated a third and fourth time in vain, and at last, despairing of accomplishing that which had clearly been so often prevented by the currents, she anchored. The *Mexicana* had moored in Aliponzoni Creek (due east of Denham Islet).

> On the twenty-third, at six in the morning, the *Sutil* renewed her effort to leave, and with the experience of the previous evening and the knowledge gained concerning the character of this place, she rowed along in calm water near the coast, made Eddy (Horn) Point, passed out of Aliponzoni Creek and on sighting the *Mexicana* at once joined her. With a fresh north wind in our favour, we then navigated along the lefthand (Sonora Island) shore.

The frustrations of the Spaniards may seem very familiar to any yachtsman who has found himself in an area with no prior knowledge of local idiosyncracies of wind and tide, no means of propulsion other than sails and oars, and no local charts. It was not until the Spaniards were able to take advantage of the offshore northeasterly wind in the early morning and a slackening in the prevailing eastward moving current along the mainland shore that they were able to successfully leave Horn Bay. Despite the very strong ebb and flood currents along the Sonora shore of Cordero Channel and through the centre of the Arran, Gillard and Yuculta Rapids, there are prevailing currents in several places in this area close to shore which flow almost all the time in one direction, no matter whether the tide is ebbing or flooding. These currents may slacken or reverse for only an hour or so in every 12 hour ebb-flood tidal cycle and are indicated by small arrows on the map at the beginning of this chapter.

Big Bay

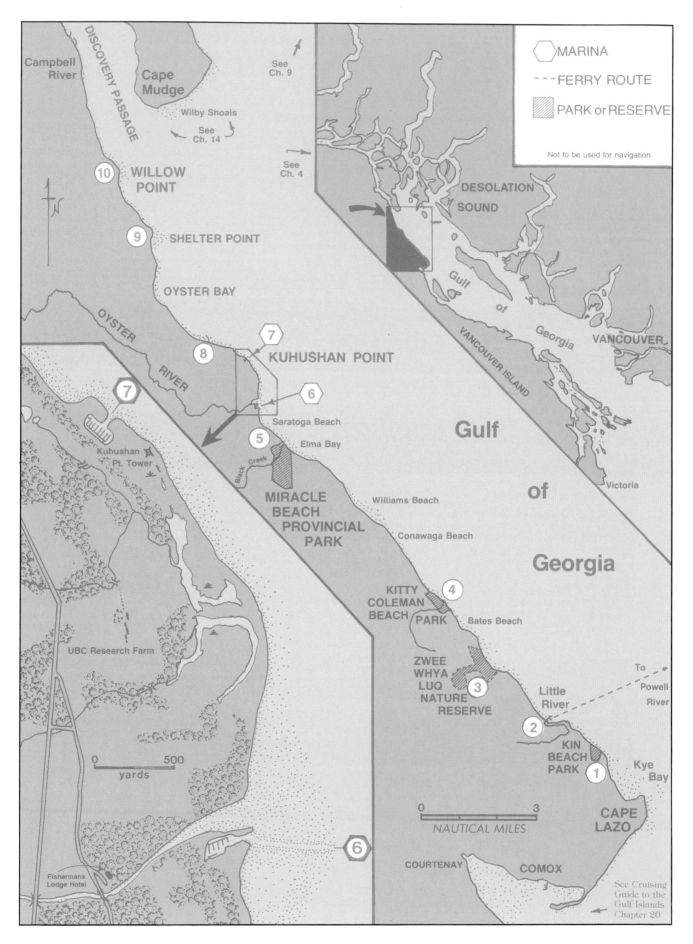

MARINA

FERRY ROUTE

PARK or RESERVE

Not to be used for navigation

Campbell River

DISCOVERY PASSAGE

Cape Mudge

See Ch. 9

Wilby Shoals

See Ch. 14

See Ch. 4

DESOLATION SOUND

N

10 WILLOW POINT

9 SHELTER POINT

OYSTER BAY

OYSTER RIVER

Gulf of Georgia

VANCOUVER ISLAND

VANCOUVER

7

8

KUHUSHAN POINT

7

6

Kuhushan Pt. Tower

Saratoga Beach

Elma Bay

5

Black Creek

MIRACLE BEACH PROVINCIAL PARK

Williams Beach

Gulf

of

Georgia

Victoria

UBC Research Farm

Conawaga Beach

KITTY COLEMAN BEACH PARK

4

Bates Beach

ZWEE WHYA LUQ NATURE RESERVE

3

To Powell River

Little River

2

KIN BEACH PARK

1

Kye Bay

0   500
yards

0   3
NAUTICAL MILES

CAPE LAZO

6

COURTENAY

COMOX

Fishermans Lodge Hotel

See Cruising Guide to the Gulf Islands Chapter 20

CHAPTER THIRTEEN

Cape Lazo to Discovery Passage

Kye Bay, Kin Beach, Little River, Seal Bay, Oyster River

Cruising yachtsmen usually avoid the 29 mile stretch of open coastline between Cape Lazo and Willow Point at the entrance to Discovery Passage because of the apparent lack of shelter. In addition the coastline is relatively low and featureless making it somewhat difficult to be sure of one's exact position. The prominent hills, points, islands or deep embayments which make pilotage easier in other areas of the coast are absent here. Southeast winds can generate large seas along this coast with an open fetch of twenty to forty miles from Lasqueti Island.

This coastline is, however, very attractive in good weather with extensive stretches of sandy beaches and is increasingly popular for small boats which can be carried or hauled out of the water and for large boats which can anchor comfortably offshore. Medium sized boats could also enjoy this area with a careful eye to weather and tidal conditions and a thorough knowledge of the location of local landmarks, drying rocks and the nearest accessible options for protected moorage or anchorage.

One should be especially wary when approaching this shoreline however, even when one's exact position is known and the sea is calm. Depths are not always exactly as charted. The shallows and beach sands, gravels, cobbles and boulders are in continual motion from one year to the next. The process of "longshore drift", caused by waves breaking along the shore at an angle and washing back down to the sea, acts in gradually transporting materials along the beach. Sand, silt and gravels move to the south during the summer when northwesterly winds prevail and to the north in winter when southeasterlies are dominant. The net motion of materials is to the north (Cape Lazo is gradually disappearing) because of the greater strength and frequency of southeast winds and seas throughout the year.

Anywhere along this coast or along similar straight and shallow coasts, composed of "softer" sedimentary or drift (glacial) deposits, one can observe how man's interference with the shoreline has disrupted normal beach processes. Artificial structures such as breakwaters, groynes, launching ramps or "protective" rip-rap tend to result in increased erosion on the downwind side (in this case, north) of the structure and increased deposition (shallowing offshore,

CHART
3591 — CAPE LAZO to DISCOVERY PASSAGE
(1:76,397)

accretion above shore) on the upwind side.

Yachtsmen can make use of this knowledge in approaching the shore as the deeper water (especially in spring and early summer) is generally to the north of launching ramps or other structures.

Winds

The winds which prevail in this area and the boating attractions and facilities of the Comox area south of Cape Lazo have been described in Chapter 20 of Pacific Yachting's *Cruising Guide to the Gulf Islands*. To recapitulate: calm winds are frequent, especially at night. Winds from the northwest quadrant blow over 30 percent of the time in summer (over 60 per cent in the early morning hours, less than 20 per cent in the afternoon). Winds from the southeast and east blow about 20 per cent of the time in summer (over 40 per cent in the afternoon, less than 15 per cent at night).

Boats leaving Comox should pass outside the bell buoy (P56), 1½ miles off Cape Lazo when southeasterly winds are blowing. At other times it is wise to keep at least a mile offshore to avoid the boulder studded spits which surround this prominent Cape.

Kye Bay

If one does not mind the occasional roar of jets taking off and landing at the RCAF base behind Cape Lazo, Kye Bay is a pleasant location for temporary anchorage in calm weather conditions with a rising tide. The preferred anchorage is in the southern, relatively boulder free, part of the bay where there is a small local park (Elks) for picnics ashore. There are also three resorts here — Cathay Cottages, Kye Bay Bungalow Motel and Kye Bay Kottages. A 546-acre provincial recreational reserve covers the beach which, at extreme low tide, extends out from the shoreline for over ½ mile. A launching ramp at the north end of Kye Bay has increased deposition to the south of it and erosion to the north of it (Krauel, Royal Roads).

1   Kin Beach Provincial Park

North of Kye Bay is 15-acre Kin Beach Park with an extensive grassy backshore. This "Class C" park is locally popular for swimming, picnicking and camping. There are 15 campsites, tennis courts, playground and a 1,200-foot long sand and gravel beach. Three rows of piling type groyne structures run perpendicular to the beach, attempting to prevent erosion of the foreshore.

2   Little River

The King Coho resort, offering campsites, coffee bar, boat rentals, fuel, launching ramp, fishing tackle and bait, laundromat and showers is located a few hundred yards east of the Little River ferry dock. This bight offers possibly the best protection from south-easterlies between Cape Lazo and Campbell River, but is open to the northwest. The ferry dock serves as the Vancouver Island terminus for the car ferry link to Powell River on the mainland. The ferry also gives periodic mid-Strait of Georgia weather reports on local radio. Good protection from northwesterlies can be found immediately south of the ferry dock. Commercial fishboats often tie between the dolphins at night when southeasterlies are infrequent. The deepest water here is found *south* of the dock structure. The northerly orientation of the shoreline south of the dock inhibits longshore drift and the outlet of the Little River is continually adding deltaic deposits north of the ferry dock. The Little River could probably be negotiated by a canoe or dinghy at high water for half a mile or so behind the beach. Portaging may be necessary as there are at least eight bridges (some low) across the river.

3   Seal Bay

Approximately 1,600-acres of undeveloped crown land behind Seal Bay have been proposed as a nature reserve by the Comox-Strathcona Natural History Society. There are two beach accesses on either side of a ravine which drains a large beaver-dammed swamp (Filbergs Marsh) about 1½ miles inland. Several miles of trails have been constructed by local volunteers. The Comox Indian name for this area is XWEE-XWHYA-LUQ, pronounced "Zway Why Luck", and meaning "a place of beauty; beauty that is not only seen, but felt."

Anchorage close to shore in Seal Bay is inhibited by the large number of drying boulders. Temporary anchorage is somewhat easier a mile to the north off Bates Beach. There are two resorts at Bates Beach which offer accommodation, showers, campsites, launching ramps, rental boats and fishing tackle.

4   Kitty Coleman Beach Provincial Park

This 24-acre park is one of the oldest on Vancouver Island (established in 1944) and includes a launching ramp, playground, picnic sites, picnic shelter and a campground with over 35 campsites. There is a small stream which bisects the park, slipping out through tall woods of virgin fir, balsam and hemlock onto the beach.

The 5-mile stretch of shoreline between Kitty Coleman Beach and Miracle Beach is the least developed, but at Williams Beach in locally known Tranquility Bay, there are a few cottages and The Alders Resort near some low pastoral land.

A "conspicuous" steep cliff of unconsolidated sands is now obscured by vegetation, but is periodically revealed by occasional landslides. Special care is necessary in approaching the shoreline south of here, especially near high tide as there are several drying boulders; but north of Williams Beach itself, the foreshore is relatively boulder free.

The Miracle Beach Resort in Elma Bay can be identified from the sea by a conspicuous building — the "Red Caboose", which serves as a diner-snack bar. This resort is at the southern end of what is claimed to be one of the finest white sand beaches on the east coast of Vancouver Island and provides housekeeping cottages, showers, laundromat, store, rental boats, launching ramp and fuel. Mooring buoys, which dry at extreme low water, are also provided for guests.

5 Miracle Beach Provincial Park

Miracle Beach Provincial Park, in Elma Bay south of the Black Creek estuary, comprises 108 acres of upland and 118 acres of foreshore. There is a large campground (over 180 campsites) here, picnic shelters and tables, and a nature house with parks branch naturalists interpreting the seashore and upland natural life at regular times throughout the summer months. At high tide, small shoal draught boats might be able to penetrate for a short distance up Black Creek to obtain shelter from any onshore winds.

Care should be exercised, if approaching the shore near high water, to avoid the two rows of concrete groyne structures which were sunk off this beach many years ago in an attempt to trap the sand which was being carried along the foreshore by longshore drift. These structures now stand about 3 to 4 feet above the level of the sand. (1980).

Between Black Creek and the Oyster River is beautiful, sandy Saratoga Beach where there are ten separate resorts — Timberlane, Killarney, Dick and Di's, Island Silver Sands, Owen's Sea-Esta, The Breakers, McLeod's, Saratoga Beach, Oyster River and Pacific Playgrounds. The resorts offer a varied range of accommodations and facilities. The hydrographic charts indicate that the bight off Saratoga Beach could be used as an anchorage for large vessels. The bight is also suitable for smaller vessels closer to shore in all but southeast weather (or northeast in winter) as Kuhushan Point offers considerable protection from northwest winds. If anchoring here, with the intention of exploring ashore, it is unwise to leave your boat unwatched, especially on summer afternoons when onshore southeasterlies are common.

6 Oyster River

South of the Oyster River outlet there is a dredged channel across the delta which leads to a small

Little River.

Oyster River estuary and dredged channel leading to the
Pacific Playgrounds marina. Saratoga beach on left.

Dredged channel to Pacific Playgrounds marina.

marina basin operated by Pacific Playgrounds Ltd. The seaward terminus of the dredged channel is marked by two pilings, the northernmost of which is covered with red fluorescent tape. Depths outside the entrance are reported to be approximately 3 feet of water below chart datum (1980), and the channel, which is about 500 yards long, is kept dredged to 4 feet below chart datum. Dredging must be an almost continual or at least annual process as longshore drift will be continually filling it in. Because the channel is not perfectly straight, it might be easier to follow when the tide is not high and the surrounding banks are completely exposed. These banks tend to cover at extreme high tide. Entrance into the marina basin approach channel is not advisable when a sea is running for boats unfamiliar with the channel course.

The marina basin can accommodate up to 130 boats and usually has space for a few visiting boats. Depths within the basin are dredged to about 6 feet below chart datum. There is a fuel dock here, accommodation, campsites, showers, laundromat, heated pool, golf course, store, fishing tackle, launching ramp, dry storage, boat rentals and charters.

The entrance to the Oyster River itself dries at low tide, but near high water, shoal-draught boats could navigate for a short distance upstream. Just below the first bridge, on the north bank of the river, is the old Fishermans Lodge Hotel and pub — a favourite haunt of river explorers and steelhead fishermen. There is also a 12-acre recreational reserve around the woods here, and behind Kuhushan Point — the extensive 1,500-acre UBC Research Farm with a herd of 350 dairy cows. Visitors are welcome.

Kuhushan Point

Kuhushan Point is low and treeless and projects further out into the Strait of Georgia than other headlands along this coast. There is a long row of tall poplar trees about 300 yards inland which (warns the *Small Craft Guide*) "in thick weather might be mistaken for the extremity of the point". The oyster pond lagoon and saltwater marsh behind Kuhushan Point, charted as being open to the sea, is now closed off and serves as a waterfowl sanctuary.

It is an incredibly beautiful area to visit, especially in winter when it serves as a haven for waterfowl. In summer, one can hike down from the Salmon Point marina; or if conditions are perfect and one's boat is small enough — portage over the gravel berm separating the lagoon from the sea. Kuhushan Point is known locally as Salmon Point. This name change could have been brought about by local people concerned about some misplaced meanings of the original word.

About 3 miles east of Kuhushan Point (4 miles south of Mitlenatch Island) the chart has a notation: "Flood tides from the North and South meet about here". In 1860, Commander Richard Mayne (*Four

Years in British Columbia and Vancouver Island) wrote:

> Coming out at the north end of Baynes Sound, and rounding Cape Lazo, Cape Mudge — so named by Vancouver, after his lieutenant, the late Admiral Zachariah Mudge — appears like an island in the middle of the Gulf, presenting a high steep face to the southward; though as it is approached, shoals will be found extending from it a long way. This part of the Gulf of Georgia forms a sort of playground for the waters, in which they frolic, utterly regardless of all tidal rules. This is caused by the collision of the streams which takes place here; the flood-stream from the south, through the Strait of Fuca, and up the Haro Archipelago, being met by that from Queen Charlotte Sound and Johnstone and Discovery Straits. The tide-rips caused by the conflict between these opponent streams are excessively dangerous to boats, and great care has to be exercised in crossing. These tide-rips exist to some extent in all parts of these inner waters, but they are certainly more dangerous here than anywhere else. A boat getting into them is almost certain to be swamped; and even a ship is so twisted and twirled about as to run considerable risk, if the passage is at all narrow, of being forced on the rocks or beach.

The central part of this quotation has been often repeated, giving this particular stretch of coastline an unwarranted reputation. In actual fact, it is not so much the meeting or "collision" of tidal streams which is dangerous, since the velocity of the current here will be close to zero, but where the flood tidal stream from Discovery Passage is still flowing strongly (some distance to the north) and is opposed by a southeast wind.

The actual meeting place of the tidal streams can vary over several miles depending on local wind and barometric conditions and is generally remarkably placid, being occasionally marked by "tide lines" of accumulated driftwood, seaweed and other debris (see Richard E. Thomson's forthcoming book: *Oceanography of the British Columbia Coast*). When a strong wind blows, there may be abrupt changes in sea state here, but nothing like the really dangerous seas occasionally encountered closer to the entrance to Discovery Passage.

If one is running north, in front of a southeast wind, and the tide tables indicate a flooding tide in Discovery Passage, it is here that one should make the decision to pass east of Quadra Island and seek shelter behind Rebecca Spit or on Cortes Island.

7 Salmon Point Resort

Five hundred feet north of the 60-foot-high Kuhushan Point "skeleton" light tower is the entrance to another dredged out marina basin. The entrance channel is much shorter and easier to negotiate than the one across the Oyster delta although there is probably only a foot or so of water below chart datum.

Two orange triangular ("slow vehicle") signs serve as range markers and at night two blue lamps serve the same purpose. The markers should be lined up one on top of the other to assist access to the marina basin. A sign inside the basin warns: "DEAD SLOW — INCOMING BOAT HAS RIGHT OF WAY". This

Salmon Point marina, with moorage for 200 boats, at low tide.

resort provides moorage for 200 boats, fuel, fishing tackle, bait, launching ramp, accommodation and campsites, showers, laundromat and winter boat storage.

8 Oyster Bay

Just south of where the Island Highway comes down to the sea is Bennett's Point Resort (accommodations, power and sailboat rentals, charter boat, launching ramp) and the "Gourmet by the Sea" restaurant. The Oyster Bay Resort has a launching ramp, dry storage, fuel, accommodations and rental boats which appear to be launched near ruined marine railway pilings which extend out over the beach for several hundred feet.

After the Second World War, old vessels which were no longer of any use were brought to the south end of Oyster Bay and grounded to serve as a break-water for a large log booming and storage area. Some of these old ships were towed here — war surplus U.S. destroyers and redundant steamships like the *Gray* and the *Lady Pam*, but one — the clipper ship *St. Paul* reportedly entered the bay under full sail and was quickly stripped of her rigging, sails and spars after grounding. Oyster Bay became known as the "bay of broken ships" as successive winter southeasterly gales battered the hulks into oblivion. What was left of the hulks has been removed now, leaving a sandy, log covered beach and one acre of newly formed (accreted) land upwind (south) of the old breakwater. This new land is protected as a recreational reserve for picnicking.

A fair amount of protection from southeast winds is afforded for temporary anchorage here, but southeasterly swells tend to curl around Kuhushan Point. The foreshore inside (north of) the old breakwater is not particularly recommended for anchorage, except for shoal draught boats near high tide. This part of Oyster Bay is also used as a resting area for murres and other diving sea birds, particularly during winter southeast gales.

There are several resorts and motels along the shorefront from here to Campbell River, catering mainly to trailer boat fishermen and tourists attracted by the opportunity for abundant salmon catches. Temporary anchorage (with reasonable protection from northwesterly winds) is available at the north end of Oyster Bay, in the lee of Shelter Point or 2 miles

160

Salmon Point marina (high tide), entrance to Oyster Lagoon in background has now been closed off.

north, in the lee of Willow Point. But special care must be exercised in avoiding drying boulders along this shore and the dangerous tide rips previously mentioned, north of Willow Point.

In 1911, the American steamship *Cottage City* was groping for the entrance to Discovery Passage in a blinding snowstorm when she grounded off Willow Point. Fred Rogers (*Shipwrecks of B.C.*) notes that passengers and crew safely reached shore but " . . . Most of the baggage was lost or left behind. Six members of a vaudeville show, en route to a booking in Alaska, lost their costumes and a quantity of theatrical equipment, most of it later being found scattered along the beaches. Oldtimers around Campbell River (recall that) some rollicking parties were held when local women and men dressed up in the salvaged costumes . . . someone (also) salvaged a piano, which 's said to still exist in the town."

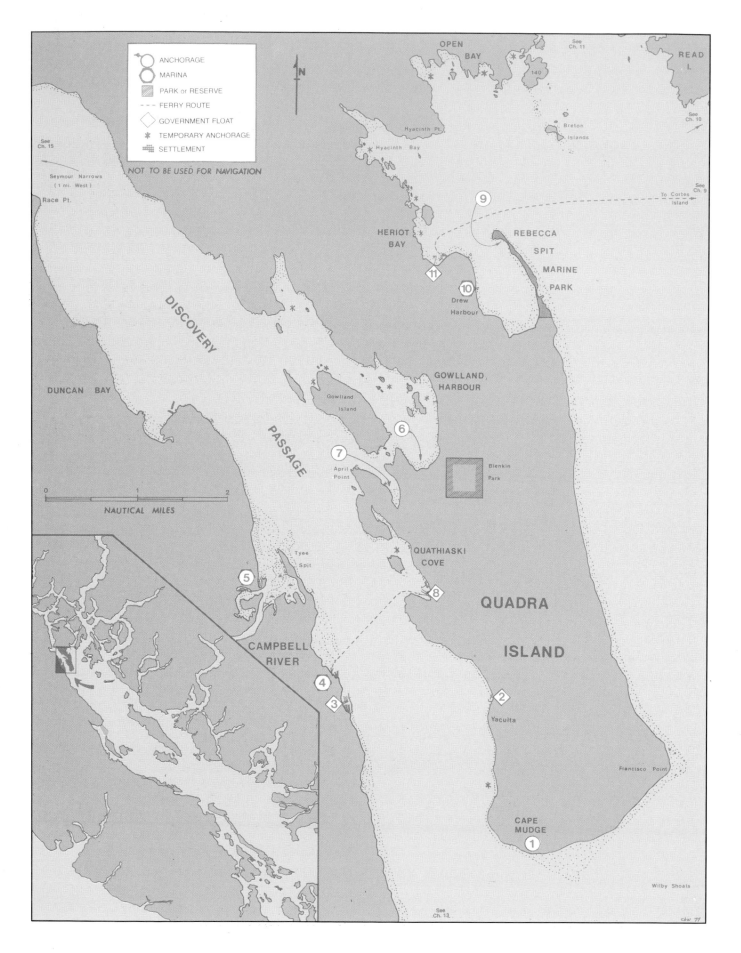

OPEN
BAY

See Ch. 11

READ
I.

See Ch. 10

ANCHORAGE
MARINA
PARK or RESERVE
FERRY ROUTE
GOVERNMENT FLOAT
TEMPORARY ANCHORAGE
SETTLEMENT

N

See Ch. 15

Seymour Narrows
(1 mi. West)

NOT TO BE USED FOR NAVIGATION

Race Pt.

Hyacinth Pt.

Breton
Islands

140

Hyacinth Bay

DISCOVERY

DUNCAN BAY

HERIOT
BAY

9

To Cortes
Island

See Ch. 9

REBECCA
SPIT
MARINE
PARK

11

10

Drew
Harbour

PASSAGE

GOWLLAND
HARBOUR

Gowlland
Island

6

Blenkin
Park

0   1   2

NAUTICAL MILES

7

April
Point

Tyee
Spit

5

Quathiaski
Cove

8

QUADRA

CAMPBELL
RIVER

4

3

ISLAND

2

Yaculta

Francisco Point

CAPE
MUDGE

1

Wilby Shoals

See Ch. 13

cbw 77

162

CHAPTER FOURTEEN

Campbell River and Southern Quadra Island

Campbell River and Quadra Island are located at the extreme northwestern end of the Strait of Georgia, about 100 miles from Vancouver. Quadra Island is the largest of the "Discovery Islands" which stretch from Discovery Passage, alongside Vancouver Island, to Desolation Sound (proper) and the mainland coast. These islands separate the Strait of Georgia from Johnstone Strait — the main inside passage leading to northern British Columbia.

Quadra Island has an interesting history as it is on the border between the Kwakiutl and Coast Salish Indian tribes. At various times members of these and other tribes, such as the northern Haidas, would fight fierce battles for possession of this strategic area. The prime locality was the southern tip of Quadra Island — atop the cliffs at Cape Mudge — overlooking the Gulf of Georgia.

Sailors approaching Cape Mudge at the entrance to Discovery Passage are approaching one of the most notoriously vicious areas in the Strait of Georgia. The combination of strong southeast winds and a flood tide (from the north) raises a very confused and dangerous sea with short, steep swells and breaking waves extending right across the entrance of Discovery Passage. Even with very light southeast winds against a flooding tide, huge rollers can be generated.

Southeast winds have a clear fetch of over 40 miles before reaching Cape Mudge where the flood tidal streams from the north shoot through Discovery Passage at rates up to 7 knots at springs. The rate of flow of this flood tide dissipates to 4 knots only a few miles south of Cape Mudge, but the southerly direction of the flood continues for several miles south of Mitlenatch Island (7 miles SE of Cape Mudge) where the north-going flood from around the south tip of Vancouver Island is met (See Chapter 13).

Some of the largest vessels to vanish in coastal waters have been lost in the vicinity of Cape Mudge: in the 1800s — the steamtugs *Standard*, 75 feet, one survivor (1892) and *Estelle*, 90 feet, no survivors (1894). Other wrecks have included the *Carlyle IV*, 26 tons (1939); *Petrel* (1954); *Eva-Di* (1957); *Daryl-D* (1958); and the *Royston* (1964). Many other ships have foundered here, but possibly none were greeted with more delight by local residents than the wreck of the American steamship *Northwestern*. Doris Ander-

---

CHARTS
3591 — CAPE LAZO to DISCOVERY PASSAGE
         (1:76,400)
3594 — DISCOVERY PASSAGE to TOBA INLET
         and connecting channels (1:75,000)
3565 — DISCOVERY PASSAGE (1:38,000)
3556 — For plans of GOWLLAND HARBOUR
         and QUATHIASKI COVE (1:18,200)

---

son (*Evergreen Islands*, Gray's, 1980) recalls:

> Excitement came to the island in 1927 when the S.S. *Northwestern*, northbound in a snowstorm about five a.m. missed the channel into Discovery Passage and foundered on the beach at Cape Mudge. Alex Mercier, former fire chief for Quadra, was a boy of nine then, living at the cape, and he ran down with the others to view the wreck. She was a huge ship and, with her lights shining through the darkness and the falling snow, he says she had the appearance of a city suddenly risen up from the sea. She had been *en route* to Alaska, laden with Christmas supplies of every sort: butter, flour, lard, cheese, hams, blankets, clothing, innumerable toys, leather goods, tools and myriad other luxury items. The animals trapped below deck were shot, and a power launch came to take off passengers and crew on the leeside. The ship itself was left untended for months.

> Settlers and Indians swarmed about the *Northwestern*, coming from as far as Heriot Bay in rowboats and gasboats and by horse and sledge to load up. In the weeks that followed, storekeepers complained to police that the island residents had stocked their homes with *Northwestern* cargo and no one was patronizing the stores. The police made an inspection tour of the island homes and there was a great scurrying about to conceal loot in root houses and hay lofts, as no one was sure of the rules of salvage. In the confusion, hams were left hanging in the attic and ship's blankets waved in the breeze on the clothes-lines, but the inspectors departed without comment and without confiscating anything. Eventually, a salvage tug came and towed away the ravished *Northwestern*. Quadra Islanders enjoyed a bounteous Christmas that lingered long in their memories.

Winds

Although there is a weather station at the Cape Mudge lighthouse, no permanent records of wind direction frequency and speeds are kept. The closest stations where this information is recorded are Comox (20 miles south) and Chatham Point (20 miles north). The data from these stations would appear to indicate that in the vicinity of Cape Mudge winds from the west and northwest occur over 50 per cent of the time in summer and over 25 per cent of the time in winter. Winds from the southeast occur approximately 20 per cent in summer and 30 per cent in winter.

If you intend entering Discovery Passage in a strong south or southeast wind and the tide is flooding or close to the change to flood, then it is best to pass east of Cape Mudge and anchor overnight at Rebecca Spit or Cortes Island before heading back around when the tide is ebbing. If the wind is favourable or calm, but the flood tide is still strong, it is possible for smaller boats to enter Discovery Passage by riding a back eddy along the edge of Wilby Shoals as far as the lighthouse.

1   Cape Mudge

If you should find opportunity to visit Cape Mudge by car ferry from Campbell River, by small boat, or by being washed ashore, you may be startled by a number of sombre faces staring out over the Gulf from innumerable boulders perched on the drying tidal flats. These faces represent spirit beings and were carved into the hard granite boulders by Indians in pre-historic times. It is likely that Cape Mudge was an important early shaman site. There are over 26 boulders carved in one fashion or another, more than at any other site on the Pacific coast. In recent years, many of these boulders have been relocated to the Indian museum at Yaculta (2).

In addition to the petroglyphs originally at Cape Mudge, there are four petroglyph boulders on Francisco Point and in Dogfish Bay, ½ mile to the north are two more. One of these — a large boulder near high tide — includes a remarkable carving of a sea serpent which bears a startling resemblance to the mythological Kwakiutl sea wolf.

On Friday, July 13, 1792, after spending a depressing few weeks exploring Desolation Sound, Captain George Vancouver anchored H.M.S. *Discovery* and *Chatham* just north of Cape Mudge and with Archibald Menzies, botanist, he was rowed ashore to visit the village atop the Cape Mudge cliffs. Vancouver notes:

> . . . we were received by a man who appeared to be the chief of the party. He approached us alone, seemingly with a degree of formality. . . . I made him such presents as seemed not only to please him excessivley, but to confirm him in the good opinion with which he was prepossessed; and he immediately conducted us to the village by a very narrow path winding diagonally up the cliff, estimated by us to be about an hundred feet in height, and within a few degrees of being perpendicular.

Menzies writes:

> . . . we found a considerable village consisting of about 12 houses or Huts planked over with large boards some of which were ornamented with rude paintings particularly those on the fronts of the houses. They were flat roofed & of a quadrangular figure & each house contained several families to the number of about 350 Inhabitants in all . . ."

> . . . They did not appear any wise shy or timerous tho we were pretty certain our party were the first Europeans they had ever seen or had any direct intercourse with, nor did they seem to regard us or the Vessels with any particular degree of curiosity.

> The women were decently coverd with Garments made either of the Skins of wild Animals or wove from Wool or the prepared bark of the American Arber Vitae Tree, but many of the Men went entirely naked without giving the least offence to the other Sex or shewing any apparent shame at their situation.

> . . . Some Fish and Curiosities were purchased from them for Beads & Small Trinkets, & in these little dealings they appeared to be guided by the strictest honesty, indeed their whole conduct during our short stay was quiet, friendly & hospitable, pressing us often to partake of their entertainment such as Fish Berries & Water, & we in return endeavourd to make them sensible of our approbation by distributing among the Women & Children some small presents, which made them appear highly gratified.

The Cape was named by Vancouver after his First Lieutenant aboard H.M.S. *Discovery*, Zachary Mudge, who, although only 22 years old, had had 12 years of sea experience since joining the Royal Navy when he was 10 years old. In 1782, at age 12, he had taken part in the celebrated naval battle in which his ship the *Foudroyant* captured the French line-of-battle ship *Pegase*. At age 79, 3 years before his death, he was made an Admiral. (Walbran).

When Captain Vancouver stopped at Cape Mudge

in 1792 he was the guest of the Salish Indians. The village he visited was TSQULOTN, meaning "playing field" after a large level pasture two miles long behind the village. (Anderson). Around the middle of the next century the Lekwiltok (pronounced Euclataw) band of the Kwakiutl Indians pushed down from the north and occupied this strategic site. The Lekwiltok established their main village at Yaculta, two miles to the north of Tsqulotn.

2   Yaculta

This Indian settlement is served by government floats with 440 feet of berthage space, used mainly by village fishermen. A log piling breakwater protects the floats from southerly winds. On an ebb tide there is a strong south-going back eddy past the government floats as far south as the lighthouse. When planning any passage in this area, either along or across Discovery Passage, it is wise to take into account the direction and strength (maximum 5 to 7 knots) of the tidal streams. Otherwise, a sail across the channel may put you 2 miles further "downstream" than you intended to be. It is considerate of power boats not to travel so fast that their wash interacts with the strong currents to make it particularly dangerous for the many small craft in the passage or moored to floats along the shoreline.

The Indians who now live at Yaculta are descendants of the former fierce and warlike Lekwiltok, and

Sandy cliffs of Cape Mudge can be seen for many miles.

are living up to the name of their ancestors, which means "unkillable thing". In 1922, the federal government had banned the potlatch — an essential part of Indian life, and confiscated valuable tribal artifacts and potlatch regalia. These Indians, proud and independent, worked over the years to regain possession of this part of their heritage. The Cape Mudge village was the first Indian village in Canada to seek municipal status. The fishing fleet grew and prospered — a small part of it can be seen on the back of the Canadian $5 bill. In 1953, Chief Billy Assu was honoured with a medal "for meritorious service" by Queen Elizabeth II.

Finally, in 1979 many of the potlatch artifacts and regalia were returned to the new sea-snail shaped Cape Mudge Kwakiutl Museum, which was formally opened at a huge potlatch to celebrate the occasion. The potlatch was given by Chiefs Jimmy Sewid of Alert Bay, Harry Assu of Yaculta and Jimmy Wilson of Kingcome Inlet. The ceremonies began with a thanksgiving service in Walker Memorial United Church, named for an early pastor of a religious community which has served the village for more than 100 years. (Mayse). Then came the welcoming of guests and emotional speeches by Sewid and other visiting chiefs as a lone bald eagle soared overhead. Traditional dances were performed before a Cape

Mudge D'entsiq board brought back by Ottawa's National Museum from the Museum of the American Indian in New York. (Anderson). Local foods, barbecued salmon and clam chowder were freely given to all in a gesture of typically lavish Indian hospitality. A park site near the museum includes petroglyph boulders, some of which have been relocated from the Cape Mudge tidal flats to protect them from erosion and vandalism.

Campbell River

Campbell River is known around the world as the home of the great Canadian conservationist and author, Roderick Haig-Brown, who died at the age of 68 in 1976. He was also a logger, artist, trapper, farmer, magistrate, guide, Chancellor of the University of Victoria, poet, judge and fisherman. It is as a fisherman and an author that he is best known. He was able to communicate the special relationship which sometimes develops between an angler, the fish he is looking for and the encompassing environment. Russel Chatham has written:

> Happily absent from his writing is that boorish, tiresome stance of the 'expert' giving his boring advice on how we might catch more fish or kill more game. Instead, Haig-

Campbell River's major interests of sport fishing and logging are apparent in this view of Tyee Spit, looking south.

Brown observes for the sake of observing, and he informs with astounding clarity, a complete lack of hysteria and no sense whatsoever of personal gain. He invites you to enter his world, and it is not so much the rather specific world of the fisherman as it is the broader, richer one of natural cycles, of wonder, gratitude and most of all, hope.
(cited in Environment Canada, SES No. 7, 1977).

Roderick Haig-Brown has left an example of life and work worth emulating.

Campbell River is also famous as the home of the Tyee Salmon. In 1896, Sir Richard Musgrave, the first sportfisherman at Campbell River, caught 19 Tyee in one week, his largest fish weighing over 70 pounds. Sir Richard fished with the Indians from a dugout canoe and wrote an article in *Field* magazine which praised the Indian skill for catching fish, their hospitality and their methods of practical conservation. The prestigious Tyee Club was officially established in 1924, the only stipulations for membership being that one must catch a Tyee salmon over 30 lbs. while fishing from a rowboat with light tackle.

Unfortunately, the majority of fishing done here now is not with light tackle from rowboats, although up until the 1930s there were hundreds of single man rowboats, many of them hand-trollers who concentrated in the area of Cape Mudge. Many of these hardy fishermen lived permanently in shacks along the beach all around the south tip of Quadra Island and in Campbell River.

3 Campbell River Gov't Wharf

Over 4,000 feet of berthage space is provided for small craft at floats north and south of the government wharf. Both boat basins are protected by a stone breakwater from southeast winds and seas. Although these basins are often crowded they offer reasonably convenient moorage for those wishing to make use of the many facilities in the town of Campbell River (population over 15,000). The southernmost boat basin is used primarily by transient recreational small craft as well as fishermen and is administered by the Comox-Strathcona Regional District. The northernmost basin is used primarily by commercial fishboats and is the location of Seaway Marine Sales, providing fuel (Esso agent) and marine supplies. McQuades marine chandlers are located nearby, as well as boat repair facilities with marine ways of 60-ton capacity.

4 Chevron Marina

This marina, half a mile north of the government wharf and immediately adjacent to the Quadra Island ferry dock, supplies fuel, showers and approximately 1,500 feet of moorage which is less crowded, more secure and closer to the centre of town than the government floats. Moorage fees are, however, considerably more expensive. The dredged channel leading to the marina is the same one used by the ferry. Range lights (strobe lights in fog) are mounted on beacons to assist passage.

The shopping centre directly across from the marina also includes the Campbell River Museum which is noted for its display of coast Indian and pioneer artifacts. Restaurants, pubs, bookstores, liquor store etc. are all located within two blocks of

View up the Campbell River estuary.

the marina. Tours of Elk Falls Paper Mill can be arranged and are conducted daily without charge.

Campbell River Estuary

The Campbell River estuary, 1½ miles further north, is protected by Tyee Spit from southeasterlies. The Spit is festooned with trailers, small marinas and seaplane docks which cater mainly to the needs of the hundreds of seasonal tourists who come every summer to Campbell River to fish, can and export their catch.

Inside the spit, small craft of shallow draught (such as canoes) which are capable of navigating the log boom-choked, narrow, shallow passages through the estuary can explore up the river for several miles. Parts of the river remain exceptionally beautiful with opportunities for viewing waterfowl, mature stands of timber, riverside wildlife and for picnicking, camping and angling. One mile up the river, just before the highway bridge, one passes the settlement of Campbellton. A few hundred yards past the highway bridge, on the same side of the river, is the homestead of Roderick Haig-Brown which has been donated to the province to be used as a retreat for authors concerned with conservation and the environment.

In writing about estuaries, Roderick Haig-Brown notes:

In general it is true that river mouths are not spectacular; one has to know and understand something of them to appreciate them. Even the youngest and wildest rivers tend to cushion their approach to immolation by building deltas of gravel and sand and mud. This then, is likely

to be the way of estuaries. Only when one has walked the flat places and heard the wind in the grasses, explored the sloughs and side channels, watched the tides and faced the storms, does a river mouth take on character and substance and reveal its dramatic power.
(From *Fisherman's Fall*, cited in SES No. 7, Environment Canada).

Two miles up the river, past the logging bridge, we come to Elk Falls Provincial Park and the Quinsam River Campground. Three miles from the mouth, the river disappears. The old river canyon contains only a trickle of water. A large powerhouse discharges water which has been carried through Penstocks from John Hart Lake. A whistle systems warns of sudden discharges. To avoid being caught in the millrace it is advisable to retreat above the high water mark if the whistle is heard.

The old canyon has interesting rock formations and sheer cliffs where waterfalls (Elk, Deer and Moose) once tumbled and is surrounded by the Elk Falls Provincial Park Nature Conservancy.

Two largest marinas in Campbell River are the government wharf complex, foreground, protected by newly-aligned breakwater, and the Chevron Marina.

5 Fresh Water Marinas

Moorage primarily for small recreational fishing boats is provided at two marinas across the estuary from Tyee Spit. Launching ramps, marine hardware, fuel, trailer park sites and charter boats for fishing are available. The famous Painter's Lodge and other fishing resort camps are located along the shore north of the estuary.

Just around the corner is Duncan Bay, home of the Crown Zellerbach Elk Falls paper mill and many log booms. The smoke stack here provides a convenient means of weather forecasting for residents of Campbell River. If you can smell the effluent, good weather is on the way; if you can't smell it, bad weather may be coming or has arrived.

A strong southeast wind against a flood tide sets up a heavy tide rip off Race Point, similar (but not as gruesome) as that encountered off Cape Mudge under similar conditions.

Quadra Island

6 Gowlland Harbour

The main entrance to this beautiful anchorage is north of Gowlland Island. Safe, well protected anchorage can be found at the south end of the harbour just off the abandoned government wharf or midway between Stag and Quadra Island. Temporary anchor-

Discovery Inn, right, and shopping center, front Chevron Marina and Quadra ferry dock.

age in all but northwest winds is also possible in a small cove at the north end of Gowlland Island or just inside the Vigilant Islets if the inside shore of Gowlland Island is not completely encumbered by log booms up to the northern tip.

These islets, as well as Wren, Crow, Fawn and the Mouse Islets, are protected as provincial park reserves and are a delight to visit especially when spring wildflowers are blooming in profusion.

Seascape Marine Chalets, just north of Fawn Islet, provides accommodations, picnic area, groceries, rental boats, canoes, fishing guides, fuel, a laundromat and a dock for guests. A restaurant and pub are planned for 1981. Camp Homewood, the Pacific Coast Children's Mission and Blenkin Memorial Community Park are also located in the Gowlland Harbour area.

A navigable boat passage, south of Gowlland Island, should not be attempted unless one is thoroughly familiar with the location of midchannel rocks and the edge of the drying bank which extends out from Quadra Island. The tidal stream through this passage is fairly strong.

7 April Point

Sheltered anchorage is possible behind April Point close to the "April Point Yacht Club" floats. The April

169

Islands in beautiful Gowlland Harbour are provincial park reserve.

Point Resort provides lodge and cottage accommodation, camping, restaurant, showers, laundry, rental of sail and motorboats, fishing guides, boat maintenance and repair (OMC agency) as well as fuel and moorage at their floats.

8 Quathiaski Cove

This cove serves as the terminus for the Quadra Island ferry which comes in almost every hour from Campbell River. Because of this, moorage at the government floats (1,300 feet of berthage space) located immediately north of the ferry dock is not always comfortable. A small store sells supplies just up the hill from the ferry landing. The Cove includes facilities for boat repair (Cove Boat Works) with a 60 ton capacity marine ways and a fuel dock.

From Quathiaski Cove, roads lead south to Cape Mudge and north to Granite Bay, Heriot Bay and Rebecca Spit. Prior to 1924, Quathiaski Cove was a larger community than Campbell River. The constable's home here was also the jail and court for the entire area. This house may still be seen on the corner of Heriot Bay and Greene Roads, with bars on the small windows of the rooms which served as the jail. (Anderson).

9 Rebecca Spit Marine Park

The best location for sheltered anchorage is just inside the northern tip of the spit. The spit was originally formed by longshore drift with southeast winds and waves moving sand and gravel from the Cape Mudge cliffs along the tidal zone to be deposited as a natural breakwater protecting Drew Harbour. In 1946, three acres of land at the end of the spit subsided beneath the sea during an earthquake which also affected other parts of the Strait of Georgia. In addition, two large cracks, still in evidence, appeared some distance back from the end of the spit. Long marsh grass and the stark, silver grey sheen of trees killed by salt water intrusions, reveal the subsidence that took place during the earthquake.

Halfway down the spit, open grassy meadows beneath tall Douglas firs have long been used by the local community as the site for the traditional Victoria Day Quadra Island Picnic. The large picnic field is surrounded by part of an old semi-circular trench embankment. Other smaller trenches are found along

170

Heriot Bay, with Rebecca Spit, centre, Read Islands and the mainland mountains, background.

April Point Bay has good sheltered anchorage, facilities ashore.

Quathiaski Cove has fish camps, processing facilities and ferry dock, top.

the spit. Archaeologists have postulated that these were fortifications built by Salish Indians defending the area against the Kwakiutl between the sixteenth and eighteenth centuries.

Rebecca Spit Park at one time contained campsites for park visitors arriving by car, but these have been removed because of the need to prevent erosion and to encourage day use visitors to discover the unique natural attractions of the park.

Campsites are provided at the We-Wai-Kai Campground owned by the Yaculta Indians and located immediately adjacent to the south end of the park.

10 Taku Resort

Directly across Drew Harbour from Rebecca Spit is the Taku Resort which provides accommodation, fuel dock, moorage, (800 feet of space for boats up to 23 feet), campsites, rental boats, outboard repairs, launching ramp, showers and a laundromat. There is a grocery store here and a restaurant and lounge are planned for 1980.

11 Heriot Bay

The government float in Heriot Bay offers almost 1,000 feet of berthage space, usually completely oc-

cupied by those who were here "first". The outer face of the float is sometimes unoccupied, but exposure to the full effects of the incoming Cortes Island ferry does not make this moorage very attractive.

Between the government floats and the ferry dock are marina floats with slightly more protection provided for patrons of the Heriot Bay Inn. Moorage, fuel and boat rentals are provided at the floats. The historic Heriot Bay Inn offers a few modest rooms, a restaurant (open from 10 am to midnight) — with very fine meals (Chinese or western) and a convivial pub. There are plans to provide showers and a small laundromat. A post office and store are nearby, providing fresh and frozen meats and other produce as well as a liquor stock at competitive prices.

One of the original Heriot Bay Hotels (several have been burned down, relocated or rebuilt) was managed by Mrs. Bull, a New Zealander, who changed the character of the old hotel into one of respectability and social nicety. Anderson notes:

> The beer parlour still flourished, offering relaxation to weary loggers and fishermen, but a gentler clientele was served by the remainder of the elegant rooms. There were 19 bedrooms and an upstairs dance hall, as well as a wide veranda on the second floor, used for summer dances. In this era (circa 1912), hanging flower baskets decorated the lower veranda, which served as a tea-room, and young girls clad in white uniforms waited on the guests. There was an aviary of rare canaries, and old-timers say a pet seal was kept in a pool behind the hotel.

Temporary anchorage is possible in Heriot Bay, Hyacinthe Bay and Open Bay, but the latter two are completely open to Strait of Georgia southeasters. If the weather is fair, Open Bay is a fascinating stretch of coastline to explore. The Bay itself is actually broken up into four smaller shallow bays by projecting peninsulas of geologically unique folded limestone.

Close examination also reveals an outstanding display of well preserved Upper Triassic fossils as well as pillow lavas (volcanic rock which has been rapidly cooled by contact with sea water into a distinctive "pillow" shape). The three westernmost bays, although too shallow for any thing but temporary anchorage, provide opportunity for warm water swimming with a rising tide flooding over the sun baked fine white sand. The remains of a limekiln, built in the 1930s, and two grassy fields for picnicking, can be found behind Open Bay.

Local Quadra Islanders and a geology professor have tried to get this area preserved as a park but only about 200 acres comprising Hyacinthe Point and the 140-foot island just outside Open Bay have been reserved from alienation.

It was possibly in Open Bay or in the bay behind the 140-foot island, just south of the Breton Islands, that the crew of the *Caprice* found a curious deserted house with glassless windows covered by chicken wire, apparently in order to keep all but the spirit of the occupant trapped inside. The heavy atmosphere of these surroundings are evocatively described by M. Wylie Blanchet in the B.C. coastal cruising classic *The Curve of Time*.

Rebecca Spit is a marine park with remnants of Indian fortifications from the 16th century.

Government wharf at Heriot Bay, right, is usually crowded. Floats for patrons of Heriot Bay Inn, centre, usually have space.

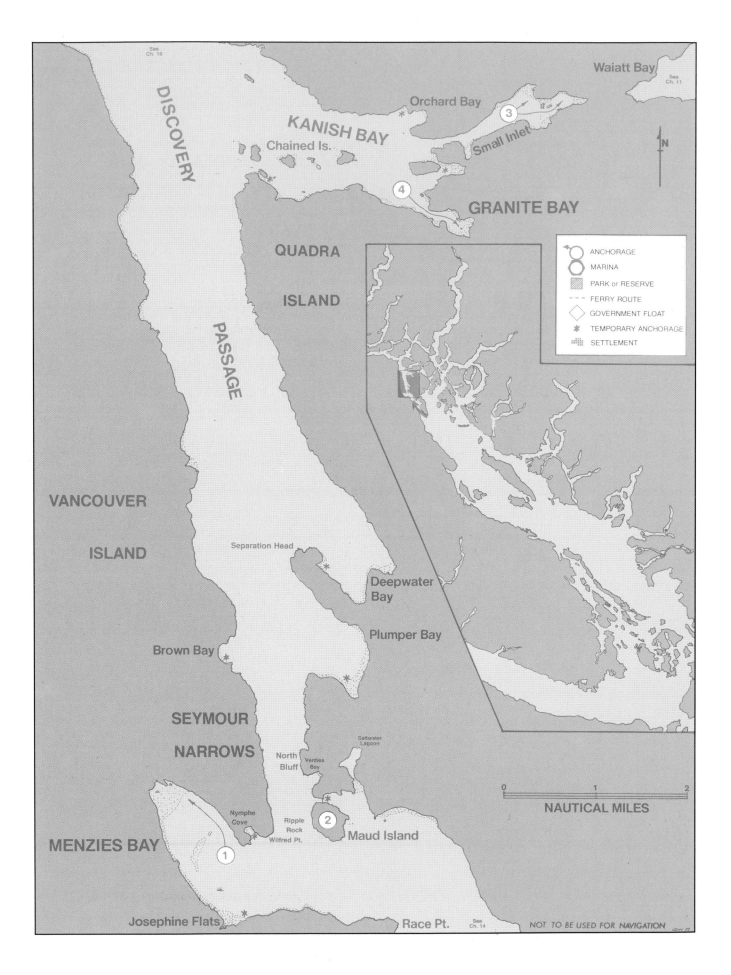

DISCOVERY

KANISH BAY

Waiatt Bay

See Ch. 16

See Ch. 11

Orchard Bay

③

Small Inlet

Chained Is.

④

GRANITE BAY

QUADRA

ISLAND

N

ANCHORAGE

MARINA

PARK or RESERVE

FERRY ROUTE

GOVERNMENT FLOAT

TEMPORARY ANCHORAGE

SETTLEMENT

VANCOUVER

ISLAND

PASSAGE

Separation Head

Deepwater
Bay

Plumper Bay

Brown Bay

SEYMOUR

NARROWS

Saltwater
Lagoon

North
Bluff

Verdies
Bay

0   1   2

NAUTICAL MILES

Nymphe
Cove

Ripple
Rock

②

Maud Island

MENZIES BAY

Wilfred Pt.

①

Josephine Flats

Race Pt.

See Ch. 14

NOT TO BE USED FOR NAVIGATION

CHAPTER FIFTEEN

Discovery Passage

Seymour Narrows to Kanish Bay

Discovery Passage, the major waterway linking the Strait of Georgia with Johnstone Strait, carries a wide variety of shipping traffic from the smallest power-boat or canoe to large passenger liners cruising to Alaska. Many of these vessels tend to move through the Passage in convoy-like concentrations at regular intervals, their timing and direction determined by the state of the tide at the narrow, half-mile wide constriction of Seymour Narrows.

Approaches to Seymour Narrows and to possible temporary anchorages which can be used while waiting for a favourable tide will depend on the strength and direction of the wind as well as the tidal stream. The blowup inset of Seymour Narrows on Chart 3565 includes tidal stream current strengths and directional arrows for flood and ebb.

With a flood tidal stream flowing south against a southeast wind it is wise to hug the Quadra Island shore to avoid the heavy rips off Race Point. A back eddy along the Quadra shore will carry one as far as Maud Island where one can make the decision of seeking partly exposed shelter behind the island, or crossing to Josephine Flats if the whirlpools and overfalls directly south of the Narrows do not look too vicious. The floodstream between Maud Island and Race Point runs at rates up to 11 knots and generates two lines of whirlpools where the rapid, southward

flowing current comes in contact with the nearly motionless waters to its east and west (Menzies Bay). (R. E. Thomson, *Oceanography of the B. C. Coast*). In calm weather it is generally safe to make use of a back eddy close to Race Point and the Vancouver Island shore can be hugged fairly close into Menzies Bay.

1   Menzies Bay

Named after Archibald Menzies, surgeon and botanist aboard H.M.S. *Discovery*, and B.C.'s first great explorer-naturalist, this bay is used primarily for the storage of log booms. Temporary anchorage is possible off Josephine Flat (named after Josephine, the captain's daughter and heroine in the operetta "H.M.S. *Pinafore*, or the Lass that Loves a Sailor" by Gilbert and Sullivan). Named by the officers of H.M.S. *Nymphe* who had seen the play acted by amateurs in Nanaimo, and the young lady taking the part of Josephine had so captured their hearts that they gave her a place on the chart while resurveying this bay in

---

CHARTS
3594 — **DISCOVERY PASSAGE to TOBA INLET**
   (1:75,000)
3565 — **DISCOVERY PASSAGE (1:38,000)**
   (includes 1:18,247 inset blowup of
   Seymour Narrows)

Anchorage at Maud Island.

Fourteeen ships, over 100 small boats and 114 lives were lost in the fierce tidal rapids of Seymour Narrows before the removal of Ripple Rock in 1958.

1895. (Walbran). With a northwest wind, more protection may be obtained by mooring in the lee of any convenient logboom or anchoring in the north end of the bay or in Nymphe Cove at the western entrance to the Narrows.

Anchorage at Nymphe Cove is not particularly recommended except in an emergency because of its southeast exposure and a rock bottom below low tide with poor holding ground. Mud deposits have been removed by the scouring action of tidal currents from nearby Seymour Narrows. Currents off Nymphe Cove tend to be unpredictable with back eddies usually causing a westward flowing ebb and a northeastward flowing flood. The shoreline from Nymphe Cove to Wilfred Point is protected as a recreational reserve and one can scramble over the cliffs for a view of Seymour Narrows, taking care not to dislodge the shattered remnants of Ripple Rock which have been plastered all over the surrounding countryside.

Seymour Narrows

Captain George Vancouver, on viewing Seymour Narrows on the 14th of July, 1792, noted:

> the tide, setting to the southward through this confined passage, rushes with such impetuosity as to produce the appearance of falls considerably high, though not the least obstruction of either rocks or sands, so far as we had an opportunity of examining it, appeared to exist.

Vancouver was obviously unaware of Ripple Rock, 9 feet below chart datum, in the centre of the Narrows. Another of Vancouver's officers is reported to have described the pass as "the most nightmarish spectacle his eyes had ever beheld." Walbran notes that the Narrows was first mentioned in an official despatch, dated 1846 as "Sir George Seymour's Narrows"; and oldtimers referred to them as "the Seymours". Arthur Mayse (*Victoria Times*, 1978) also recalls first hearing them while working 12 miles inland from Menzies Bay as "a low continuous muttering too deep for wind in the trees . . ." An old logger explained . . . "That's the tide, a big tide booming through the Seymours."

> . . . Of all the many tidal passes that thread the island archipelago of the British Columbia coast, this is the mightiest. True, there is at least one saltwater rapids — the Nakwakto draining out of and into Slingsby Channel — that belts along at a more furious pace. Sectionally, the Yuculta and the Skookum Chuck may be more spectacular. But there is none that gives such a sense of power unleashed . . . of destructive and hostile forces at work . . . as Seymour Narrows.

A large part of the destructive nature of Seymour Narrows could formerly be attributed to the presence of Ripple Rock and to the ferocious currents, whirlpools and overfalls around it. At least 14 large vessels have sunk or been severely damaged here and over 100 small boats and 114 lives have been lost. The first recorded sinking was the USS *Saranac*, 1,484 tons, in 1875. The *Saranac* was a three-masted gunboat (10 guns) sailing north from San Francisco on what was politely referred to as a "Centennial Exposition voyage to collect curios and native artifacts." The vessel may well have been jinxed by Lekwiltok shaman who discerned her real mission as she sailed past their Cape Mudge village. At this time, these Narrows were also known as the Euclataw Rapids and enterprising Indians requested tolls for safe passage. A seaman aboard described the rapids . . . "here the contending currents take a vessel by the nose and swing her from port to starboard and from starboard to port as a terrier shakes a rat." Although the *Saranac* sank within minutes of striking Ripple Rock she was able to make the Vancouver Island shoreline and none of her crew of over 200 were lost. Other vessels which sank or were severely damaged (as listed by F. Rogers, *Shipwrecks of B.C.*) included:

- In 1881 the USS *Wachusett*. She crashed onto Ripple Rock causing considerable damage to her false keel.
- In 1884 the steamer *Satellite* from Victoria. She missed slack tide and also lost part of her keel.
- 1902 — steamer *Bonita* damaged and almost sank.
- 1904 — steamer *Danube* damaged but escaped.
  - American cable ship *Burnside*: extensive damage.
- 1906 — steamer *Themis*. She grazed rock, struck North Bluff.
- 1911 — American luxury excursion steamer *Spokane* sailing to Alaska from Seattle with 165 prominent passengers aboard. She safely passed Ripple Rock but sheered toward North Bluff where she crashed against the rocks. The captain grounded the *Spokane* in Plumper Bay before she sank but . . . "realizing that the ship was sinking, some passengers panicked. Like a staggering drunk, she swayed and rolled as she limped into shore and then came to an abrupt stop. By this time the screaming passengers were fighting to get into the boats. They had gathered portside, which was higher above water, but suddenly the ship rolled over to starboard. Fearing she would capsize, many passengers wearing lifejackets leaped overboard; the others made a wild rush for the other side, causing the ship to roll again." Incredibly, only two passengers died. The survivors were later rescued by the steamship *Prince George*.
- 1914 — American cargo hulk *Gerald C. Tovey*; Sunk.
- 1916 — barges *Henry Villard* and *Palmyra*: damaged.
- 1918 — *Steamer Queen* damaged.
- 1919 — *Princess Edna* strikes rock.
- 1920 — *Prince George* strikes rock.

Because so many of the casualties in Seymour Narrows were American vessels, the U.S. government was the first to suggest that Ripple Rock be removed. Although Ottawa favoured removal, many local people did not. It was argued that the Rock provided one of the few "feasible" foundations on which to build the central pier of a bridge linking Vancouver Island to Quadra Island. This link would be part of the railway connection down Bute Inlet originally proposed by Alfred Waddington (see Chapters 7 and 8). Several schemes to remove the rock were studied over many years.

In 1942, the first attempt was abandoned after a workboat carrying nine men ashore from a drill barge anchored over the rock, was sucked into a whirlpool with the loss of everyone aboard.

In 1953, the National Research Council renewed a proposal previously thought to be too expensive, to tunnel under the Narrows from Maud Island. Finally, at 9:31 a.m. on April 5, 1958, the Rock was blown up in the world's largest non-atomic explosion. Ripple Rock, now 45 feet below chart datum, is no longer a major hazard to navigation but the strong currents continue to flow through Seymour Narrows, undiminished in strength at rates up to 15 knots. Seymour Narrows remains one of the most dangerous passages on the B.C. Coast.

Boats unfamiliar with the vagaries of tidal rapids should pass through as close to slack water (preferably high water slack if travelling north) as possible. One should stay fairly close to Maud Island until past Ripple Rock, then steer for centre channel opposite North Bluff. A notable feature on the ebb is that one hour after maximum current, the turbulence on both sides of the channel has greatly diminished, in fact the change is quite remarkable. (Captain Lillies Coast Guide).

Slack water can sometimes be dangerous for small boats when there is a long lineup of larger, more powerful craft waiting to shoot through the Narrows at the moment the tide turns. They all seem to take off at once like racers after the starting gun and the confusion of wakes and turbulent seas left behind is almost worse than what can be experienced at full flood or ebb.

Like other rapids on the coast, the times of High and Low water are delayed by about two hours, and Lower High water south of the Narrows is Higher High water north of the Narrows.

2   Maud Island

If the weather is favourable, anchorage is possible to the north of Maud Island. From here one can explore the nearby saltwater lagoon by dinghy or hike across the rockfill dam which joins Quadra Island to Maud "Island". This dam was constructed to provide road access from the miners' encampment to the shaft and underground tunnel which was constructed from Maud Island under Seymour Narrows and up into Ripple Rock. Maud Island and Verdies Bay, ¼ mile to the north, are now protected as a recreation reserve. All that is left of the miners' encampment are the concrete bunker foundations and piles of drill cores on Maud Island.

One can watch from Maud Island as the occasional vessel attempts to run through Seymour Narrows, a perilous procedure at the best of times, but if travelling with the current, the progress they seem to make is almost unnatural. Commander Mayne, while serving as a surveying officer in H.M.S. *Plumper* relates in his book *(Four Years in British Columbia and Vancouver Island,* 1862) that:

> the stream turns almost instantaneously . . . (and) there is an incessant turmoil and bubble going on. On the Monday after we moved from Baynes Sound to Quathiosky Cove, just inside Cape Mudge, Pender and I started for these narrows. I had to stop at them while he was going further on for a distance of 40 or 50 miles. We pulled up to them with the young ebb: my boat keeping close inshore to prevent its being carried through; Pender in the midstream. As we approached we watched his boat quickening her pace every second. When close to the entrance we shot into a little pool of still water (Verdies Bay?), and jumping on a rock I was just in time to see him shoot through at a tremendous speed, laying on his oars, for they were quite useless, and flying up the Strait. In about an hour from the time we parted he had reached Point Chatham, about 15 miles up. This is very well so long as a boat is going with the stream, but when working against it it is not so pleasant, particularly if, as frequently happens, a strong wind is blowing with (or even against) the current. For, as the mountains are mostly very high on each side and the Strait (Discovery Passage) nowhere more than two miles wide, the wind blows up and down it with great force.

North of Seymour Narrows, there are several possible temporary anchorages which can be used while awaiting a favourable tide when proceeding south. If a southeasterly is blowing, Plumper Bay or the head of Deepwater Bay offer the best protection, while Brown Bay and the small anchorage area just inside Separation Head provide fairly good protection with a northwest wind. Brown Bay and Plumper Bay are also subject to back eddies opposite to the direction of current in Discovery Passage. A private float in Brown Bay is used by patrons of Adam's Resort, identified by the prominent red roofed buildings. The ebb tidal stream tends to be strongest (and flood weakest) along the starboard (east) side of the middle of Discovery Passage, as is the case in many other narrow passages and inlets along the Coast.

Because Discovery Passage is bounded by fairly steep sides (as noted by Mayne), the prevailing summer "westerly" wind is often funneled by the topography into a sometimes brisk "northnorthwester". This can have a decidedly unpleasant effect on a strong ebb tide and the welcome shelter of Kanish Bay does not appear soon enough for those who dislike such conditions.

Kanish Bay

While the wind and tide outside may be raging, Kanish Bay is often incredibly calm despite its openness to the west. Although the Chained Islands do not offer particularly good anchorage, safe temporary anchorage is possible just inside a small islet near Bodega Point. Safer anchorage is available in several small bays and inlets at the head of Kanish Bay. This area was extensively used by early Indians. Will Dawson *(Coastal Cruising),* reports that Indian kitchen

middens or mounds of shell, bone, stone and flint utensils covering many acres up to 25 feet deep and the remnants of at least 16 villages indicate the antiquity of primitive settlements. The Haida and Kwakiutl Indians to the north raided these villages so frequently that the Bay was finally abandoned.

Orchard Bay at the extreme northeastern end of Kanish Bay and the small islet at the entrance to Granite Bay provide easily visible evidence of this early Indian occupation as well as the efforts of later-day white settlers to hack out a home in the wilderness. Orchard Bay has a glistening white shell beach and is backed by a thick uncut grass meadow and a variety of introduced fruit and deciduous trees.

3   Small Inlet

Safe anchorage with good protection from all dangerous winds and seas is available through the narrow but navigable ingress into Small Inlet. Bald eagles perched in eyries high above the narrows have an excellent view of anything passing through the shallow waters. The head of this Inlet is only ½ mile from Waiatt Bay on the other side of Quadra Island. Anchorage is also available within a small bay bet-

Remnants of at least 16 Indian villages dot the area around Kanish Bay anchorage in Granite Bay.

Small bay between Small Inlet and Granite Bay has protection from west winds.

ween Small Inlet and Granite Bay with fairly good protection from the west.

4   Granite Bay

The government float here offers convenient moorage but no place to walk to. The float is not attached to the shore but moored to pilings in the centre of the bay. Access to the shore must be by dinghy. This bay was a thriving community around the turn of the century, with a population of over 500 engaged in logging, farming and mining. Many of these early settlers came from Finland. Possibly fewer than five or six families live here today. Granite Bay is linked to southern Quadra Island by road and a walk along this road reveals the remains of this former activity. Huge stumps marked with springboard notches, an old log schoolhouse, farm meadows, and three miles up the road — the remains of the Lucky Jim gold and copper mine are to be found. A large steam engine wheel stands quietly remote in the forest, and the right of way for what was one of the first logging railways on the coast is now obscured by vegetation. "Curly" the steam engine, preserved in a historical park on the lower mainland, once hauled logs along these right of ways.

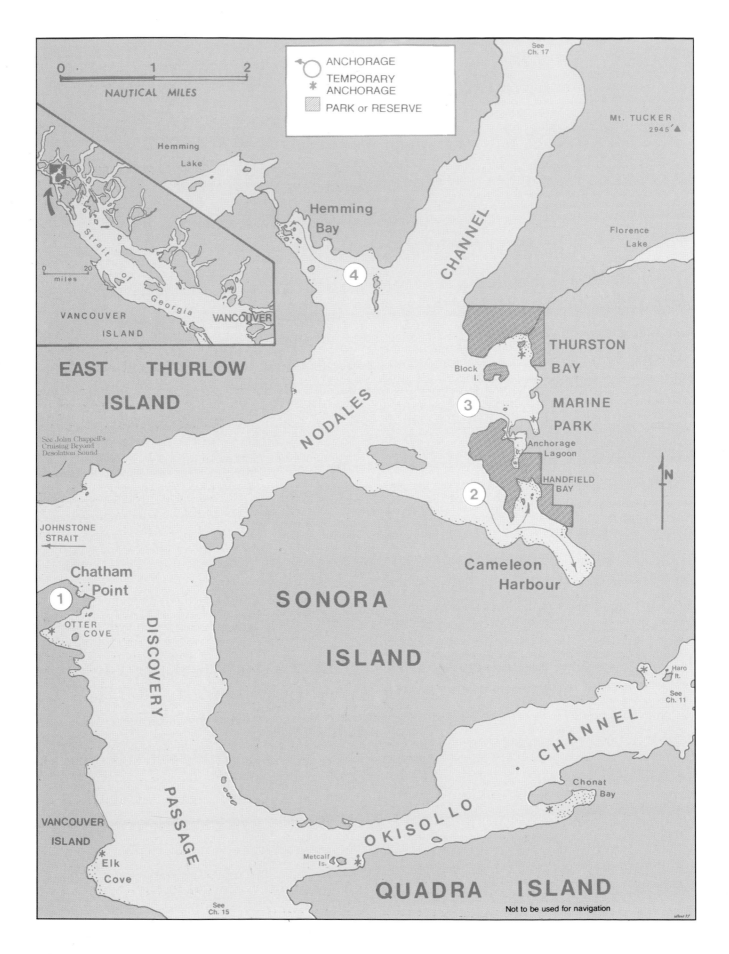

ANCHORAGE
TEMPORARY ANCHORAGE
PARK or RESERVE

NAUTICAL MILES

0   1   2

Hemming Lake

Strait of Georgia

0   miles   20

VANCOUVER ISLAND

VANCOUVER

EAST   THURLOW

ISLAND

See John Chappell's
Cruising Beyond
Desolation Sound

JOHNSTONE
STRAIT

Chatham
Point

①

OTTER
COVE

DISCOVERY

VANCOUVER

ISLAND

PASSAGE

Elk
Cove

Hemming
Bay

④

See
Ch. 17

Mt. TUCKER
2945'▲

Florence
Lake

CHANNEL

NODALES

Block
I.

THURSTON
BAY

MARINE

③

PARK

Anchorage
Lagoon

②

HANDFIELD
BAY

Cameleon
Harbour

N

SONORA

ISLAND

Haro
lt.

See
Ch. 11

Chonat
Bay

CHANNEL

O K I S O L L O

Metcalf
Is.

QUADRA   ISLAND

See
Ch. 15

Not to be used for navigation

180

CHAPTER SIXTEEN

Okisollo to Nodales Channel

Chatham Point, Thurston Bay Marine Park

Okisollo, the name of the channel which encircles the northeast coast of Quadra Island, is derived from the Kwakiutl word for "pass", which is unusual in that most other Indian place names in this area are derived from the Salish. Although well known by the Indians, this passageway was unknown to the chartmakers until the late 1800s and Quadra, Sonora and Maurelle Islands were all thought to be one island, known as "Valdes Island".

There are a few possible temporary anchorages within this northern section of Okisollo Channel where one can await a favourable tide before proceeding through the Lower and Upper Rapids. Good protection is available in a small cove just west of Haro Islet. Chonat Bay, located beneath a conspicuous cliff on the north shore of Quadra, is somewhat exposed to westerlies and shallows quickly with several drying boulders at the edge of the tidal flat. Slightly more protection is afforded in the lee of Metcalf Islands near the entrance to Okisollo Channel.

Okisollo Channel enters Discovery Passage directly across from Elk Bay where Captain George Vancouver anchored for the night of July 15, 1792 before proceeding into Johnstone Strait. This Bay, and Otter Cove to the north, offer good temporary anchorage and shelter from the prevailing summer westerly winds. Otter Cove is named after the Hudson's Bay Company steamer *Otter*, the "second historical craft on this coast" (after the *Beaver*). She was built at Blackwall, London, 1852; length, 122 feet; beam, 20 feet. Her powerplant, consisting of two direct-acting, condensing engines 26 x 18 inches, had taken first prize in the Great Exhibition, London, 1851 (Walbran). It is quite likely that this cove and the rock

CHARTS
3594 — DISCOVERY PASSAGE to TOBA INLET (1:75,000)
3566 — JOHNSTONE STRAIT (Eastern Portion) (1:36,500)
3521 — OKISOLLO CHANNEL (1:24,354)
3522 — CHATHAM POINT to STUART ISLAND (1:24,330)
3556 — PLAN of ELK BAY (1:18,350)
— PLAN of OTTER COVE (1:12,300)

Looking up Johnstone Strait to Chatham Pt. light, with Beaver Rock beacon on the right.

Chatham Pt. lighthouse float, with Sonora Island in background.

north of Chatham Point were named in association with the two other vessels which also had a very prominent part in the survey of this coast.

1 Chatham Point

Chatham Point was named by Vancouver after H.M.S. *Chatham*, the small but heavy consort of the *Discovery*. Walbran notes that she was probably named after the Earl of Chatham who, when Vancouver sailed from England, was First Lord of the Admiralty. The *Chatham* was built at Dover as an armed tender, mounting four three-pounders and six swivels; sheathed with copper and rigged as a brig. Although less than 60 feet in length she rated 135 tons burthen and carried a crew of 55. The *Chatham* was described as being top heavy and slow in sailing, "the most unsuited vessel that could have been chosen for this dangerous and lengthy voyage". In contrast to the *Chatham*, H.M.S. *Discovery* (after which Discovery Passage was named) was ship-rigged, 340 tons burthen, 100 feet long, copper fastened, sheathed with plank and coppered. She mounted ten four-pounders and ten swivels, with a crew of 134 all told.

Due north of Chatham Point is Beaver Rock named after the Hudson's Bay Company's paddle steamer *Beaver*, the first steam vessel on this coast.

It is possible to visit the lightstation at Chatham Point, either by anchoring in Otter Cove and hiking around the Point, or by tieing up to the very small float in the cove just below the station. A 4-foot drying rock is located only a few boat lengths from the end of the float.

Chatham Point marks the entrance to Johnstone Strait and in fairly strong tidal currents (generally 1 to 3 knots but reaching 6 knots where the strait narrows), a knowledge of what wind patterns one can expect helps to avoid unpleasant sea conditions. This is especially true when the prevailing westerly wind is blowing against the ebb tide, which in Johnstone Strait tends to be stronger and of longer duration than the flood. On neap tides it is not uncommon for the ebb to continue for several days with no apparent interruption by a flood current at all. This phenomenon is probably the result of less dense, fresher surface waters from land drainage flowing seaward on top of the more saline ocean waters. What is surprising, is that it is largely the influence of the Fraser River, discharging into the Strait of Georgia over a hundred miles away, which induces this net seaward moving current. (R. Thomson, *Oceanography of the B.C. Coast*).

The anemometer at Chatham Point is protected somewhat from southwest, west and northwest winds by a densely wooded ridge to the west. Nevertheless, winds in summer tend to be predominantly from these directions (blowing over 70 per cent of the time). There appears to be a diurnal trend as the westerly decreases in frequency during the afternoon hours to less than 40 per cent. Winds from the east and southeast tend to have an average frequency of 20 per cent in the summer months, blowing most frequently in the afternoon.

The monthly mean speed of the wind at Chatham Point is stronger during the summer months (12.4 mph, for July) than for the winter months (8.5 mph for January), an unusual difference possibly due to the relatively good protection afforded by the Discovery Islands from winter southeast storms. The most frequent wind in the winter months is from the northeast (28 per cent in January), but winds from east and southeast also occur relatively frequently (15 to 20 per cent for each direction).

Summer fogs are common in Johnstone Strait due to colder surface waters (approximately 10° C colder than Desolation Sound and 3° C colder than Queen Charlotte Sound to the north). These fogs occasionally spill into Discovery Passage and up Nodales Channel to Cordero Channel. Yachts proceeding

through Johnstone Strait should refer to John Chappell's *Cruising Beyond Desolation Sound*.

Nodales Channel, named by the Spaniards Galiano and Valdes in 1792, is the major waterway linking Frederick Arm with Discovery Passage. Because of this, it is usually deserted. After all, who wants to visit Frederick Arm? (See Chapter 17).

2 Cameleon Harbour

Part way up Nodales Channel, the curious explorer can find several delightful anchorages in some out of the way harbours. The first of these, Cameleon Harbour, was named in 1863 by Captain Daniel Pender after H.M.S. *Cameleon*, 17 guns, who was engaged in

Boiling down Discovery Passage in a brisk westerly under jib alone, Chatham Point astern.

the original detailed survey of this area. All place names in the vicinity were named after the Captain and officers aboard the *Cameleon*, including Piddell Bay after Alfred H. Piddell, RN, secretary's clerk. The surrounding land at this time was still known as Valdes Island.

Safe anchorage, protected from all seas and winds, is available within Cameleon Harbour. Just inside Greetham Point there is a delightful deserted farmstead which seems to hold the evening sun on its grassy meadows long after the surrounding landscape has faded into shadow.

Thurston Bay Marine Park

The south end of Thurston Bay Marine Park includes Handfield Bay at the north end of Cameleon Harbour. It is possible to walk across the low lying, narrow isthmus to the head of Anchorage Lagoon. Sunlight filtering through the trees onto a forest floor with surprisingly little underbrush reveals the unused pathways of long departed former residents.

Anchorage Lagoon (3) is very shallow and swampy at its head, and although providing good anchorage inside, one should beware of boulders 2 feet below chart datum in the entrance. The middle part of Thurston Bay has been used as a base for logging activities on this side of Sonora Island.

Reasonably safe anchorage is available behind Block Island. From here one can visit the site of the

LEFT: Cameleon Harbour, lower right, with Handfield Bay above, looking over Thurston Marine Park. BELOW: Middle of Thurston Bay is being used for log booming.

abandoned Ministry of Forests Ranger Station. Virtually nothing of the station remains, as floats and buildings have been removed since the land was transferred from the Forest Service to the Parks Branch. An old logging trail leads east from here to Florence Lake — a pleasant mile and a half hike. At Florence Lake there is reported to be good cutthroat trout fishing and a spectacular 1,400-foot high cliff drops to the north shore of the Lake.

A more arduous hike leads west from the station 4 miles up the ridge from above Davis Point to the old Forestry lookout on top of Mount Tucker. Magnificent views are possible across Cordero Channel to the spire-like peak of Mount Estero, down to the Yuculta Rapids at the entrance to Bute Inlet, and west down Johnstone Strait towards the north end of Vancouver Island.

4 Hemming Bay

Good anchorage is available north of the 145-foot islet near the head of Hemming Bay. Anchorage for shoal-draught small craft is also possible to the southwest of this islet in an almost totally enclosed nook. Active logging is still carried on in the vicinity and the outlet of Hemming Lake, a few hundred yards from salt water, is clogged with logging debris as far as one can see.

East Thurlow Island was named by Vancouver after the Lord Chancellor, Edward Lord Thurlow. Although of relatively humble origin (he was the son of a parson) he was raised to the peerage and became a noted orator, being greatly assisted by his "singularly majestic appearance." It was said of him that "no man ever was so wise as Thurlow looks." (Walbran).

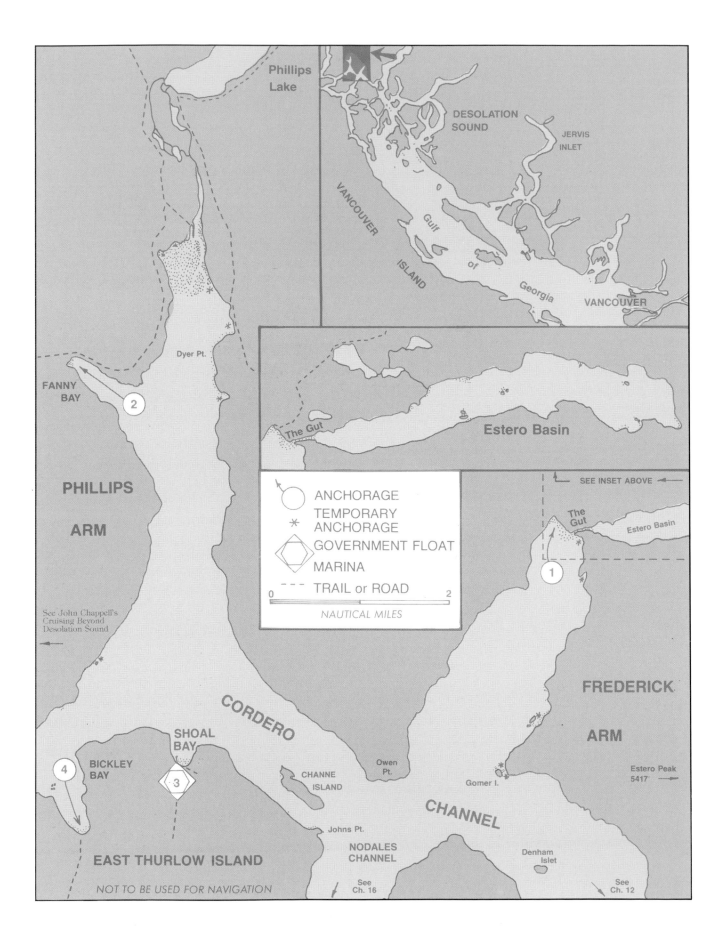

Phillips Lake

DESOLATION SOUND

JERVIS INLET

VANCOUVER ISLAND

Gulf of Georgia

VANCOUVER

The Gut

Estero Basin

SEE INSET ABOVE

The Gut

Estero Basin

ANCHORAGE

TEMPORARY ANCHORAGE

GOVERNMENT FLOAT

MARINA

TRAIL or ROAD

0   2
NAUTICAL MILES

Dyer Pt.

FANNY BAY

②

PHILLIPS

ARM

See John Chappell's Cruising Beyond Desolation Sound

①

FREDERICK

ARM

SHOAL BAY

④ BICKLEY BAY

③

CORDERO

CHANNE ISLAND

Owen Pt.

Gomer I.

Estero Peak 5417'

CHANNEL

Johns Pt.

NODALES CHANNEL

Denham Islet

EAST THURLOW ISLAND

NOT TO BE USED FOR NAVIGATION

See Ch. 16

See Ch. 12

186

CHAPTER SEVENTEEN

Frederick and Phillips Arms

Cordero Channel, Shoal Bay

Cordero Channel serves as a less congested, more protected waterway than Discovery Passage for many small boats using the "inside passage" between northern B.C. and the Strait of Georgia. Passage through the Yuculta, Gillard, Dent and Greene Point rapids must be carefully timed to coincide with local slack water from the Tide and Current Tables (described further in Chapter 7 of John Chappell's guide *Cruising Beyond Desolation Sound*). Unless one has a very fast boat, this usually necessitates a stopover between slack waters at Dent and Greene Point. One can either wait at Shoal Bay or spend a few hours exploring up Frederick or Phillips Arm.

In July of 1792, the Spaniards Galiano and Valdes were considerably relieved to have escaped the clutches of the tidal rapids south of the "Brazo de Quintano" (Bute Inlet) as they proceeded westward along Cordero Channel against a westerly wind (See end of Chapter 12).

> After leaving these dangerous places we met other natives who came alongside the *Sutil* in two canoes and pointed out the course we ought to follow. The confidence they displayed was as great as if they had been among their best friends, and when we had shown them the chart of our surveys they pointed out on it by means of a pencil the direction of the channels opening to the W, and those which had their outlet to the sea. As they did not understand the manoeuvre of tacking, which some-times turned us away from the direction we ought to follow, they advised us not to sail towards the Ensenada del Estero (literally "the bay of the estuary" — Frederick Arm and Estero Basin) as it was closed. This they indicated by arching their arms, but seeing at last that we disregarded their advice they went ashore. We continued on our tack to the end of the Estero, which we found to be closed . . . (Voyage of the *Sutil* and *Mexicana*).

It is unlikely that the Spaniards sailed to the end of Estero Basin itself as this would have required more than one tack and the entrance channel has only 3 or 4 feet of water at high tide (although it may have been deeper 200 years ago). "Estero" means "estuary" or "lagoon" in Spanish, so it is quite possible that they sailed to the end of Frederick Arm and the edge of the "estuary mouth" of what is now known as Estero Basin; while their small boats made a brief exploration into the basin (see chart page 23).

Temporary anchorage is possible around the

CHARTS
3522 — CHATHAM POINT to STUART ISLAND
(for Cordero Channel) (1:24,330)
3594 — DISCOVERY PASSAGE to TOBA INLET
(1:75,000)
— inset of Frederick and Phillips Arms
(excludes Estero Basin)

Estero Peak sits like a fortress over Frederick Arm.

The Narrow "Gut" leads into Estero Basin from Frederick Arm.

perimeter of the estuary delta. Old logging roads lead past an abandoned logging camp and several small lakes northeast of Estero Basin's outlet. Since the basin is uncharted, one can experience how the early explorers must have felt by venturing (with some trepidation) into these "unknown" waters. Although tug boats have been hauling log booms out of the basin for many years, entrance is only possible close to high water slack (about one to two hours after local high water). The tidal stream rushes into and out of Estero Basin like the streams that run into the Desolation Sound lagoons such as at Squirrel Cove, but on a much larger scale.

In 1901, the Union Steamship *Comox* experienced some difficulty landing at the wharf (still shown on Chart 3594, 1978 edition) and got stuck in the narrows or "the Gut" as it is known locally. Gerald Rushton (*Whistle Up the Inlet*) records this account:

> Usually there is a light on the float, but this time there was no lantern there, although a man was lying asleep on the wharf ostensibly waiting for the steamer. Just beyond the float the current begins to run swiftly and there are times when the tide through the little narrows runs at twelve (sic) miles an hour. On this occasion, mistaking a light away up on shore for the one that should have been on the wharf, the *Comox* passed by the end of the float and got in the force of the current . . . The engines were promptly reversed but the propellor struck a rock and was stripped of its blades, and the steamer, with the way she had on, was carried aground in the Gut hard and fast.
>
> The Postmaster, it turned out, had apparently gone to sleep with the light on in his bedroom, and it was quipped that the *Comox* obligingly came ashore right

Gomer Island is connected to the mainland by a tombolo spit at low tide.

View up Phillips Arm from Shoal Bay.

Shoal Bay Lodge is at head of government wharf in Shoal Bay.

Steep cliffs plunge into Estero Basin, where few boats dare to venture.

The Gut into Estero Basin in a quiet mood. .

under his window." The basin was sealed off by two scows serving as a breakwater and the *Comox* was repaired and refloated two weeks later.

There is an eerie stillness inside the basin with an almost sheer cliff dropping down into the southern shoreline, several tiny islets and many uncharted rocks. The basin extends in an easterly direction for over 5 miles to within a mile or so of Bute Inlet.

Frederick Arm and Owen Point at the western entrance are named after the same surveying officer who is honoured on the east side of Read Island (Chapter 10), Staff Commander Frederick John Owen Evans, R.N. (Walbran).

Temporary anchorage is also possible in a few shallow nooks along the eastern shore of Frederick Arm; particularly just inside the 160-foot islet, a mile north of Gomer Island. Temporary anchorage while waiting for slack water at Dent Island might also be available on either side of the tombolo spit which joins Gomer Island to the mainland. This anchorage is not ideal because of its somewhat exposed location and the large quantities of kelp (in season) over the shallows. Currents east of Gomer Island tend to flow east most of the time, reversing to a westerly direction for only 3 hours near the end of the ebb. Currents in the vicinity of Denham Islet run at rates up to 4 knots at springs.

Estero peak is not particularly spectacular when viewed from the south, but becomes an increasingly prominent landmark, dominating the eastern skyline as one proceeds to the west down Cordero Channel.

After confusing the Indians by their desire to "tack" to the end of Frederick Arm to see what was there, the Spaniards turned up Cordero Channel.

> . . . (we) then tacked to look for the narrow Canal del Engano, which trended NW, and succeeded in reaching the mouth of it. When we were passing inside, however, the canoe with our Indian pilots arrived, and told us that this was closed. The favorable tide was coming to an end so we proceeded to the west shore to seek anchorage in the Canal de los Nodales. We anchored in the roadstead of that name at a cable length from land.
>
> The information of the Indians did not tally with that we had received from the English about this place, and it was therefore indispensible for the smaller vessels to go and survey the Canal del Engano. So Salamanca went out for that purpose in the longboat at 2:30 in the afternoon, with a favorable tide just beginning to make to the north along the shore.

Salamanca explored Phillips Arm, Fanny Bay and Loughbrough Inlet before returning to the *Sutil* and *Mexicana* in Nodales Channel. The Spaniards then left for the sea, assisted by a strong ebb, via the "Canal del Engano" — now known as Cordero Channel (named by Royal Navy surveyors after Josef Cordero, the draughtsman of Galiano's expedition).

Just inside Johns Point there is a small sawmill operation. Huge veins of quartz appear like waterfalls in the cliffs above Channe Passage.

Phillips Arm

Many years ago, Phillips Arm was one of the prime fishing areas on the coast. One can only guess as to why this is not so today, but a sail to the head of this Arm may give a few clues. The river which runs into the head of Phillips Arm has built an extensive delta almost a mile from shore. This river which was earlier described as 40 miles long, shallow, treacherous, and difficult to navigate (Colonist, 1897) became a route for mineral prospectors and loggers, in search of rich resources in the hinterland.

The Matsayno Indian Reserve covers a large part of the estuary mouth and there are a few houses and a boat basin on the west bank of the river. Phillips Lake, only 16 feet above sea level, is about 2 miles long and can be reached by river or by logging roads.

2   Fanny Bay

Fanny Bay offers anchorage or moorage on log booms, well protected from the prevailing westerly winds. There is a large logging camp here. Temporary anchorage is also possible on the other side of Phillips Arm at the mouth of Shirley Creek (somewhat exposed to westerlies), north of Dyer Point, or at the edge of the estuary delta (beware of snags).

3   Shoal Bay

At Shoal Bay on East Thurlow Island there is a government wharf which extends out along the west side of the Bay with floats at the end providing about 650 feet of moorage space. Fuel and water is available at these floats and at the head of the wharf, accessible by a boardwalk over the marshy delta, is the Shoal Bay Lodge. The lodge is located on the old townsite of "Thurlow". A few of the 100-year-old buildings still exist. In 1889 Thurlow was "the most important establishment on the coast, it being a point of supply for (logging) camps, timber cruisers and also for the numerous hand-loggers working in the neighbourhood". (Rushton).

Around the turn of the century, Shoal Bay became the centre for intense mineral prospecting activity. Several small mines opened in the Phillips Arm area, two on Channe Island (the Yuclaw and the Puddle Dog) and one 1,000 feet up the mountainside east of Shoal Bay (the Douglas Pine). Keith Hammond (Pacific Yachting, March 1977) notes that this latter mine is accessible by an old cedar skid road: "This is a hard two hour hike. One can enter the uppermost of three horizontal tunnels, but take a flashlight because vertical shafts to the lower levels open directly in the floor."

The Shoal Bay Lodge provides accommodation, showers, laundry, restaurant, charter boats and guide service and a pub(lounge) with a pleasant view up Phillips Arm.

Bickley Bay, (4) just around the corner is backed by an extensive grassy meadow similar to the one behind Shoal Bay, and provides well protected anchorage.

This is the end of this guide — but one can cruise from here into another fascinating world of intricate waterways; isolated hideaways; ferocious rapids and more beautiful, mist enshrouded scenery; and still further beyond, the open sea . . .

Indeed, the cruising of a boat here and there is very much what happens to the soul of man in a larger way. We set out for places which we do not reach, or reach too late; and, on the way, there befall us all manner of things which we could never have awaited.

. . . the sea presents, upon the greatest scale we mortals can bear, those not mortal powers which brought us into being . . . sailing the sea we play every part of life: control, direction, effort, fate; and there can we test ourselves and know our state. All that which concerns the sea is profound and final . . sailing the sea . . . is a beckoning from powers outside mankind.
— Hilaire Belloc, On Sailing The Sea, 1951

To find one's way to lands already discovered is a good thing.
— Joshua Slocum, Sailing Alone Around the World, 1899

BIBLIOGRAPHY

Akrigg, G. P. V. and Helen B. Akrigg. *1001 British Columbia Place Names*. Vancouver: Discovery Press, 1973.

———— *British Columbia Chronicle, 1778-1846: Adventures by Sea and Land*. Vancouver: Discovery Press, 1975.

———— *British Columbia Chronicle, 1848-1871: Gold and Colonists*. Vancouver: Discovery Press, 1977.

Anderson, Doris. *Evergreen Islands*. Sidney, B.C.: Gray's Publishing, 1980.

Appleton, Thomas E. *Usque Ad Mare: A History of the Canadian Coast Guard and Marine Service*. Ottawa: Dept. of Transport, 1968.

Ashwell, Reg. *Coast Salish*. Saanichton, B.C.: Hancock House, 1978.

Bancroft, J. Austen. *Geology of the Coast and Islands Between the Strait of Georgia and Queen Charlotte Sound, B.C.* Ottawa: Dept. of Mines, 1913.

Barnett, Homer G. *The Coast Salish of British Columbia*. Oregon: Univ. of Oregon Press, 1955.

Barrett-Lennard, Capt. C. E. *Travels in British Columbia with the Narrative of a Yacht Voyage Round Vancouver's Island*. Toronto: Canadiana House, 1969.

Begg, Alexander. *History of British Columbia from its Earliest Discovery to the Present Time: 1894*. Toronto: McGraw-Hill Ryerson, 1972.

Bergren, Myrtle. *Tough Timber: The Loggers of British Columbia — Their Story*. Toronto: Progress Books, 1967.

Berssen, William. *Sea Boating Almanac*. Costa Mesa, U.S.A.: Sea Magazine, 1980.

Blanchet, M. Wylie. *The Curve of Time*. Sidney, B.C.: Gray's Publishing, 1968.

Bodsworth, Fred. *The Pacific Coast*. Toronto: Natural Science of Canada Ltd., 1970.

Calhoun, Bruce. *Northwest Passages: A Collection of Pacific Northwest Cruising Stories, Vol. I.* San Francisco: Miller Freeman Publications, 1969.

———— *Northwest Passages: A Collection of Northwest Cruising Stories, Vol. II.* San Francisco: Miller Freeman Publications, 1972.

Canada, Hydrographic Service. *British Columbia Small Craft Guide, Vol. I, Gulf Islands: Sooke to Campbell River*. Ottawa: 1978.

———— *British Columbia Small Craft Guide, Vol. II, Boundary Bay to Cortes Island*. Ottawa: 1980.

———— *Sailing Directions: British Columbia Coast (South Portion)*. Ottawa: 1979.

Capt. Lillie's British Columbia, Puget Sound and S.E. Alaska Coast Guide and Radiotelephone Directory. Vancouver: Progress Publishing, 1979.

Carefoot, Thomas. *Pacific Seashores: A Guide to Intertidal Ecology*. Vancouver: Douglas & McIntyre Ltd., 1977.

Carl, G. C. *Guide to Marine Life of British Columbia, Handbook #21*. Victoria: B.C. Prov. Museum, 1971.

Chappell, John. *Cruising Beyond Desolation Sound: Channels and Anchorages from the Yuculta Rapids to Cape Caution*. Vancouver: Naikoon Marine, 1979.

Childerhose, R. J., and Marj Trim. *Pacific Salmon*. Vancouver: Douglas & McIntyre Ltd., 1979.

Clark, Cecil. *Tales of the British Columbia Provincial Police*. Sidney, B.C.: Gray's Publishing, 1971.

Clark, Lewis J. *Wild Flowers of British Columbia*. Sidney, B.C.: Gray's Publishing, 1973.

Clutesi, George. *Potlatch*. Sidney, B.C.: Gray's Publishing, 1969.

Cornwall, I. E. *The Barnacles of British Columbia*. Victoria: B.C. Prov. Museum Handbook #7, 1970.

Cuddy, Marylou and James J. Scott. *British Columbia in Books*. Vancouver: J. J. Douglas, 1974.

Dawson, George. *Report on a Geological Examination of the Northern Coast of Vancouver Island and Adjacent Coasts*. Montreal: Dawson Bros., 1887.

Dawson, Will. *Coastal Cruising: An Authoritative Guide to British Columbia, Puget Sound-San Juan Islands Waters and the Waterways of Southeast Alaska*. Vancouver: Mitchell Press, 1973.

De Volpi, Charles P. *British Columbia a Pictorial Record: Historical Prints and Illustrations of the Province of British Columbia, Canada 1778-1891*. Don Mills: Longman Canada, 1973.

Douglas, Gilean. *The Protected Place*. Sidney, B.C.: Gray's Publishing, 1979.

Duff, Wilson. *The Indian History of British Columbia, Vol. I: The Impact of the White Man*. Victoria: B.C. Prov. Museum of Natural History and Anthropology, 1969.

Espinosa y Tello, Jose. *Account of the Voyage Made by the Schooners Sutil and Mexicana in the Year 1792*. Trans, by G. F. Barwick, London, 1911. From 1802 ed., Madrid Royal Printing Office.

———— *Spanish Voyage to Vancouver Island and the Northwest Coast of America*. Trans. by Cecil Jane. London: Argonaut Press, 1930. From 1802 ed., Madrid Royal Printing Office.

Farley, A. L. *Atlas of British Columbia: People, Environment and Resource Use*. Vancouver: Univ. of British Columbia Press, 1979.

Farrow, C. M. *Nobody Here But Us: Pioneers of the North*. Vancouver: J. J., Douglas, 1975.

George, J. David and Jennifer J. *Marine Life: An Illustrated Encyclopedia of Invertebrates in the Sea*. Vancouver: Douglas & McIntyre Ltd., 1979.

Hacking, Norman and W. Kaye Lamb. *The Princess Story*. Vancouver: Mitchell Press Ltd., 1974.

Geddes, Gary. (ed.) *Skookum Wawa: Writings of the Canadian Northwest*. Toronto: Oxford Univ. Press, 1975.

Gough, Barry M. *The Royal Navy and the Northwest Coast of North America. 1810-1914: A Study of British Maritime Ascendancy*. Vancouver: Univ. of British Columbia Press, 1971.

Gould, Ed. *Logging: British Columbia's Logging History*. Saanichton, B.C.: Hancock House, 1975.

Griffiths, Garth. *Boating in Canada: Practical Piloting and Seamanship*. Toronto: Univ. of Toronto Press, 1969.

Guiget, C. J. *The Birds of British Columbia: Gulls, Terns, Jaegers and Skua*. Victoria: B.C. Prov. Museum, Handbook #13, 1967.

———— *The Birds of British Columbia: The Shorebirds*. Victoria: B.C. Prov. Museum, Handbook #8, 1973.

———— *The Birds of British Columbia: Waterfowl*. Victoria: B.C. Prov. Museum, Handbook #15, 1973.

———— *The Birds of British Columbia: The Woodpeckers; the Crows and Their Allies*. Victoria: B.C. Prov. Museum, Handbook #6, 1973.

Haig-Brown, Roderick. *Fisherman's Fall*. Toronto: William Collins Sons, 1964.

———— *The Living Land*. Toronto: Macmillan, 1961.

———— *Measure of the Year*. Toronto/London: Collins, 1969.

———— *A River Never Sleeps*. Toronto: Collins, 1965.

———— *Woods and River Tales*. Toronto: McClelland and Stewart, 1980.

Hancock, David and David Stirling. *Birds of British Columbia.* Saanichton, B.C. Hancock House, 1973.

Hart, J. L. *Pacific Fishes of Canada.* Bulletin *#180.* Ottawa: Fisheries Research Board of Canada, 1973.

Henderson, Lydia and Phil Capes. (eds.) *A Naturalist's Guide to the Comox Valley and Adjacent Areas Including Campbell River.* Courtenay: Comox-Strathcona Natural History Society, 1973.

Hewlett, Stefani and K. Gilbey. *Sea Life of the Pacific Northwest.* Toronto: McGraw-Hill Ryerson Ltd., 1976.

Hill, Ray and Beth Hill. *Indian Petroglyphs of the Pacific Northwest.* Saanichton, B.C.: Hancock House, 1974.

Hill-Tout, Charles. Ralph Maud, (ed.) *The Salish People – Volume IV – The Sechelt and the South Eastern Tribes of Vancouver Island.* Vancouver: Talon Books Ltd., 1978.

Holland, Stuart S. *Land Forms of British Columbia.* Victoria: Bulletin #48, B.C. Dept. of Mines, 1964.

Howay, F. W. and E. O. S. Scholfield. *British Columbia from Earliest Times to the Present.* Vancouver: Clarke, 1914.

Hutchinson, Bill and Julie Hutchinson. *Rockhounding and Beachcombing on Vancouver Island.* Victoria: Tom and Georgie Vaulkhard. The Rock-Hound Shop, 1971.

Jackman, S. W. *Vancouver Island.* Toronto: Griffin House, 1972.

Kochanek, D. B. McLean and B. Burkhardt. *Sailors and Sauerkraut.* Sidney, B.C.: Gray's Publishing, 1978.

Landale, Zoe. *Harvest of Salmon: Adventures in Fishing the B.C. Coast.* Saanichton, B.C.: Hancock House, 1977.

Langlois, W. J. (ed.) *Navigating the Coast: A History of the Union Steamship Company.* Victoria: Prov. Archives of B.C., Sound Heritage, Vol. 6, #2, 1977.

Leslie, S. (ed.) *In the Western Mountains, Early Mountaineering in British Columbia.* Victoria: Prov. Archives of B.C., Sound Heritage, Vol. 6, #4, 1980.

Lindsay, F. W. *Outlaws in British Columbia.* Quesnel: F. W. Lindsay, 1963.

Lowther, Barbara J. *A Bibliography of British Columbia: Laying the Foundations, 1849-1899.* Victoria: Social Sciences Research Centre, Univ. of Victoria, 1968.

Luxton, Norman Kenny. *Tilikum: Luxton's Pacific Crossing.* Edited by Eleanor Georgina Luxton. Sidney, B.C.: Gray's Publishing, 1971.

Lyons, C. P. *Milestones on Vancouver Island.* Vancouver: Evergreen Press, 1958.

————— *Trees, Shrubs and Flowers to Know in British Columbia.* Revised Edition. Toronto/Vancouver: J. M. Dent, 1965.

Lyons, Cicely. *Salmon: Our Heritage.* Vancouver: British Columbia Packers, 1969.

Mark, David M. *Where to Find Birds in British Columbia.* New Westminster, B.C.: Kestrel Press, 1978.

Mayne, Richard Charles. *Four Years in British Columbia and Vancouver Island.* London: J. Murray, 1862.

Meade, Edward. *Indian Rock Carvings of the Pacific Northwest.* Sidney, B.C.: Gray's Publishing, 1971.

————— *The Biography of Dr. Samuel Campbell, R.N.* Campbell River: E. Meade, 1980.

Meany, Edmond S. *Vancouver's Discovery of Puget Sound: Portraits and Biographies of the Men Honoured in the Naming of Geographic Features of Northwestern America.* Portland, Oregon: Binfords and Mort, 1957.

Middleton, Lyn. *Place Names of the Pacific Northwest: Origins, Histories and Anecdotes in Bibliographic Form About the Coast of British Columbia, Washington and Oregon.* Victoria: Eldee Publishing, 1969.

Mitchell, Helen A. *Diamond in the Rough.* A history of Campbell River, 1966.

Mohoney, Russ. *The Dogfish Cookbook.* Sidney, B.C.: Gray's Publishing, 1976.

Mountain Access Committee. *Mountain Trail Guide for S.W. Mainland Area of British Columbia.* Vancouver: Federation of Mountain Clubs of B.C., 1972.

Macfie, Matthew. *Vancouver Island and British Columbia. Their History, Resources and Prospects.* Toronto: Coles Publishing, 1972.

McConkey, Lois. *Sea and Cedar: How the Northwest Coast Indians Lived.* Vancouver: J.J. Douglas, 1973.

McCormick, John A. *Cruise of the Calcite.* Everett, Wash.: B. & E. Enterprises, 1973.

McKechnie, Robert E. II. *Strong Medicine: History of Healing on the Northwest Coast.* Vancouver: J. J. Douglas, 1972.

McKervill, Hugh W. *The Salmon People.* Sidney, B.C.: Gray's Publishing, 1967.

McTaggart Cowan, Ian, and C. J. Guiguet. *The Mammals of British Columbia.* Victoria: B.C. Prov. Museum, Handbook #11, 5th edition, 1973.

Newcombe, C. F. *The First Circumnavigation of Vancouver Island.* Victoria: Cullin, 1914.

Norcross, E. Blanche and Doris Farmer Tonkin. *Frontiers of Vancouver Island.* Courtenay: Island Books, 1969.

Ormsby, Margaret A. *British Columbia: A History.* Toronto: Macmillan, 1958.

Paterson, T. W. *Shipwreck! Piracy and Terror in the Northwest.* Victoria: Solitaire Publications, 1972.

————— *Hellship!* Langley: Stagecoach Publishing, 1974.

Peake, Frank A. *The Anglican Church in British Columbia.* Vancouver: Mitchell Press, 1959.

Pearse, Theed. *Birds of the Early Explorers in the Northern Pacific.* Comox: Theed Pearse, 1968.

Pethick, Derek. *James Douglas: Servant of Two Empires.* Vancouver: Mitchell Press, 1969.

————— *S.S. Beaver. The Ship that Saved the West.* Vancouver: Mitchell Press, 1970.

Pratt-Johnson, Betty. *141 Dives in the Protected Waters of Washington and British Columbia.* Vancouver: Gordon Soules, 1977.

Quayle, D. B. *The Intertidal Bivalves of British Columbia.* Victoria: B.C. Prov. Museum, Handbook #17, 1973.

Reid, R. L. *Alfred Waddington.* In the Royal Society of Canada. Proceedings and Transactions; third series. 1932, Vol. 26, section 2.

Richards, Sir George Henry. *The Vancouver Island Pilot.* Great Britain, Hydrographic Office, 1864.

Rogers, Fred. *Shipwrecks of British Columbia.* Vancouver: J. J. Douglas, 1973.

Rogers, John. *Shorebirds and Predators of B.C.* Vancouver: Douglas & McIntyre Ltd., 1978.

Rothenberger, Mel. *The Chilcotin War: The True Story of a Defiant Chief's Fight to Save His Land from White Civilization.* Langley, B.C.: Stagecoach Publishing, 1977.

Rushton, Gerald A. *Whistle Up The Inlet.* Vancouver: Douglas & McIntyre Ltd., 1976.

Scagel, R. F. *Guide to Common Seaweeds of British Columbia.* Victoria: B.C. Prov. Museum, Handbook #27, 1972.

Shanks, R. N. *Waddington: A Biography of Alfred Penderill Waddington.* Port Hardy: North Island Gazette, 1975.

Smith, Ian. *The Unknown Island.* Vancouver: J. J. Douglas, 1973.

Stewart, Hilary. *Looking at Indian Art of the Northwest Coast.* Vancouver: Douglas & McIntyre, 1979.

Stirling, David. *Birds of Vancouver Island for Birdwatchers.* Saanichton, B.C.: Hancock House, 1972.

Strathern, Gloria. *Navigations, Traffiques and Discoveries, 1774-1848: A Guide to Publications Relating to the Area Now British Columbia.* Victoria: Univ. of Victoria, 1970.

Taylor, Harry, comp. *Powell River's First 50 Years.* Powell River: Powell River News, 1960.

Texada Centennial Committee. *Texada Island.* Texada Island: C. May, 1960.

Thomson, Richard E. *Oceanography of the B.C. Coast.* Ottawa: Canadian Special Publications, Ocean and Aquatic Sciences, (forthcoming).

Turner, Nancy J. *Food Plants of British Columbia Indians.* Victoria: B.C. Prov. Museum, Handbook #34, 1975.

Vancouver, George. *A Voyage of Discovery to the North Pacific Ocean and Round the World.* Amsterdam, N. Israel: Bibliotheca Australiana No's. 30, 31, 32, 33, 1967.

Van der Ree, Freida. *Exploring the Coast by Boat.* Vancouver: Gordon Soules, 1979.

Waddell, Jane. *Hiking Trails III: Central and Northern Vancouver Island.* Victoria: Outdoor Club of Victoria, Trails Information Society, 1979.

Waddington, A. P. *The Fraser Mines Vindicated; or, the History of Four Months.* Victoria: De Garro, 1858.

Wagner, Henry R. *Spanish Explorations in the Strait of Juan de Fuca.* New York: AMS Press, 1971.

Walbran, John T. *British Columbia Coast Names.* Vancouver: The Library's Press, 1971.

White, Charles and Nelson Dewey. *How to Catch Bottomfish!* Sidnery, B.C.: Soltaire Publishing, 1971.

White, Howard (ed.) *Raincoast Chronicles First Five.* Madeira Park, B.C.: Harbour Publishing, 1975.

——————*Raincoast Chronicles #8.* Madeira Park, B.C.: Harbour Publishing, 1979.

Wolferstan, W. H. *Marine Recreation in the Desolation Sound Area of British Columbia.* Unpublished M.A. thesis, Simon Fraser Univ., Burnaby, 1972.

—————— *Cruising Guide to the Gulf Islands and Vancouver Island from Sooke to Courtenay.* Vancouver: Interpress, 1976.

Wood, Daniel and Betty Campbell. *Kids! Kids! Kids! and Vancouver Island: Hundreds of Places to Visit in Victoria and Vancouver Island.* Vancouver: Fforbez Publications, 1977.

PERIODICALS:

Beautiful B.C. (Quarterly), Parliament Buldings, Victoria, B.C.
B.C. Outdoors, #202 - 1132 Hamilton Street, Vancouver, B.C.
Pacific Yachting. #202 - 1132 Hamilton Street, Vancouver, B.C.
Raincoast Chronicles, Box 119, Madeira Park, B.C.
Radio Aids to Navigation (Quarterly), Ministry of Transport, Ottawa, Ont.
Notices to Mariners (Weekly), Ministry of Transport, Ottawa, Ont.
Pacific Coast Tide and Current Tables (Annual), Ministry of Transport, Ottawa, Ont.

ILLUSTRATION CREDITS

All photographs, except those listed below, were taken by George McNutt or the author. Aerial photographs taken from planes piloted by George McNutt and Al Nairne (Ch. 8, 13).
Page 4, Jim Dudley; page 16, Deadeye Photography; page 18, Ken Alexander; page 24, Phillipe M. Dore; page 89, Alvin Fairhurst; pages 108, 153, Cathi Robinson.
All maps and sketches, except those listed below, were draughted by Clementien Wolferstan or the author.
End papers, Chart index and guide index base map — courtesy of Canadian Hydrographic Service; page 12, reproduced with the permission of the Department of Energy, Mines and Resources, Ottawa; page 21, drawn by W. Alexander from a sketch taken on the spot by T. Heddington, engraved by J. Landseer for "A Voyage of Discovery" . . . George Vancouver, London, 1798, courtesy of Provincial Archives, Victoria; page 22, chart base courtesy of Canadian Hydrographic Service; pages 22,23, explorers charts courtesy of Provincial Archives, Victoria; page 26, base map courtesy of Surveys and Mapping Branch, Victoria.

QUOTATION CREDITS

Quotations on pages listed below are reproduced with the kind permission of: page 6, Charles Scribners Sons Ltd., New York; pages 23,24, G.P.V. Akrigg, Discovery Press, Vancouver; pages 161,177,189, J.J. Douglas Ltd., Vancouver; pages 128,164,172, Gray's Publishing Ltd., Sidney; page 191, A.D. Peters & Co. Ltd.

INDEX